Brassey's *History of Uniforms*

Brassey's *History of Uniforms*

Current titles

American Civil War: Confederate Army
American Civil War: Union Army
Napoleonic Wars: Wellington's Army
Napoleonic Wars: Napoleon's Army
Mexican-American War 1846-48
English Civil War

Forthcoming titles

Roman Army: Wars of the Empire
Barbarian Warriors: Saxons, Vikings, Normans

Brassey's *History of Uniforms*

Mexican-American War 1846-48

By Ron Field

Colour plates by Richard Hook

Series editor Tim Newark

For Joseph Hefter

First English Edition 1997

UK editorial offices: Brassey's Ltd, 33 John Street, London
WC1N 2AT
UK orders: Marston Book Services, PO Box 269, Abingdon,
OX14 4SD

North American orders: Brassey's Inc,
PO Box 960, Herndon, VA 22070, USA

Ron Field has asserted his moral right to be identified as the
author of this work.

Library of Congress Cataloging in Publication Data available
British Library Cataloguing in Publication Data
A catalogue record for this book is available from the British
Library

ISBN 1 85753 210 4 Hardcover

Originated, printed and bound in Singapore under the
supervision of M.R.M. Graphics Ltd., Winslow,
Buckinghamshire.

Contents

Introduction

One hundred and fifty years ago the thunder of guns was first heard along the banks of the Rio Grande. The causes of the conflict, known as the Mexican-American War to some, and *La Intervencion Norteamericana* to others, were numerous and spanned at least a decade. In the spirit of 'Manifest Destiny', many Americans, and particularly those of Democratic persuasion, were convinced that it was the God-given right of the United States to spread its presumed political, social and economic power over the whole of the North American continent. This would prove a direct challenge to Mexican possession of the West Coast and southwest, which included Alta California with its soon-be-discovered gold seams, and trade links with the Orient.

Tension between the U.S. and Mexico first grew over possession of Texas in the 1830s, and reached breaking point after the slaughter of the Alamo garrison during the Texan War of Independence in 1836. Further friction developed as Mexico failed to pay her war debts after defeat at San Jacinto, and American citizens in Texas claimed several million dollars in damages for property destroyed during those tumulteous days. Mexico finally agreed to pay the United States $2 million compensation, but it was not long before she defaulted on her payments.

Mexican anger and resentment towards the U.S. reached a head when Texas was annexed by the U.S. in 1845. As a Mexican province, the southern boundary of Texas had not extended beyond the Nueces River, but Americans began to claim land as far south as the Rio Grande. Determined to uphold this claim, President James K. Polk sent 3,500 U.S. regulars known as the 'Army of Observation', under General Zachary Taylor, into the disputed area during the summer of 1845. The reaction in Mexico was to demand war.

Polk was also determined to acquire California Territory (including the modern states of Nevada, Utah, Arizona, and parts of New Mexico, Colorado and Wyoming) and, in November 1845, sent John Slidell, a Louisiana politican, as special envoy to Mexico in a last attempt to persuade the Mexicans to sell this land. Slidell was authorised to cancel the unpaid damage claims against Mexico in return for the Rio Grande boundary, and was to offer $25 million for California. Arriving in Mexico City as a new anti-American government came to power under President Mariano Paredes, Slidell was not even received.

On learning of the failure of the Slidell mission in January 1846, Polk ordered General Taylor to advance his force to the Rio Grande. This amounted to a U.S. attempt to entice Mexico across the river, which would give America the excuse she needed to declare war. But Mexico did not react. By 9 May, Polk's patience expired and he decided to ask for a declaration of war on the grounds that Mexico had refused to pay her debts, and had insulted the U.S. by refusing to negotiate with Slidell. That same evening, before the message could be sent, news arrived that Mexican troops had crossed the Rio Grande, and that sixteen U.S. dragoons had been killed and wounded. This was the excuse that Polk had been waiting for. His message to Congress now claimed that 'after reiterated menaces', Mexico had 'shed American blood on American soil', and claimed that 'war exists by act of Mexico itself'. On this false pretext, he asked for a declaration, and on 13 May 1846 both houses of congress voted overwhelmingly for war and for a bill authorising the President to raise 50,000 volunteers to fight alongside the small U.S. Regular Army.

Not all Americans wished for war. Some Congressmen, such as John C. Calhoun, Thomas Hart Benton, and John Quincy Adams, saw the war as one of U.S. aggression. Calhoun even suggested that Polk had violated the Constitution by giving himself war-making powers. While early U.S. victories were warmly greeted in the expansionist Southwestern States, they were coolly received in the Northeast, particularly in New England. This area supplied

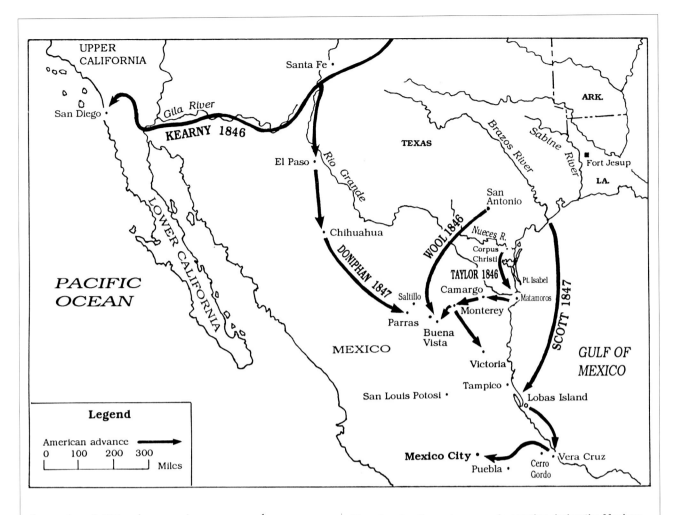

UPPER CALIFORNIA

Santa Fe

San Diego

Gila River

KEARNY 1846

Rio Grande

El Paso

TEXAS

ARK.

Fort Jesup

LA.

Brazos River

Sabine River

San Antonio

Nueces R.

Corpus Christi

WOOL 1846

TAYLOR 1846

Pt. Isabel

Camargo

Matamoros

DONIPHAN 1847

Chihuahua

Saltillo

Monterey

Parras

Buena Vista

SCOTT 1847

MEXICO

Victoria

Tampico

San Louis Potosi

Lobas Island

Mexico City

Puebla

Cerro Gordo

Vera Cruz

PACIFIC OCEAN

LOWER CALIFORNIA

GULF OF MEXICO

Legend

American advance →

0   100   200   300

Miles

Map showing the main areas of operation during the Mexican-American War.

fewer than 8,000 volunteers in answer to the President's call, in comparison with 20,000 from the South, and 40,000 from the West. Anti-slavery spokesmen, such as Ralph Waldo Emerson, Henry David Thoreau, and James Russell Lowell, denounced the war as a plot to acquire more slave territory. In reality this was far from the case, as most Southern planters regarded New Mexico and California as unsuitable for slavery, and Mexico as being even more so.

Others opposed the war for purely political reasons. The Democrats feared that it might split their party, and were jealous of the success of two Whig generals, Zachary Taylor and Winfield Scott. The Whigs in turn became increasingly critical of the costly progress of the war, and mounting casualties, and labelled it 'Polk's War'.

In the face of American internal divisions, Mexico entered the war confident of victory, and full of doubt that the U.S. had either the will or the way to win the war. The Mexican regular army was four times the size of that of the United States, but was composed mainly of native conscripts who were badly led, poorly organised, and armed with antiquated weapons. The U.S. had much greater reserves of manpower with a population of 17 million, which was twice the size of

that of Mexico. The U.S. economy was also much stronger, and capable of supporting a prolonged war.

America also had more competent generals in Taylor and Scott, and was also fortunate in possessing approximately 200 subordinate, or junior officers, who had been trained thoroughly in the art of war at the U.S. Military Academy at West Point. These included Robert E. Lee, Ulysses S. Grant, Thomas J. Jackson and George B. McClellan, all of whom later fought either side by side, or against each other, in the American Civil War of 1861-65. Nonetheless, these officers led a largely amateur, volunteer army which did not always stand the test of fire. Command of the high seas by its modest size navy gave the U.S. a marked advantage over Mexico, who had little navy to speak of. For this reason, the U.S. was able to supply troops across the Gulf of Mexico, and regularly imported war supplies from Europe. It was also able to establish a blockade, thereby starving Mexico of her lifelines of trade.

The campaign in northern Mexico

The first major clash between Mexican and American

'Battle at the Plains of Buena Vista, February 23, 1847', painted by Samuel Chamberlain, 1st U.S. Dragoons, who took part in the battle. Chamberlain's unit is at right, advancing by the U.S. Regular battery of Captain Thomas W. Sherman. The mounted officer in the foreground is General Zachary Taylor, astride 'Old Whitey' and wearing his non-regulation brown frock coat. San Jacinto Museum of History Association.

forces occurred six days before the U.S. officially declared war on Mexico. At Palo Alto, on 8 May 1846, a small army of 2,300 U.S. Regulars under General Taylor crushed a larger Mexican force of 6,000 under General Mariano Arista. This was followed up the next day by further American success at Resaca de la Palma, after which an exhausted Mexican 'Army of the North' retreated south to Linares. On both occasions superior use of U.S. light artillery drove the Mexicans from the field.

Taylor followed up these two victories by demanding and receiving the surrender of Matamoros, which U.S. forces entered on 18 May 1846. As a result he was breveted a major general and named commander of the 'Army of the Rio Grande'. Meanwhile his victorious army began to die from diseases such as cholera, measles, and yellow fever. Fifteen hundred soldiers in his army died during the summer of 1846. Despite this, recruits and volunteers continued to flood into his camp swelling his army to 20,000.

Taylor next advanced on Monterey, the nearest Mexican city, where he found a fortified garrison awaiting under Pedro de Ampudia, a Mexican general noted for his cruel treatment of prisoners and hatred of Texans. Arriving on 20 September 1846, Taylor commenced his attack the next day as the Texas Rangers, assisted by Regular Infantry, stormed the hills surrounding Monterey and captured Mexican cannon which they turned on the city. Only after four days fighting did the 'impregnable' Monterey finally fall to Taylor's army. But American losses, amounting to 120 killed and 368 wounded, were heavier than those suffered by the Mexicans. Feeling himself dangerously overextended, Taylor permitted Ampudia's troops to withdraw with arms and declared an eight-week armistice. Meanwhile another American force of 3,000 under Brigadier General John E. Wool, known as the 'Army of the Centre', gingerly felt its way through the Mexican province of Chihuahua from San Antonio, Texas.

Although Taylor's victory at Monterey was greeted with wild celebrations throughout the U.S., Polk was critical of Taylor's leniency with Ampudia, and alarmed by growing talk of nominating Taylor as Whig candidate for the presidency. Hence, on 26 January 1847, he ordered Taylor to remain at Monterey, whilst four-fifths of his army was to be sent to aid General Winfield Scott in the planned invasion of Mexico at Veracruz. Ignoring orders, Taylor advanced his much reduced army of 5,000 men further inland towards Saltillo, capital of the Mexican province of Coahuila, thereby extending his line of communications from Matamoros to 400 miles in length. Learning of this, Santa Anna, the 'villain of the Alamo', who had returned from exile in 1846 to immediately be appointed president and commander of the newly-styled Mexican 'Army of Liberation', rushed north with 20,000 hastily recruited troops in hope of achieving a decisive victory.

The two armies clashed at the hacienda of Buena Vista on 22 February 1847. Outnumbered four to one, the Americans came close to defeat during the two-day battle. But once again superior artillery fire, and the fighting ability of the U.S. volunteer soldiers, won the day and at sunrise on 24 February Taylor learned that Santa Anna had retreated proclaiming a 'victory'. However, Taylor's run of success in the Mexican War was over. Despite being awarded three gold medals, and a vote of thanks from Congress, he continued to be criticized and neglected by Polk, and returned to the U.S. in late 1847 to campaign for the presidency.

The campaign in New Mexico & California

President Polk hoped for a few quick victories and a short and limited war in 1846. Thus he quickly ordered U.S. troops to occupy the Mexican provinces of New Mexico and California - for which he went to war. During June 1846, Colonel Stephen W. Kearny, 1st U.S. Dragoons, assembled a rag-tag army, designated the 'Army of the West', at Fort Leavenworth. It numbered some 2,700 men, and included a battalion of Mormons, enlisted at Brigham Young's request as their army pay would help finance the sect's move westward to the Great Salt Lake. Kearny set out on 26 June 1846, and after a march of 565 miles reached Bent's Fort on the upper Arkansas River. Manuel Armijo, governor of New Mexico province, awaited the American attack at Santa Fe. Kearny sent James W. Magoffin, a Santa Fe trader and old friend of the New Mexican governor, who successfully bribed Armijo into surrendering. Thus the U.S. army entered Santa Fe on 18 August without a shot being fired.

After appointing Charles Bent territorial governor and Colonel Sterling Price commander of the army of occupation in New Mexico, Kearny divided his forces and sent Colonel Alexander W. Doniphan and the Missouri Mounted Volunteers south down the Rio Grande to El Paso. Doniphan next crossed the desert to Chihuahua City, and then turned east to link up with Taylor in northern Mexico. Enroute Doniphan marched 6,000 miles without any supplies, uniforms, or pay from the U.S. government, and won two important battles - El Brazito, just north of El Paso, on Christmas Day, 1846, and Sacramento, near Chihuahua City, on 28 February, 1847.

Meanwhile, Kearny led the third part of his army north to California, but before his arrival on the West Coast, a bizarre tale of personal ambition and intrigue had already begun to unfold. Brevet Captain John C. Frémont, U.S. Topographical Engineers, had penentrated California from the east several months before hostilities commenced along the Rio Grande, supposedly on a surveying expedition to Oregon country. At Frémont's instigation, American settlers in the territory revolted against Mexican colonial government, which was already in factional disarray. This so-called 'Bear Flag revolt' occurred in June, 1846, with the raising of the Bear Flag in Sonoma on the 14th of that month. Frémont declared himself governor of the 'Republic of California', and falsely suggested that he was acting on U.S. authority.

Shortly after this, U.S. Navy Commodore John D. Sloat put a force ashore at Monterey, capital of Alta California (not be be confused with Monterey in northern Mexico), on 7 July, 1846 and declared California U.S. territory. Following this he sent naval expeditions to other key points on the coast to claim them for the U.S.A. The warring Mexican, or Californio, factions put aside their differences in order to expel the hated *americanos*. In ill health, Sloat was succeeded by Commodore Robert F. Stockton who, in turn, proclaimed an American regime in California with himself in charge. He subsequently appointed the disgruntled Frémont as military governor in the north, whilst another Yankee adventurer, U.S. Marine Lieutenant Archibald Gillespie, was given similar responsibility in the south. Meanwhile, the united Californios seized key points in the south and proclaimed their own regime.

Into the middle of this cauldron stepped Colonel Kearny and his small force of 100 U.S. Dragoons and two mounted howitzers. Learning of the Californio opposition to U.S. rule, he fought his way through a Mexican force at San Pascual on 6 December, 1846, losing about 30 of his party, and reached San Diego six days later. Joining forces, Stockton and Kearny led a 560-strong army consisting of dragoons, sailors,

Entitled 'Battle of Sacramento – Terrible Charge of the Mexican Lancers', this lithograph by Ferdinand Bastin was published in 1850. In reality, this charge never took place. The Mexican cavalry from Durango and Chihuahua, under General Pedro Garciá Conde, lost all order and dispersed before they could be brought into action at Sacramento on 28 February 1847. DeGolyer Library.

marines and volunteers, north to Los Angeles to crush the Californios. This was accomplished in two clashes on the San Gabriel River on the 8th and 9th January, 1847, after which the American conquest of California was complete.

The campaign in central Mexico

Despite a series of American victories in the north, the Mexicans refused to surrender. Polk thus decided to order his forces to strike at Mexico City. Because of a difficult 500 mile overland approach, Polk ordered a seaborne expedition under command of Winfield Scott to capture Veracruz . Beaching his force of 9,000 in wooden landing craft at Anton Lizardo on 9 March 1847, Scott captured the city after an eighteen day siege. By early April 1847, Scott's army was marching inland along the National Highway over a 240 mile route through difficult terrain. In the face

of determined resistance, this force encircled and defeated a Mexican army of 13,000 under Santa Anna at Cerro Gordo the 17th and 18th April. Despite lack of support and supplies from Polk, Scott had by August reached the high Mexican plateau and on the 20th of that month the Battle of Mexico City began. After two American victories at Contreras and

Opposite.

Top.

'Pillow's attack advancing through the woods of Chapultepec', by James Walker. An Englishman, Walker emigrated to America in 1823, and was resident in Mexico City when war broke out. Escaping through the lines, he joined the U.S. army as a guide and interpreter and accompanied Scott till the end of the war. Pillow's division, consisting of the Voltigeurs and Regular Infantry deploys at the double, whilst Mexican infantry in the woods give covering fire to their retreating red-coated cavalry on the right. Chapultepec Castle is seen in the distance. Dept. of Defense Still Media Records Center – SDAN: CC-21823.

Bottom.

Map of the assault on Chapultepec Castle, 13 September, 1847; from N. C. Brooks, *A Complete History of the Mexican War,* Philadelphia, 1849. Peter Newark's Western Americana.

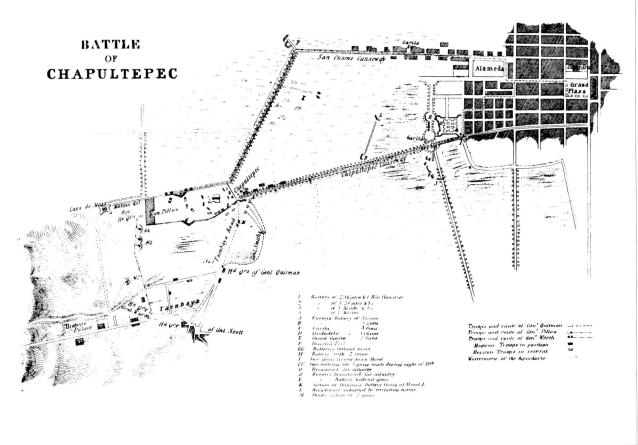

BATTLE
OF
CHAPULTEPEC

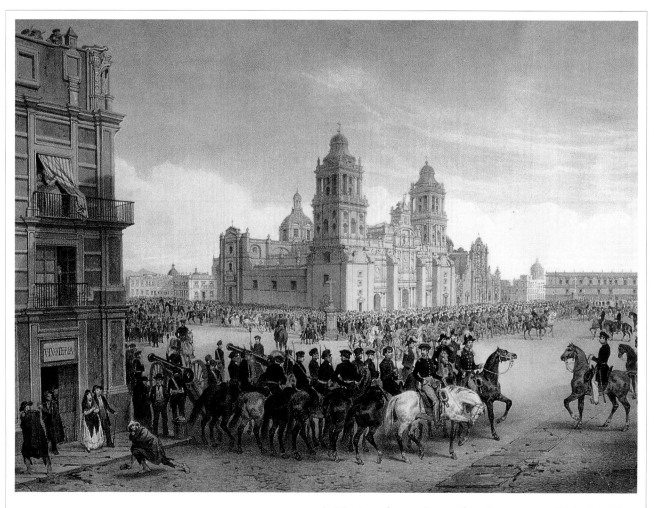

'General Scott's Entrance into Mexico City'. This toned lithograph published in 1851, after Carl Nebel's illustration, depicts Scott's triumphal entrance into the main plaza of Mexico City on 14 September 1847. There is no doubt war is still on here. Loaded cannon of Steptoe's Battery are posted to sweep the streets, while a body of dragoons in the foreground gathers tensely with drawn sabres near General Scott and his staff. An artillery officer on a white horse in the centre foreground glares as a Mexican prepares to throw a rock. Also note the Mexican snipers on the roof top. The building at the right is the Palacio National, or seat of the Mexican government, which the Americans called 'the Halls of Montezumas'. In the centre is the Cathedral of Mexico. San Jacinto Museum of History Association.

Churubusco, Scott granted a Mexican request for an armistice in order to negotiate. Taking advantage of what they saw as American weakness, the Mexicans used this time to reinforce their positions. Hence fighting resumed on 8 September at Molino del Rey and by 13 September the Castle of Chapultepec had fallen, and the Americans were at the gates of Mexico City, which was abandoned by Santa Anna the next day.

Within six months, a small US army of approximately 10,000 had defeated a much larger Mexican force. Soon after the capture of Mexico City, Santa Anna retreated to Guadalupe Hidalgo, where he renounced the presidency on 22 September 1847. A new Mexican government came to power firstly under Manuel de la Peña y Peña, and subsequently under Pedro María Anaya, both of whom were prepared to make peace. Several months earlier Polk had appointed Nicholas P. Trist, chief clerk of the State Department, as peace commissioner and had authorized him to offer terms similar to those proposed by the Slidell mission of 1846. Several months passed before Trist could persuade the Mexicans to negotiate, by which time Polk had run out of patience and ordered Trist's recall, adding the terms offered were too generous. Believing that a break down in negotiations would lead to further anarchy and bloodshed, Trist, with Scott's backing, ignored Polk's orders and concluded a settlement based on his original instructions. By the Treaty of Guadalupe Hidalgo, signed on 2 February 1848, Mexico ceded to the U.S. about half her national territory by giving up California and New Mexico, and agreeing to recognise the Rio Grande boundary of Texas.

Meanwhile the US agreed to pay $15m for the ceded territories, and to pay the damage claims still

owned to American settlers by Mexico, which amounted to $3¼m. This treaty gave the US everything she had gone to war for. Despite demands from expansionists who desired the annexation of the whole of Mexico, Polk forgave Trist for disobeying orders, and decided to recommend ratification of the treaty by the Senate. The Treaty of Guadalupe Hidalgo was thus ratified by a vote of 38 to 14 on 10 May 1848.

Thus between the years 1845 and 1848 the U.S. gained half a million square miles of additional territory, completed its expansion to the Pacific Coast, and secured its boundaries with Mexico and Canada. However, the Mexican War had cost the U.S. nearly $100m and more than 13,000 soldiers had died, mostly from disease. The number of Mexicans casualties is not known. A far more tragic consequence for the U.S. was the revival of the controversy over the extension of slavery into the territories. This ushered in a period of strife between north and south which eventually culminated in civil war in 1861. As Ralph Waldo Emerson prophesied, 'The United States will conquer Mexico, but it will be as the man who swallows the arsenic which brings him down. Mexico will poison us.'[1]

Brigadier General John Ellis Wool and staff in the Calle Real, Saltillo, in 1847. Various evidence suggests that this daguerreotype, and others in the same collection, were taken by Philadelphia photographer J.H. William Smith. Wool is the figure in the caped overcoat, and the bearded officer second from the right might be Brevet Captain Irwin McDowell, Wool's aide-de-camp, who would achieve notoriety in the Civil War for losing the First Battle of Bull Run, or Manassas. Other officers in this image may include Inspector General Sylvester Churchill, Captain William W. Chapman, an extra aide to Wool, and Captain David Hunter, who may be the man in light-coloured trousers on the left. Most of the officers are dressed in regulation forage caps and dark blue frock coats. Dragoon escorts are barely visible behind them. Note the Mexican civilians in the background. Amon Carter Museum, Fort Worth: accession #81.65.22.

U.S. Regular Army

On the eve of the conflict with Mexico, the United States Regular Army consisted of a mere 8,613 officers and men, of which only about 6,562 were present for duty. These men were organised into eight regiments of infantry, four of 'artillery', and two of dragoons. The 'artillery' regiments, which were theoretically expected to serve in fortifications with heavy guns, were armed, equipped and drilled as infantry; but one company of each regiment had a field battery, and under the instruction of well-trained officers had reached a high standard of proficiency in that arm of service. The infantry and dragoons were also well drilled, though separate postings among coast and frontier stations, besides impairing discipline and efficiency, had provided limited experience for manoeuvring in large bodies. A few well-trained

Entitled 'American volunteer infantry standing along a street in Saltillo', this compelling outdoor scene taken in 1847 may well depict the Virginia Regiment taking advantage of shade during the mid-day Mexican heat. Whoever the troops are, they appear to wear the regulation U.S. sky blue infantry fatigue uniform eventually issued to most volunteer regiments, aswell as the regular army. Note the company officer eighth from the right, distinguished by his dark blue frock coat, and broad white trouser seam stripe. Amon Carter Museum, Fort Worth: accession #81.65.25.

topographical engineers, an ordnance department, a small medical staff, and a quartermaster's department completed this miniature army.

An Act of Congress dated 23 August 1842 had reduced company sizes to 42 men per infantry and 'artillery' company, 64 men per field artillery company, and 50 men per dragoon company. In reality, company sizes always ran approximately 15 per cent below what the law allowed. After the commencement of hostilities, Congress approved legislature between 13 and 19 May 1846 which theoretically boosted regular troop levels to 17,812 by increasing company size to 100 men in each branch of service, and creating the Regiment of Mounted Rifles, and the Company of Sappers, Miners and Pontoniers. Nonetheless, by November 1846 there were still no more than 10,690 officers and men with the colors under Regular command.

Enlistment was for five years or the war's duration. Recruitment was slow as men were reluctant to risk life and limb for $7 a month. In desperation, the government relaxed physical requirements and paid $2 per head to anyone who brought in suitable cannon fodder. Eventually, recruits were offered a $12 bounty, but none of the measures were particularly effective.

On 11 February 1847 the Regular Army was augmented to 31,000 via the 'Ten Regiment Bill'

which authorised ten new regiments - the 3rd U.S. Dragoons, the 9th, 10th, 11th, 12th, 13th, 14th, 15th, and 16th U.S. Infantry, and a regiment of 'voltigeurs and foot riflemen ... provided with a rocket and mountain howitzer battery'. Recruits for these new regiments were to serve during the war and then be disbanded. Altogether, 1,016 officers and 35,009 men served in the Regular Army between 13 May 1846 and 5 July 1848, making a total of 42,587 for the war. Of this number, 30,954 saw active service.

Some of the senior officers in the regular army had received their commissions during the War of 1812 and had no West Point education. Since there was no retirement system, they tended to remain in the

Captain Wiliam Chapman, 5th U.S. Infantry, and friend, possibly Captain Moses Merrill of the same regiment. This quarter plate daguerreotype is one of only about fifty surviving images of American soldiers actually taken in Mexico during the war. Chapman served throughout the whole war and received brevets to Major and Lieutenent Colonel. If the man on the right is Merrill, he was killed at Molino det Rey on 8 September 1847. Hence this image may tentatively be identified to sometime before that date. Both men are dressed in a most casual and non-regulation manner. Chapman wears a Model 1830 army frock coat, whilst his friend wears a 'New England' style overshirt popular in the 1840s. Both wear shirts of ribbed linen material issued to army officers during the war with Mexico. William Dunniway collection.

Major General Winfield Scott was still wearing his Model 1847 dress uniform when he was painted by artist Robert W. Weir in 1856. West Point Museum Collections, United States Military Academy.

Although Brigadier General Henry Storms was not a regular, he was entitled to wear a uniform based on that prescribed for brigadier generals of the Regular Army. Rank is shown by the single star on his epaulette straps, and coat buttons placed in twos, although he has 12 in each row, as oppose to the regulation eight. Note his buff or white gloves, and white-tipped-with-red hat plume. USAMHI/photo by Jim Enos.

service as long as possible. Thus many were not physically fit, hence junior officers commanded in the field. Zachary Taylor was sixty-two in 1846. His brigade commanders and other leading subordinates ranged in years from fifty-five to sixty-six. Their command experience dealing with large bodies of men was also hampered by dispersion at frontier posts.

In comparison, there were about 500 graduates of West Point Military Academy serving in the junior officer corps, mostly as captains and lieutenants. Their tactical knowledge and experience as Indian fighters was to prove invaluable in getting the U.S. Army ready for large-scale war in 1846.

According to Ulysses S. Grant, who served as a young second lieutenant in the 3rd U.S. Infantry, recruits to the Regular Army '... were principally foreigners who had enlisted in our large cities'. About 47 per cent of the regulars under General Zachary Taylor were foreign - with 24 per cent Irish and 10 per cent German. Anti-foreigner riots sweeping the large centres of population in the States during the period

forced many of them into the Army for their own safety. Most went into the ranks of the infantry and artillery regiments. Scotsman George Ballentine, who enlisted in Company I, 1st U.S. Artillery, in 1845, recalled that his company consisted of sixty men, including non-commissioned officers and privates; of these, two were English, four Scottish, seven German, sixteen Americans, and the remainder Irish.[2]

The Dragoon regiments were generally filled with 'natives' who looked down on the infantry and artillery. Samuel E. Chamberlain, who served in Company E, 1st U.S. Dragoons, boasted:

'...I came to the conclusion that the Dragoons were far superior in materials to any other arm of the service. No man of any spirit and ambition would join the "Doughboys" and go afoot, when he could ride a fine horse and wear spurs like a gentleman. In our Squadron were broken down Lawyers, Actors and men

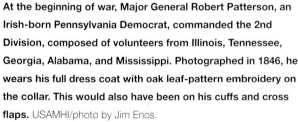

At the beginning of war, Major General Robert Patterson, an Irish-born Pennsylvania Democrat, commanded the 2nd Division, composed of volunteers from Illinois, Tennessee, Georgia, Alabama, and Mississippi. Photographed in 1846, he wears his full dress coat with oak leaf-pattern embroidery on the collar. This would also have been on his cuffs and cross flaps. USAMHI/photo by Jim Enos.

William Jenkins Worth already had an illustrious military service record before entering the Mexican War. He was First Lieutenant, 23rd Infantry in 1813; Colonel, 8th U.S. Infantry in 1838; and Brevet Brigadier General by 1842 for his services as a commander against the Seminole in Florida. Commanding the 2nd Division of Taylor's army in 1846, he was promoted to Brevet Major General after Monterey. He died on 7 May, 1849. Worth wears the regulation undress frock coat for a major general, with dark blue velvet collar and cuffs, and two gold stars on his shoulder straps. USAMHI/photo by Jim Enos.

of the world, Soldiers who had served under Napoleon, Polish Lancers, French Cuirassiers, Hungarian Hussars, Irishmen who had left the Queen's service to swear allegiance to Uncle Sam and wear the blue.'[3]

The uniforms worn by U.S. Regulars during the Mexican War were based on various regulations going back to 1832. During that year the army completely redesigned the uniform worn by all ranks, and restored to use the facing colours worn by the Revolutionary Army. These were buff for generals and staff; white for infantry; and red for artillery. With the exception of some minor changes, these regulations remained in effect until the war's end. All ranks were authorised three sets of uniforms - a dress uniform; a winter fatigue uniform; and a summer fatigue uniform. According to Private Barna Upton, 3rd U.S. Infantry, enlisted men were 'allowed three uniform coats and

caps in the five years [of service], the first, third and fifth years; one fatigue jacket every year; four pair boots and stockings every year; two pair woolen pants; one pair cotton ditto; one cotton jacket; one pair drawers; two flannel shirts [and] two cotton ones in a year; three blankets in the five years.'[4]

Although the winter fatigue uniform was worn by all ranks on campaign during the conflict with Mexico, sufficient evidence exists to suggest that individual officers, and certain units, occasionally wore full dress. Indeed, a return for clothing on hand at a large quartermaster depot established at Veracruz, dated 6 December, 1847, lists 79 dress coats, 81 shoulder straps (worn by enlisted men on dress coats only), and 7 epaulettes (for corporals and sergeants).[5] Hence that

Storming of Chapultepec

The assault on the Castle of Chapultepec, key to the capture of Mexico City, took place on 13 September 1847. The storming party which first scaled the ten feet walls included 250 volunteer officers and men from General William J. Worth's division, under Captain Samuel McKenzie of the 2nd U.S. Artillery; and a similar force from the division of General David E. Twiggs. The personnel in this assault party consisted of Regular Infantry, plus Volunteers, who were supported by members of the U.S. Regiment of Voltigeurs, plus a detachment of U.S. Marines. The plate opposite depicts the moment the first wave of the American assault force reached the top of the Castle parapet. The figure at top left wears the dark blue uniform issued to the Voltigeurs during 1847, whilst others are in sky blue U.S. fatigues. They are armed with Model 1835 flintlocks. Accoutrements consist of M1839 cartridge boxes attached to buff shoulder belts, and M1839 waist belts with oval 'US' plates.

The defending Mexican garrison was composed of members of the Active Militia or National Guard, plus the Cadets of the Military Academy situated within the Castle. The figure at right is a member of the Angostura Battalion, whilst others belong to the San Blas Battalion. Note the officer wears the French-style kepi introduced to the Mexican Army in 1845. The latter unit was wiped out during its defense of Chapultepec. The men are armed with British Tower Muskets, whilst accoutrements have been improvised from various sources, including some captured American equipage. Painting by Richard Hook.

aspect of U.S. Army uniform regulations is also considered in full.

The Schuylkill Arsenal in Philadelphia had been supervising the design and manufacture of clothing for enlisted men for the U.S. Quartermaster's Department since the War of 1812. The outbreak of war with Mexico found this establishment with only the scantiest of clothing supplies on hand. The reduction of clothing appropriations in the years immediately preceding the war had permitted this Department to do no more than provide the annual clothing supply for the small peacetime Army, and to accumulate clothing stocks sufficient to supply that force with only a half year's allowance.

In the spring of 1846, the Arsenal was therefore in no position to furnish clothing to the 45,000 volunteers called into service, and it was not expected to do so. Realising the situation, Congress enacted legislation on 18 June requiring volunteers to furnish their own clothing in return for a commutation allowance. However, the increased number of Regulars in the field still put a tremendous pressure on the clothing establishment at Philadelphia.

The system of procurement and production instituted by Callendar Irvine, Commissary General of Purchases from 1812 until his death in 1841, still functioned in 1846 under the direction of Brigadier General Thomas S. Jesup as Quartermaster General. Cloth was purchased from manufacturers, cut into garments at the Arsenal by government cutters, and distributed to seamstresses and tailors who returned the finished garments to the Arsenal for inspection and approval. The Schuylkill establishment was capable of rapid expansion to meet the demands of war. Increased cloth production, and growing numbers

This unidentified major displays his staff officer designation via the insignia on his forage cap, consisting of the 'U.S.' within a laurel wreath. This device was first proposed for staff officers by Major General Alexander Macomb in 1839. Although not officially approved on that occasion, it was clearly in use soon after. He holds across his lap an ornate staff officer's sword with Phrygian helmet pommel and ivory grip. Michael F. Bremer collection.

Top left.

This unidentified infantry lieutenant wears his full dress coat with white summer trousers. The M1839 infantry officer's plate is clearly visible on his white shoulder belt. He holds a distinctive militia officer's sword. Michael F. Bremer collection.

Top right.

Captain Henry Lewis Little, 7th U.S. Infantry, in his 1832 regulation full dress coat, circa 1847-48. Little had previously behaved bravely as a lieutenant of the 5th Infantry during Taylor's assault on Monterey in September 1846. USAMHI/photo by Jim Enos.

Left.

Brass eagle and M1834 silver metal bugle horn insignia. From artefacts, by Ron Field.

of outworkers ensured delivery of over 85,000 assorted garments per month before the end of the war.

To relieve some of the pressure upon the Schuylkill Arsenal, a branch of the clothing establishment was set up toward the end of 1846 in New York. Run by Daniel Stinson, an experienced clerk who had served in the Quartermaster's Department at that station for nearly 25 years, operations of the New York branch could also be enlarged to meet any emergency. By

Top left and right.

Front and rear of U.S. Infantry dress coat. One of many Mexican-American War period uniforms preserved in the collection of the Smithsonian Institution, it conforms perfectly to the 1847 regulations. Made of fine dark blue cloth, it is lined and trimmed with infantry white. White epaulettes with half-fringe and two loops on the cuffs indicate the rank of private.

Courtesy Smithsonian Institution/photos by Ross M. Kimmel.

Bottom right.

M1839 infantry officers' shoulder belt plate. Measuring about 2.50 x 3.30 inches, it was brass with silver letters and wreath.

From artefacts, by Ron Field.

mid-January 1847, Colonel Henry Stanton, who served as Assistant Quartermaster General while Jesup went on a tour of inspection of the western posts, was certain that the Department was able not only to meet the demands of the regular service, but could now fill requisitions made for destitute volunteers who had quickly been reduced to wearing rags after several months of Mexican service. Despite attempts to carry through Congress a resolution authorizing the issue of clothing to volunteers, it was not until 26 January 1848, a week before the treaty of peace was signed,

Top left.

The embroidered eagle on the shoulder straps of this U.S. infantry officer indicates the rank of colonel, although he wears a single-breasted frock coat instead of the double-breasted one specified for field grade officers. He also wears the regulation silver metal bugle horn insignia on the front of his forage cap. This man has tentatively been identified as **Colonel Jones Mitchell Withers, 9th U.S. Infantry.** Amon Carter Museum, Fort Worth: accession # 81.65.9.

Top right.

Lieutenant Colonel John H. Savage, 11th U.S. Infantry, wears a double-breasted frock coat of the undress uniform, possibly indicating that this image was taken towards the end of the war. Note the two smaller buttons visible on his slash cuff, and a top button missing on his breast. His fatigue cap bears the silver embroidered horn insignia with regimental number '11' in gold within. Courtesy of William J. Schultz, M.D.

Left.

This image of an unidentified major or lieutenant colonel, again wearing a double-breasted frock coat, is one of a few surviving full-length daguerreotypes of the Mexican War period. He holds a variation of the 1815-1830 mounted artillery officer's **sabre.** Courtesy of William J. Schultz, M.D.

Second Lieutenant Parmenas Taylor Turnley, 1st U.S. Infantry, 1847. Turnley wears the single-breasted frock coat, and M1839 forage cap which constituted the standard field dress for U.S. infantry officers in the Mexican War. USAMHI/photo by Jim Enos.

First Lieutenant William Root, 5th U.S. Infantry, was photographed by Meade Brothers, of Albany, New York, in 1845. Root, who resigned his commission on 18 May, 1846, has the collar of his frock coat neatly clasped together. Courtesy of William J. Schultz, M.D.

that the measure was accepted in principle, but money was not finally made available for the scheme until the following July!

If clothing could not be issued directly to the volunteers in 1846, it could, by order of General Taylor, be made available illegally to them for purchase in the field. Despite the law, several thousand suits of clothing, sent to New Orleans and the Veracruz depot in Mexico for the supply of the 'old Army' under Scott, were issued not only to the new Regular regiments raised in1847, but also to volunteers under the command of Generals Patterson, Butler and Marshall. A return for clothing issued to volunteers, dated 6 December 1847, includes 1,290 'Uniform Caps', 1,939 'Wool Jackets', 2,111 'Wool Overalls [trousers]', 1,124 'Cotton Shirts', 2,272 'Flannel Shirts', and 303 'Great Coats'. As a result, Scott complained that his regiments had to remain 'naked', or be supplied with inferior garments procured locally. The manufacture of uniforms in

Mexico was confirmed by the report of Captain James R. Irwin, chief quartermaster with Scott's Army, dated 27 September, 1847: 'I have now a thousand people engaged in making clothing; the quality of the material is not so good as our own, and the price, on the average, is fifty per cent higher. Still... I think the government will lose little, if anything, by purchasing here. I shall be able to fill, in a very short time, every requisition which has been made on me, with clothing, which, though not exactly of our uniform, will be comfortable and good.'[6] Stimulated by over extended supply lines, as much as anything else, Irwin's efforts were unfortunately short lived. By December, 1847, costs far higher than anticipated caused him to recommend that all clothing in future be drawn from the U.S.

At the beginning of the Mexican War, shoes or bootees for the U.S. Army were obtained exclusively by contract. By the summer of 1847, private contractors were failing to keep up with wartime

demand, and the Quartermaster's Department consequently set up its own shoe-making establishment at the Schuylkill depot. By the end of the war, it was turning out 12,000 pairs a month. Tents manufacture was also begun at Schuylkill, and by 1848 its employees were producing over 700 common, wall, and hospital tents per month.

While much of the procurement of clothing, shoes, and tents was centralised at Philadelphia, other items of equipage, such as knapsacks, haversacks, and canteens, were obtained via contract in Pittsburgh and Cincinnati. Some regiments were furnished with 'vulcanized india rubber' bags, or canteens, to carry

Officers' shoulder straps, U.S. Army. The infantry had silver borders, whilst all other branches had gold borders, to their straps. Top left: second lieutenant, plain. Middle left: first lieutenant, single bar the same colour as the border. Bottom left: captain, two bars the same colour as the border. Top centre: major, oak leaves. The leaves were silver where the border was gold, and gold where the border was silver. Centre: lieutenant colonel, oak leaves. The embroidered leaf was the same colour as the border. Bottom centre: colonel, eagle. The embroidery of the eagle was silver where the border was gold, and gold where the border was silver. Generals' straps had gold borders and silver embroidered stars. Top right: brigadier general. Middle right: major general. Bottom right: major general commanding the army.

water. While their use permitted a quiet approach to the enemy, the water carried in them became warm as in tin canteens. Many men threw away their issue canteens, preferring to use a Mexican gourd because water in it remained cool through the hottest day.

Despite regulations, and ample quartermaster

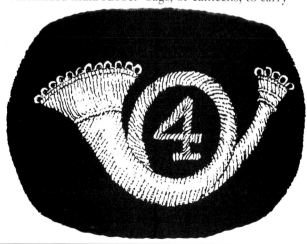

The infantry officer's fatigue cap device, circa 1839, consisted of a silver embroidered horn with number of regiment embroidered in gold within the loop of the horn, all upon a black velvet background. From artefacts, by Ron Field.

Private Sam Hickox was a 23-year-old harness maker from Connecticut when he enlisted 'for the war' in Co. I, 9th U.S. Infantry on 1 April 1847. Later transferring to Co. G, he served in all the major engagements of Scott's army, and was finally discharged in Rhode Island on 21 August 1848. He wears the regulation winter fatigue uniform and holds the Type I version of the M1839 fatigue cap. Courtesy of Herb Peck, Jr.

supply, the American officer on campaign in Mexico tended to wear a great variety of non-regulation, old-issue, and civilian clothing. Lieutenant Napoleon J. T. Dana offered the following uniform descriptions to his wife, dated 8 June 1846, during Taylor's march to Monterey:

'We wear all kinds of uniforms here, each one to his taste, some shirtsleeves, some white, some blue, some fancy jackets and all colours of cottonelle pants, some straw and some Quaker hats, and that is just the way, too, that our fellows went into battle.'

Later, on 13 July 1846, he commented:

'...I have on my old straw hat, those blue-checked pants, made by your dear hands, which are torn in both legs and pretty well worn out, and that loose coat you made which you recollect washed white. I don't

26 U.S. Regular Army

Opposite and top left.

Front and side view of the U.S. Infantry winter fatigue jacket. Made of sky blue kersey to match the trousers with which it was worn, this was the standard garb of regular infantry, and subsequently of many volunteer units, in Mexico. Edged in white lace, it is unlined except for the sleeves, and this example has two functional pockets. There is a rear cuff vent with a single button set high. The infantry accoutrements seen here consist of - a M1839 cartridge box with buff shoulder belt and stamped brass 'eagle' plate; a M1839 buff waist belt, with circa 1841 bayonet scabbard in a buff frog; this scabbard was introduced to accommodate the longer socket bayonet of the M1835/40 flintlock or the M1842 percussion musket. Courtesy Smithsonian Institution/photos by Ross M. Kimmel.

An unidentified soldier in infantry uniform. Although he wears a Type I M1839 fatigue cap, his jacket departs from regulations, being minus shoulder straps and breast pockets. This may indicate he belonged to a state volunteer regiment. Courtesy of William Schultz, M.D.

think there is much danger of a ranchero shooting me for an officer of high rank. My trimmings don't show much. Both pairs of those check pants I have worn pretty well out.'

This same officer also made further passing references to his 'purple-coloured shirt', and 'three hickory shirts', which he believed were 'first rate for marching in'.[7] A 'hickory shirt' was made of a heavy twilled cotton with thin blue stripes or checks, and was so called because of its durability.

Albert G. Brackett, a surgeon with Lane's brigade in central Mexico, recalled that, when not on duty:

'I threw Uncle Sam's blue uniform frock-coat, and my handsome foraging cap, in the corner of my tent, and enjoyed the luxury of a coarse pair of tow pantaloons, a red calico shirt, and a very high-crowned and broad brimmed Mexican hat.'[8]

Enlisted men did not have the discretion, or the funds, to indulge themselves with quite so much non-regulation clothing. As Taylor's army marched deeper into the highlands of northern Mexico, the appearance of his men began to show the effects of campaign life. John R. Kenly, captain of Company E, Battalion of Baltimore and Washington Volunteers, remarked shortly after the capture of Monterey:

'Our men begin to need clothing, particularly shoes; the long marches have been very destructive to the latter; and many ... have made sandals from raw hide, which look right well; on parade, there are a good many without jackets, yet they look soldier-like and trim with their cross- and waist-belts'.[9]

On 31 March 1847, Quartermaster General Jesup wrote of Scott's army that several thousand men were reportedly bare-footed in Veracruz. The same army, whilst marching to the interior, was reported to be shabby, with their sky blue uniforms liberally patched with red flannel.[10]

To compensate for such shortages, the Quartermaster Department established clothing stations where worn-out gear could be exchanged for new. Wool jackets and overalls, forage caps, flannel shirts and drawers, wool stockings, bootees, great coats, cotton shirts and blankets, were issued to Regulars at the Camargo depot in October, 1846. The fact that captured Mexican clothing was distributed, particularly to volunteers, at Jalapa on 1 May, 1847,

Left.
This unidentified infantryman is presumably a noncommissioned officer. Although chevrons are absent from his sleeves, he holds a M1840 NCO's sword. Courtesy of William Schultz, M.D.

Bottom.
Pattern-of-1847 chevrons for non-commissioned officers to be worn on fatigue jackets. Top left: corporal. Top centre: sergeant. Top right: first sergeant. Bottom left: Quartermaster sergeant. Bottom right: sergeant major.

Top left and right.

Reconstruction: (*front and rear views*) U.S. regular sergeant in full marching order. Rank is indicated by white chevrons and trouser stripes, red worsted sash, and M1840 NCO's sword suspended from a whitened buff leather shoulder belt. His weapon is the M1816 flintlock; leather accoutrements are M1839. On his left hip are the white cotton haversack, and grey-painted metal canteen with leather sling. Little is known about period knapsacks, though the regulation U.S. type is believed to have been a double-leaf pattern of black-painted canvas, as shown here; the overcoat was carried inside the knapsack and the blanket rolled on top. Photos by Ross M. Kimmel.

illustrates the serious nature of the supply situation on occasions.[11]

A quite different sort of clothing problem presented itself after the army had occupied Mexico City in September 1847. Possibly some men were trying to impress the natives, particularly the dark haired señoritas of the capital, but Scott's inspector general, Ethan Allen Hitchcock, remained unimpressed, reporting that:

'... the Army dress appears to be continually diverging from the prescribed pattern. Some latitude has been rendered necessary from the absence of proper materials in this country, particulary in the colors of cloth, but this affords no excuse for officers, not entitled to them, wearing gold and silver lace on their pantaloons and there is no reason why the prescribed shoulder insignia of rank should be departed from. The evil in this latter case has found its way to non-commissioned officers & particularly to hospital stewards some of whom are wearing lace upon their shoulders & adopting fancy dress of all kinds.'[12]

Hitchcock went on to complain that some Army campfollowers, such as teamsters and wagon masters, were so fancifully dressed as to be hardly distinguishable from officers.

GENERALS AND STAFF OFFICERS

For full dress, the Major General commanding the Army was prescribed a dark blue, double-breasted tail coat, with two rows of eight equally-spaced buttons. The distance between the rows was four inches at the top and three at the bottom. The stand-up collar, cuffs, facings, and linings, were of buff cloth or cassimere. The buff collar, which came up to just below the chin, met and was hooked together at the front. The buff parallel cuffs were two and a half inches deep, and fastened by three small buttons at the

Top left and right.

Reconstruction: (*front and rear views*) U.S. regular infantryman in overcoat, with cap flap down over collar. Photos by Ross M. Kimmel.

under seam. The coat tails, which reached to the bend in the knee, bore pointed cross flaps with four buttons equally distributed, and buff turn-backs fastened by small buff patches bearing a gold embroidered star.

At the option of the General, the collar, cuffs, and cross flaps, could be embroidered with an oak leaf pattern, in which case they were to be the same colour as the coat. Epaulettes were gold, with a solid crescent and dead and bright gold bullion fringe, with three silver embroidered stars placed in a row on the strap.

Headgear consisted of a black chapeau bras, or cocked hat, minus binding, with black ribbons on the two front sides, and decorated with a black silk cockade, over an eleven inch-long gold loop, ornamented with a silver spread eagle, and a drooping, yellow swan feather plume. Winter trousers were dark blue cloth, with a buff or gold lace seam stripe. Summer trousers were plain white linen or cotton.

The sword was straight with a gilt hilt, silver grip, and a brass or steel scabbard. The sword belt, which was worn over the coat, was of Russian leather with

three stripes of gold embroidery. The gilt belt plate had the letters 'US' with a sprig of laurel leaf either side in silver. The waist sash was buff silk net, with silk bullion ends. At the option of the General, it could also be made of silk and gold mixed. Gloves were either buff or white.

For undress, the Major General commanding the Army wore the same style of coat as prescribed for full dress, minus buff facings, and with plain skirt minus turnbacks. Trousers were dark blue minus seam stripes. Headgear consisted of a dark blue Model 1839 forage cap. Remaining detail was the same as for full dress.

All other major generals wore the same dress and undress uniform as the major general commanding the army, excepting that the nine buttons in each row on the breast of the coat were placed in threes; only two stars graced the epaulette straps; and the hat plume was white topped with black. A brigadier general wore the same dress and undress uniform as a major

Opposite top and bottom.

A U.S. Model 1842 percussion rifle used in the Mexican-American War. (*detail of same*) The stamp on the lock reveals that this particular weapon was made by N. Whitner of New Haven, Connecticut, in 1844. North Carolina Museum of History.

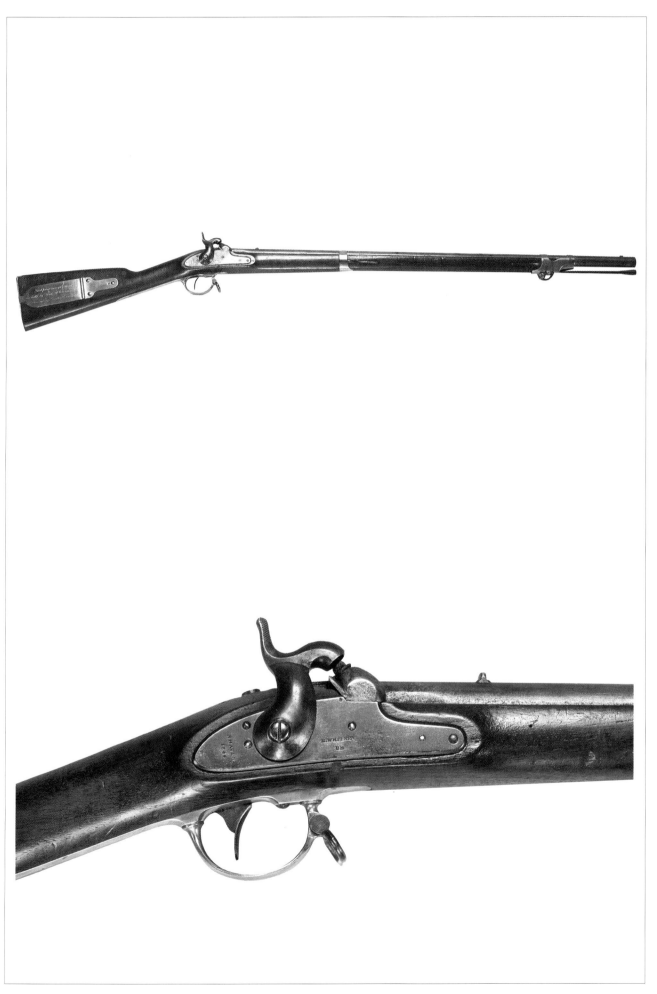

32 U.S. Regular Army

general, excepting that the coat had eight buttons placed by twos in each row on the breast; only one star appeared on the epaulette strap; and the plume was white topped with red. General officers could also wear a dark blue frock coat with two rows of buttons, placed according to rank, with stand-up dark blue velvet collar and cuffs.

For full dress, officers of the general staff wore tail coats fastened by a single row of either eight or ten buttons, depending on length of waist; a dark blue stand-up collar with a four-inch long buff patch either side; and plain blue cuffs. Their chapeau bras bore plumes corresponding to the different departments of staff, e.g. adjutant-general - white; inspector-general - green; quartermaster - light blue; subsistence - white topped with light blue; aides-de-camp - same as worn by their Generals, except that they were an inch shorter.

Undress worn by officers of the general staff consisted of a plain dark blue tail coat and trousers. Plain dark blue frock coats with a single row of eight buttons were also prescribed for general officers and staff on campaign duty. Rank was indicated by shoulder straps, with gold embroidered edging around a dark blue background, on which were three silver stars for the major general commanding the army; two stars for a major general; and one for a brigadier general. The cloak worn by General and Staff Officers was dark blue lined with either buff or blue. All buttons for generals and staff were gilt and convex, with spread eagle and stars.

The full dress for generals and staff officers was seldom worn on campaign or in action during the Mexican War. Even Major General Winfield Scott, nick-named 'Old Fuss and Feathers', was not known for over dressing in the Mexican heat. An eyewitness painting depicts him reviewing troops wearing a

Model 1839 forage caps type I, front and side views, with neck flap up. type II, characterised by shallower angle of visor, and neck flap down. Caps were made of dark blue woollen cloth with black patent leather visor and chin strap. The wide crown was made stiff and puffed out with horsehair wadding, which was often removed in order to achieve a more rakish appearance. Courtesy Smithsonian Institution/photos by Ross M. Kimmel.

Opposite top and bottom.
A 'stand' of colours. According to regulations, and also by tradition, a U.S. regiment of infantry had two colours: a national colour which was after 1841 the stars and stripes, and a regimental colour which bore the embroidered arms of the United States or some other device. Both flags had silken fields and measured 6 feet on the staff by 6 feet 6 inches on the fly. (*above*) The national colour of the 10th Regiment U.S. Infantry. The stars were silver, in line with branch colour. (*below*) The regimental colour of the 6th Regiment U.S. Infantry. The names of ten Mexican War battles were painted on its dark blue folds. Strangely this unit was not present at Palo Alto or Resaca de la Palma! It is not certain when these 'battle honours' were added, or when the practice began. West Point Museum.

broad-brimmed slouch hat with undress tailcoat and pants. A written account describes him alighting from a coach 'with his blue forage cap in his hand'.[13]

Regarding other generals, a regular captain of infantry near Saltillo described the following scene on Christmas Eve 1846:

'Winding down a hill, our column was halted to let a troop of horse pass. Do you see, at their head, a plain-looking gentleman, mounted upon a brown horse, having upon his head, a Mexican sombrero, dressed in a brown, olive-coloured, loose frock coat, gray pants, wool socks and shoes; beneath the frock appears the scabbard of a sword... Reader, do you know who this plain-looking gentleman is? No! It is Major General Zachary Taylor.'[14]

A Tennessee volunteer mounted rifleman remembered that he never once saw Taylor, who was nick-named 'Old Rough and Ready', with 'his uniform on, for he was commonly dressed in citizen's clothing of brown color'.[15] Others remember him wearing full dress at Point Isabel on 11 May 1846 to confer with one of 'the dandies of the naval service', Commodore David Conner. On this occasion, the latter deliberately dressed down in deference to Taylor's aversion to uniforms! In the comic opera situation which ensued, apologies were exchanged before the two men agreed on a joint operation to cross the Rio Grande.

A few other examples exist of officers wearing full dress in Mexico. A volunteer officer in Puebla described the arrival of Brigadier General of Volunteers Thomas F. Marshall on 10 January 1848:

'General Marshall rode through the streets of Puebla in full uniform, to the no small astonishment of a gaping crowd of Mexicans who followed him around the city, thinking, no doubt, that he was in fact the supreme head of the Americans. Marshall

A U.S.-issue haversack - this style dates as far back as 1806, and was still in use during the Civil War. Made of white cotton, it is 11½ in. high and 14in. wide; the strap is nearly 30in. long, and the haversack would ride well up under the wearer's left arm. Les Jensen collection.

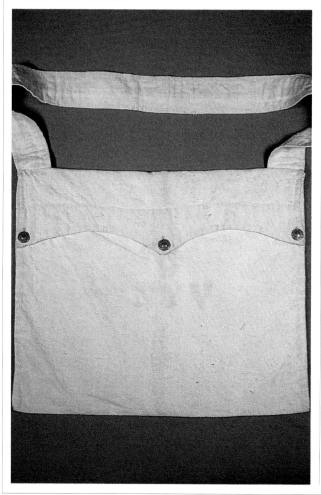

was the only man I ever saw in Mexico, in full uniform, by which I mean cocked-hat, feathers and epaulettes.'[16]

U.S. REGULAR INFANTRY

In 1845 the U.S. Regular Infantry was composed of the 1st through 8th Infantry regiments, all of which were heavily involved throughout the entire conflict. These were supplemented on 11 February 1847 with the 9th through 16th regiments, which saw extensive action under Scott in central Mexico. The field and staff of each of these regiments consisted of a colonel, a lieutenant-colonel, a major, an adjutant with the rank of lieutenant, a sergeant-major, a quartermaster-sergeant and two principal musicians. During the war, Taylor added the post of quartermaster, also ranked as a lieutenant. Surgeons were either from the Medical Corps or were hired civilians.

Each regiment consisted of ten companies. According to Scott's *Infantry Tactics* published in 1840, two of these were denominated flank companies and the remaining eight were battalion companies. One of the flank units was a grenadier company, being posted on parade, or in battle, at the right of the battalion; the other was a rifle company, or light infantry, and was placed on the left. Each company had a captain, a 1st lieutenant, two 2nd lieutenants, four sergeants, four corporals, two musicians, and 100 privates (after 19 May 1846). One man per company was designated a pioneer, and a corporal commanded the regimental pioneer section. Each company was also authorised to be accompanied by three laundresses.

Each regiment had a full band which lifted the spirits of the men with stirring martial music in camp and on the march, but served as stretcher-bearers during battle.

Regimental pride was evident throughout the Regular Army. Private Barna Upton wrote from his camp in New York, 'The Third Regiment is acknowledged to be the best disciplined regiment in the United States... Every finger and toe and joint must be placed exactly according to custom, and I rather conclude that I can come it equal to the old buck'.[17] On arrival in Mexico during September 1846, John R. Kenly, of the Baltimore Volunteer Battalion, watched Worth's Division of Regulars leave camp and remarked: '...that division of regular troops presented an appearance which wil never be effaced from my mind. It was thoroughly military and soldierlike; they looked so clean, their arms and accoutrements in such good order, that all my enthusiasm for soldiers was greatly gratified.'[18]

Officers' full dress and fatigue uniform

The dress uniform for infantry officers consisted of a dark blue tail coat, edged with white piping, with two rows of ten equally-spaced silver buttons; a white-edged standing collar with two white lace loops and buttons either side; white kerseymere turnbacks and skirt lining; and silver embroidered bugle skirt ornament. Rank was indicated on epaulettes as follows - a colonel wore silver straps with a gold eagle on each strap, silver crescent, and a half-inch silver bullion fringe, 3½ inches long. A lieutenant-colonel's was the same, minus eagles. Majors wore gold straps with silver crescent and silver bullion fringe. Captains' epaulettes had a quarter-inch silver bullion fringe, 2½ inch long. Lieutenants' epaulettes were the same, with eighth-inch bullion fringe. The regimental number was displayed in gold metal (silver for a major) in a circle in the centre of the crescent on the straps. Rank was also indicated by the number of silver loops, or false lace button holes with small silver buttons, on the slashed sleeve flap, as follows - four for field officers; three for captains; two for subalterns.

The infantry officer's dress cap was of 'black beaver, seven and a half inches deep, with lackered [sic] sunk tip seven and a half inches diameter, with a band of black patent leather to encircle the bottom...' The peak and chin strap were also of black patent leather. This was ornamented on the front with M1834 silver metal bugle horn, over which was the regimental number, and a gilt spread eagle. The whole was surmounted by a white cock-feathers plume, falling from an eight-inch upright stem with a gilt socket.

Winter trousers were sky-blue wool with one and a half inch wide white seam stripes, whilst summer trousers were white linen or cotton, without seam stripes. Waist belts were white leather, two inches wide, with a sliding frog, and fastened in front with an oval clasp. Waist sashes were crimson silk net, with silk bullion fringe ends. Shoulder-belts were two and a half inches wide with a M1839 breast plate.

For fatigue duty, infantry officers were prescribed a dark blue, single-breasted frock coat, with 'not less than eight nor more than ten (depending on the size of the officer) large silver regimental buttons down the front at equal distances'. Towards the end of 1847, officers above company grade were authorised to wear double-breasted coats. Plain slash cuffs were fastened by two small silver buttons. The low stand up collar was plain, whilst two large buttons were attached to each pocket in the skirts, one at the hip and the other at the fold at the bottom of the pocket. The coat lining was blue.

This dress cap, worn by Lieutenant D. E. Hale, 1st U.S. Artillery, bears the regulation cross cannon insignia and eagle, but has an enlisted man's red worsted pompon. West Point Museum Collections, United States Military Academy.

Rank was indicated on frock coats by shoulder straps, with a silver embroidered edging around a dark blue background. A colonel had a large gold eagle; a lieutenant colonel, a silver oak leaf at each end; a major, gold oak leave at each end; a captain, two gold bars at each end; a first lieutenant, a single gold bar at each end; and a second lieutenant, plain straps.

Infantry officers' fatigue headgear consisted of the M1839 forage cap made of dark blue cloth, with patent leather fittings. Type I of this cap had an almost vertically-angled visor, whilst that on Type II was set at a shallower angle. Infantry buttons for all ranks, from 1827 until 1851, were of convex white metal with a spread eagle and shield bearing the letter 'I'.

NCOs, Musicians, and Privates - full dress

For full dress, the sergeant-major wore the same pattern of coat and trim, and cap as prescribed for field officers, trimmed with white worsted. Trousers were also sky blue, with one and a half inch-wide white seam stripes. Epaulettes were the same as for junior officers, trimmed with white worsted fringe. The plume in the cap was a twelve inch white upright hackle. An aiguillette of white wosted with silver tags was worn on the left shoulder. A red worsted sash was worn under a white buff sword belt supporting a short sword, and secured by a two-piece 'US' plate. The chief infantry musician wore the same pattern of full dress uniform as the sergeant major, except that the coat was red with white lining and turnbacks.

Infantry sergeants wore a single-breasted dark blue tail coat with one row of nine buttons, with three buttons and loops on the sleeves. Epaulettes were of white worsted. The First Sergeant wore a red worsted waist sash. Trousers were the same as for the sergeant major. The white cap plume was shorter than that for the sergeant major, being only eight inches in height.

Infantry corporals wore the same pattern uniform as sergeants, except that there were only two buttons and loops on each sleeve, and the sky blue trousers were minus seam stripes. Privates were issued the same as corporals, except that instead of epaulettes they wore a white strap with a pad and worsted half-fringe on each shoulder.

NCOs, Musicians, and Privates -winter campaign or fatigue uniform

Winter campaign or fatigue duty uniforms for infantry N.C.O.s and privates consisted, after 1839, of a sky blue kersey shell jacket with a single row of nine white metal 'eagle-I' buttons. The front and rear of this jacket was to 'come down in a peak'. The stand-up collar was trimmed with white lace in the same style as the dress coat. The shoulder straps were also edged with white lace and secured at the base of the collar with a small button. Cuffs had a rear vent with a single small button set high. Two functional exterior side pockets were attached to some garments. These jackets were worn with the sky blue full dress pants. Infantry fatigue headgear was the same as that worn by officers, with the addition of a neck flap. All U.S. Regular Infantry serving in the conflict with Mexico wore this fatigue uniform pattern. Many of the volunteer regiments were also issued with it once their original state-issue had worn out.

Summer fatigues consisted of white cotton jackets and trousers, worn with the dark blue cap. There is little evidence that this uniform was worn in Mexico. A return of clothing issued to volunteers at Veracruz dated 6 December 1847 shows the presence of enough suits of white cotton to outfit 6-7,000 men, although none seem to have been issued, probably due to cold night time desert temperatures in the Mexican highlands.[19]

As a badge of distinction when in campaign or fatigue dress, N.C.O.s wore white lace, upward-pointing chevrons on both sleeves as follows: sergeant-major, three bars and an arc; quartermaster sergeant, three bars and a tie; First Sergeant, three bars and a lozenge; sergeant, three bars; corporal, two bars. When on campaign or fatigue duty, the First Sergeant wore a red worsted sash with this uniform.

Infantry Arms and Equipage

At the beginning of the war, the flintlock musket was still the standard weapon of the U.S. infantryman, though its effective range was only about one hundred yards, and it was unreliable when flint and powder became wet. No less than nine models of smoothbore flintlocks were produced after 1800. Most of these were used in Mexico - the most popular being the Model of 1822, which was made in large quantities by both Springfield and Harper's Ferry arsenals. These weapons were both smoothbore and rifled, and made in various calibres, although the .69 calibre was the most widely accepted. Also popular was the .53 calibre Model 1819, Hall breech-loading flintlock rifle.

The percussion system of ignition came into the U.S. in 1841, and resulted in the Model 1842 percussion musket, also known as the Mississippi rifle,

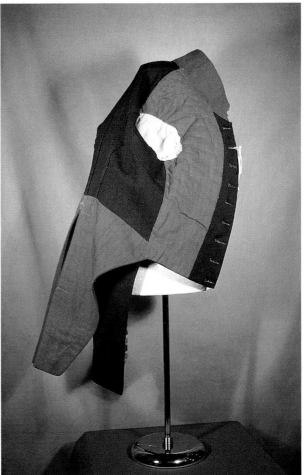

Opposite, top left and right.

Front, rear and interior of a dress coat of the U.S. Artillery. This was identical to the infantry coat apart from being trimmed with red, and partially lined with red kerseymere. Note the padding in the interior view. Courtesy Smithsonian Institution/ photos by Ross M. Kimmel.

Kentucky rifle, Harper's Ferry Yager, and the Windsor rifle. A .54 calibre weapon, it was originally designed to fire a half ounce spherical lead ball. Although the watertight percussion cap used overcame problems caused by dampness, this weapon was unpopular with many due to the unreliable supply of percussion caps. Despite the preference for flintlocks, the percussion musket did see widespread use in both Regular and volunteer American forces. Some 38,000 muskets and 10,000 calibre .54 rifles were issued during the war.

U.S. REGULAR ARTILLERY

Prior to 1842 this branch of service, which consisted of the 1st, 2nd, 3rd, and 4th Artillery Regiments, was mostly confined to garrison duty in coastal fortifications where occasional instruction in the use of heavy guns was received. During the different Indian wars, detachments were often ordered into the field as infantry, a duty not designed to increase their proficiency as artillerists.

During the 1830s it was realised that the U.S. Artillery was far behind the nations of Europe in the use of 'flying' or light artillery, in which each man had his own mount. In 1838 to remedy this, Secretary of War Joel R. Poinsett converted Company C, 3rd U.S. Artillery, commanded by Bvt. Major Samuel Ringgold, into a light battery. The following year Poinsett established a 'camp of instruction' near Trenton, New Jersey, where Ringgold's battery could train and manoeuvre alongside dragoon and infantry units. The experiment was so successful that Congress duly authorised three more light batteries, one from each of the other three Artillery Regiments. These consisted of Captain Francis Taylor's Company K, 1st Regiment; Captain James Duncan's Company A, 2nd Artillery; and Captain John M. Washington's Company B, 4th Artillery. These batteries, and others formed subsequently, did not operate as pure 'flying' artillery. Although the officers, NCOs and musicians, plus the drivers, were mounted, the other enlisted men walked or, for rapid movement over short distances, rode the limbers and caissons.

These four batteries served apart from their parent units, and subsequently came to be addressed in reports and orders by their commanders' names rather

38 U.S. Regular Army

than by regimental and company designations.

The opening battles of the war with Mexico quickly established these units as a military elite combining the manoeuvrability of cavalry with a devastating firepower and accuracy. Subsequently, on 3 March 1847 Congress authorised the formation of a second light artillery company in each artillery regiment. However, commanders in the field already recognised the need for more light artillery, and had activated additional batteries from whatever units, guns, horses and equipment were available. Captain Braxton Bragg's Light Battery (Company E, 3rd Artillery) was formed in Texas in 1845. Captain Lucian B. Webster's Battery (Company A, 1st Artillery) was

organised shortly thereafter. General Scott established three batteries. That under Captain Edward J. Steptoe was formed at Veracruz, apparently from several companies of the 3rd Artillery; Captain John B. Magruder's Battery (Company I, 1st Artillery) served Mexican cannon captured at Cerro Gordo; Captain Simon H. Drum's Battery (Company G, 4th Artillery) was formed around two American 6-pounders 'lost without dishonour' by Washington's Battery at Buena Vista. Other detachments or companies, including ordnance men and Voltigeurs, were used as artillery on various occasions.

The number of field guns in these batteries varied from four to eight. The pieces used included bronze Model 1840 6-pounder guns and 12-pounder howitzers, which had the same carriages. As 'flying' artillery, Ringgold had four new 6-pounder guns. Washington added two captured Mexican 4-pounders to his four 6-pounder guns and two 12-pounder howitzers. Steptoe's Battery served 12-pounder guns

Thomas J. Jackson entered the war as First Lieutenant of Company I, 1st U.S. Artillery. Subsequently commanded by Captain John B. Magruder, this unit was converted to a light battery in June 1847. His rock steady nerve during the assault on Chapultepec Castle and Mexico City gained him the rank of major that year. Fourteen years later on the plains of Manassas, he would earn the nickname 'Stonewall' as his brigade of Virginians halted Federal forces sweeping back the Confederate left flank at Bull Run. Jackson wears his dark blue frock coat, prescribed for fatigue duty, with collar rolled down. His rank is indicated by the single bar at either end of his shoulder straps. USAMHI/photo by Jim Enos.

Captain John Macrae Washington, a kinsman of the first President, commanded Company B, 4th U.S. Artillery, which was one of three units converted into a light battery in 1839. Washington's Battery marched with General Wool from San Antonio to Saltillo, and formed part of Taylor's army at Buena Vista, where it directed effective fire against Santa Anna's failed assault on the American left flank. Washington appears to be wearing the 'Ringgold'-pattern dress coat, with solid red collar and cuffs underneath the gold lace. The rank of captain is signified by three gold loops on the cuffs and the thickness of strands on his epaulette fringe. He holds a Model 1840 light artillery sabre with Phrygian helmet pommel and single branch guard. Amon Carter Museum, Fort Worth: accession # 81.65.4.

and 24-pounder howitzers. Although heavier and slower than a light battery, this unit successfully provided field support for infantry. Webster's had the heaviest guns to accompany Taylor south of the Rio Grande. His two 24-pounders and one 10-inch mortar were consequently treated as siege artillery.

The remaining companies of the four Artillery Regiments either served as light infantry, or manned heavy siege guns within the artillery train. An artillery infantry battalion, commanded by Lieutenant Colonel Thomas Childs, was established in Worth's 2nd Division of Taylor's army during 1846. By March

1847, a battalion from each artillery regiment served as light infantry in Scott's army.

Officers' full dress and fatigue uniform

The full dress uniform for officers within the four artillery regiments was essentially the same as that worn by the infantry, with certain differences in branch service trim colour. All artillery officers' epaulette straps were gold lace, as were collar and cuff lace. The dark blue coat collar was edged with red. The slashed flaps on the sleeves and skirt were also edged with red on the ends and indented edge. Coat turnbacks and skirt linings were red kerseymere. A gold-embroidered 'shell and flame' insignia decorated the bottom of the coat skirt. All artillery buttons were gilt, convex, and displayed a spread eagle with shield bearing the letter A.

The artillery officer's dress cap was the same pattern as that worn by infantry, with brass cross cannon insignia in lieu of the bugle horn. The plume consisted of red cock feathers. A blue cloak with scarlet *shalloon* or light woollen lining, and fastened with 'a clasp ornament, gilt eagle, with chain', was also prescribed for winter dress. Winter trousers were sky-blue, with one and a half inch wide red stripe down the outer seam. Plain white linen or cotton pants were worn in the summer. Shoulder and waist belts, and waist sashes were the same as for infantry. Artillery officers' wore the same pattern frock coat and cap as infantry for fatigue wear.

Artillery NCOs, Musicians, and Privates - full dress

The sergeant-major wore the same full dress uniform as established for field officers, except that worsted replaced gold binding and lace on collar and epaulette straps. The cap plume was a twelve inch long upright red hackle. A yellow worsted aiguillette with gilt tags graced his left shoulder. The quartermaster-sergeant wore the same uniform except the plume, which was light blue. The chief musician and bandsmen wore the same pattern of red coat, lined with white, as his infantry counterpart, with a white cap plume.

Artillery sergeants' and corporals' frock coats and rank distinction were the same as that for infantry N.C.O.s. Winter trouser seam stripes were red. Artillery privates wore yellow shoulder straps with pad and worsted half-fringe. Cap pompons were red worsted and eight inches long.

N.C.O.s and enlisted men's winter campaign or fatigue uniform

Foot artillery N.C.O.s and enlisted men wore a fatigue uniform very similar that of infantry. Scotsman George Ballentine was issued a 'forage cap, leather stock, jacket, and trousers of coarse blue cloth, two cotton shirts, two pairs of socks, one pair of half boots, a blanket, a great-coat, a knapsack, and a havresack [sic]' when he enlisted in Co. I, 1st U.S. Artillery in 1845. This jacket would have been sky blue trimmed on collar and shoulder straps with yellow worsted braid. N.C.O.s' chevrons were also yellow. Although regulations prescribed plain sky blue trousers for artillery privates, evidence suggests that enlisted men

Winter fatigue jacket, sergeant, U.S. Artillery: a 'sky blue' jacket identical to the infantry model, except for yellow lace and buttons. The downward-pointing cuffs are post-Mexican War additions. Curiously, instead of the artillery button, this garment bears the yellow metal button of the Ordnance Department, which possibly indicates that Ordnance men were also issued artillery fatigue wear. Courtesy Smithsonian Institution/photos by Ross M. Kimmel.

of foot artillery companies did not conform to this rule. Maryland volunteer John R. Kenly described the Artillery Battalion under Lieutenant Colonel Childs at Monterey as 'the red-legged infantry' due to the broad red stripe running down the seams of their blue pantaloons.[20] The paintings of James Walker indicate that the artillery also wore non-regulation red bands around their dark blue fatigue caps. This feature would probably have required the removal of ear flaps.

Foot artillery were provided with muskets and cartridge boxes identical to those issued to infantry. However, in place of bayonets they were armed with the M1834 foot artillery sword which was a two-edged thrusting weapon with an all-brass hilt, copied from the French M1831 infantry sidearm. These were carried in a black leather scabbard suspended from a white leather frog on a white buff leather waist belt.

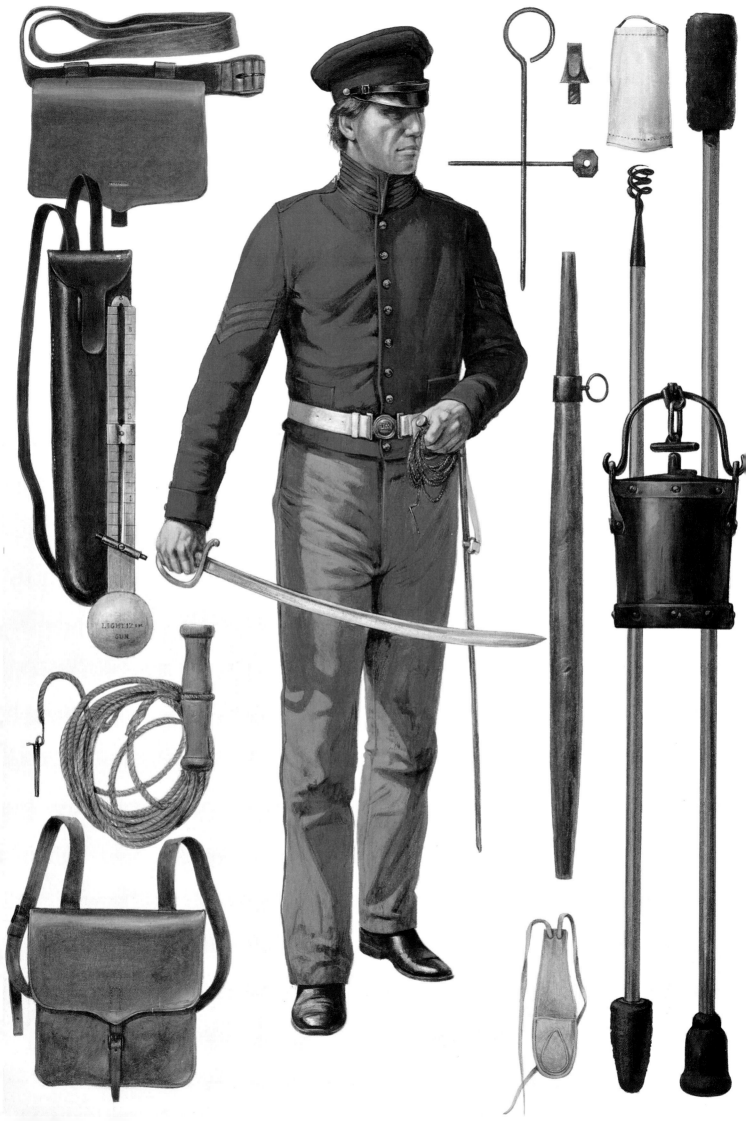

U.S. Regular Artilleryman from Ringgold's Battery

Light, or 'flying', artillery was the decisive branch of the U.S. Regular Army during the conflict with Mexico, and played a particularly prominent role at the battles of Palo Alto and Resaca de la Palma. The plate opposite features a light artilleryman wearing the distinctive fatigue uniform issued to Major Samuel Ringgold's Battery in 1838. His dark blue woollen cloth fatigue jacket is trimmed around the collar with red worsted braid and has two red loops with yellow metal buttons. Shoulder straps were also edged with red. Non-commissioned officer's rank is indicated by red chevrons with point down. His Model 1839 Type 1 fatigue cap is embellished with non-regulation red band. Sky blue trousers with 1½ inch wide red seam stripes are those worn with full dress. He is carrying a Model 1840 Light Artillery sabre, whilst around his waist is fastened a white buff leather sword belt secured by a M1836 two piece plate with letters 'US' on the centre piece.

The surrounding tools and equipage consist of: (top right) a vent pick (or priming wire); vent clearing punch; brass fuse plug to hold fuses in shells; and sponge cover. (right) Sponge and rammer; and worm-and-brush for cleaning the gun barrel; trail handspike; and water bucket and sponge. (bottom right) Leather finger stall. (bottom left) Gunner's haversack used to carry rounds; and lanyard and friction primer for firing gun. (left) Pendulum hausse and case, used to aim the gun. (top left) Gunner's pouch and belt. Painting by Richard Hook.

Each regiment of Regular Artillery carried a stand of colours consisting of a national colour and a regimental colour. The former resembled that of the infantry except its stars and regimental designation were embroidered in gold, and its tassles were red and yellow silk, intermixed. The national colour had a yellow field of the same size, with the same fringe, cords, and tassles. It bore in the centre two golden crossed cannon with a red scroll above bearing the letters 'U.S.' and another below bearing the regimental designation, e.g. 'THIRD / REGIMENT / ARTILLERY'. All edging, lettering, and ornamentation was gold embroidered.

Light Artillery dress and fatigue uniforms

The light artillery companies wore a totally different dress uniform and fatigue jacket to other Regular Artillery units, although these distinctions were never reflected in uniform regulations. In 1838, as a stimulus to both unit morale and public interest, Ringgold's newly-established battery of 'flying' artillery received uniforms modelled on those of the dragoons. Dress coats were dark blue satinette with a double row of nine gilt buttons, and a skirt 'three-quarters' in length. The standing collar was solid red and edged with strong yellow (almost orange) braid, with two yellow loops and buttons. Pointed cuffs, lining and turnbacks were also solid red and edged with yellow. There were three false buttonholes on each coat tail. Winter trousers were sky blue, with double red stripes for officers and NCOs, and single stripes for enlisted men. Dress hats, also known as the 'Ringgold cap', were patterned after those worn by the dragoons (for which see U.S. Dragoons). That worn by Ringgold's unit had in front a brass eagle over cross cannon and the numeral '3', the latter referring to regimental

Captain Lucian Bonaparte Webster commanded Company A, 1st U.S. Artillery, which was given charge of a heavy battery in 1846. A 10-inch mortar manned by this unit played havoc on the Mexican garrison of Monterey during September of that year. Webster may also be wearing the 'Ringgold'-pattern coat, although his dress cap with red cock feather plume is that prescribed for foot artillery officers. His white buff leather sword belt is fastened by a Model 1839 plate bearing an eagle and shield. USAMHI/photo by Jim Enos.

designation. This was topped with a scarlet horsehair plume. Officers' caps bore a gold cordon and cap line, whilst those of enlisted men were scarlet. Officers wore gold epaulettes; sergeants' wore scarlet worsted; corporals and privates had scarlet shoulder knots. Schabraques were dark blue, trimmed with scarlet.

Instead of the customary 'reversed colours', buglers' scarlets coats had white cuffs, collars, linings and turnbacks, all laced with yellow. Epaulettes were apparently white. Bugle cords may have been either white or scarlet.[21]

This dress uniform seems to have been issued to at least the other three original light batteries. A painting by Sam Chamberlain shows Washington's Battery in similar garb, with red-plumed caps and dark blue coats faced with red.[22]

Fatigue jackets originally issued to Ringgold's Battery were of dark blue woolen cloth, with red worsted braid around collar, and two red loops with yellow metal buttons. Shoulder straps were also edged with red braid. These were presumably worn with dark forage caps, and full dress trousers. This is the uniform most likely worn in combat by Ringgold's unit, and possibly the other three batteries, during the first few months of war service, although

Top left and right and opposite.

Reconstruction: Enlisted man of the Regular foot artillery, 1847 (front, left and right views). He wears the non-regulation red band around his forage cap. His trouser also have a broad red seam stripe normally reserved for officers and NCOs. He has discarded his fatigue jacket, and wears an issue cotton shirt. His M1816 musket and M1839 cartridge box are identical to the infantry issue. In place of a bayonet he has the M1834 foot artillery sword placed in a frog on his whitened buff waist belt. In the background is a U.S. M1841 6-pounder gun, a light mobile field piece used so effectively during the war. Photo by Ross M. Kimmel.

Chamberlain's artwork indicates that full dress may have been worn by at least one battery on occasions.

By July 1846, these uniforms were wearing out. Captain Randolph Ridgely, who took command of Co. C, 3rd U.S. Artillery, after the death of Ringgold at Palo Alto, wrote on the 3rd of that month: 'the company at the present time is much in want of clothing, and as the clothing allowed horse artillery is different to any worn by other corps, there can not be any obtained except from the Clothing Bureau'.[23] To judge from the paintings of Scott's army by Carl Nebel and James Walker, some light batteries were in undress uniform similar to that worn by the foot

artillery by 1847. Red flannel shirts were also common wear.

U.S. DRAGOONS

There were two dragoon regiments of ten companies each on the eve of war. These regiments were well mounted, and thoroughly trained to fight on foot or on horse-back. The companies of these regiments had never served all together, but were usually assigned to duty in ones, twos or threes among the posts that comprised America's frontier defense line. The first U.S. Regiment of Dragoons was formed at Jefferson Barracks, Missouri, in 1833 and subsequently saw service against the Plains Indians along the Santa Fe Trail. The 2nd Regiment of Dragoons was organised for the Florida campaign of 1836, fighting against the formidable Seminole until 1842. Within a year of being redeployed west, this regiment suffered the ignomy of redesignation as a dismounted Rifle Regiment in the cut-backs following the ending of hostilities in Florida. After much lobbying, their horses were returned to them in 1844, and six companies joined Winfield Scott in his campaign to Mexico City during the spring of 1847. A 3rd Regiment of Dragoons was organised in 1847 to serve until the end of the war.

Officers' full dress and fatigue uniform

The dragoon officer's dark blue dress coat was double-breasted, with two rows of ten buttons (although two surviving examples have two rows of nine), and a shorter skirt than that worn by other branches of service, referred to as 'three-quarters' in length, which was minus a central vent. According to surviving specimen Dragoon jackets in the Smithsonian Institution, the material used in these garments was a high-quality, knapped and grained broad-cloth. Buttons were gilt, convex, and bore the spread eagle device with the letter 'D' on the shield. Collar, cuffs, and turnbacks were yellow kerseymere. Slashes on the sleeve designated rank in the same manner as that for infantry. The collar was framed with gold lace, and had two loops on each side which terminated in small uniform buttons. For full dress, fringed epaulettes followed the established rule where the button was gilt, e.g. gold strap and bullion, silver regimental number; silver eagle for colonel; silver strap with gold border and number for major.

Trousers for mounted service were reinforced by extra pieces of material on the insides of the legs, sometimes called 'saddled' trousers. Those for colonel, lieutenant-colonel, major, and adjutant, were dark blue with two ¾ inch-wide stripes of gold lace down the outside seam. Company grade officers wore trousers of a blue-grey mix with two ¾ inch-wide yellow stripes. All dragoon officers wore plain white cotton or drill pants in the summer months.

Dragoon officers' dress caps were made from the same material as those worn by the infantry, but were based on a different pattern which incorporated a narrower crown. Ornamentation consisted of a M1833 brass eight-pointed sunburst star on which was an eagle struck in brass and silvered. The eagle was basically the Napoleonic type adopted by the British after the Battle of Waterloo and altered by omitting the lightning in the talons and adding a wreath to its breast. The drooping white horse-hair pompon was placed in a socket bearing a 'shell and flame' device. Field officers had a small strip of red hair, 'to show in front of their pompons'. A letter to a prospective supplier described this headgear thus:

'The tops of the uniform caps are of pretty stout jacked leather made to fit ... precisely. They extend down the bodies of the caps one inch and are neatly stitched to the lower edge ... The Dragoon cap is level on top, the poke ... is *patent* leather. The bodies ... are made of imported materials, so said, from South America, and coney fur or wool is the principal thereof. There is a strap of *patent* leather with a slide ..., so fixed as to be brought under the chin to secure

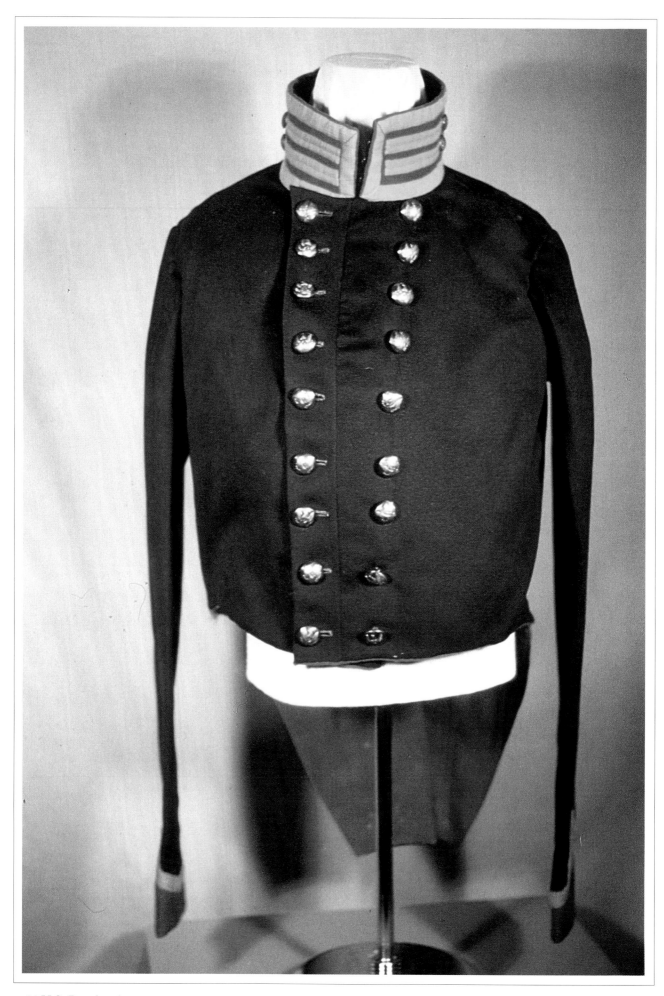

46 U.S. Regular Army

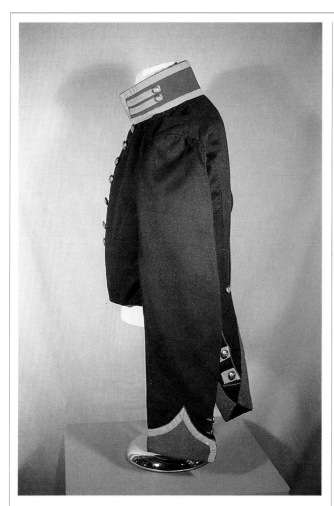

Opposite and top left and right.

Front, side and rear of a 'Ringgold'-pattern dress coat for an enlisted man of the horse artillery. Courtesy Smithsonian Institution/photos by Ross M. Kimmel.

the cap to the head.'[24]

Dragoon officers were also permitted to wear a plain, dark blue cloth frock coat, based on the same pattern as that worn by other branches of service. In this instance, rank was indicated by blue cloth epaulette straps edged with gold lace, minus bullion fringe, with the number of the regiment embroidered within a solid gilt crescent. The strap of the colonel bore a silver embroidered eagle; that of lieutenant colonel, two gold leaves; and that of major, two silver leaves. Captains' straps displayed two gold bars; a 1st lieutenants', one bar; and a 2nd lieutenant, plain.

Waist belts were black patent leather, one and a half-inches wide, and fastened by a brass plate with an Old English letter 'D' set within a wreath. A deep orange waist sash tied on the right hip was to be worn on duty when in full dress, or with the frock coat or shell jacket.

For ordinary stable duty, marches, or active service, officers were permitted to wear a blue shell, or stable jacket, adopted in 1833, with gold piping along

bottom collar seam and around the edge of two sloping breast pocket flaps. A white cotton, or drill, jacket was allowed during hot weather. The 1839 regulations prescribed that officers could wear on their forage caps a six-pointed gold star, embroidered on a dark blue background. The regulations provided that the number of the regiment should be placed in the centre of the star, and that the whole star be placed on an embroidered sunburst. Photographs of the period show that only the six-pointed star was worn.

Not all dragoon officers kept to these regulations. On the eve of war, Second Lieutenant John P. Hatch, 3rd U.S. Infantry recalled: 'You would laugh to see some of the dragoon officers, their hair hanging down their backs, immense mustaches, and beards six or eight inches long. And dressed in the most fantastic style.'[25]

Dragoon NCOs, Musicians, and Privates - full dress

Dark blue short-tailed coats were double-breasted, with yellow collar, cuffs, turnbacks, and brass shoulder knots or scales. Dragoon NCOs were permitted to wear yellow lace sleeve chevrons of yellow with point down for full dress - three for a sergeant, and two for corporal. The collar of the chief musicians' and sergeants' coats were also trimmed with gold worsted binding, after the style of officers. Musicians' coats were red with yellow trim.

Reinforced trousers were blue-grey. Sergeants had two ¾ inch-wide yellow seam stripes; corporals and privates, one yellow stripe set in advance of the seam.

Dragoon N.C.O.s and enlisted men's winter campaign or fatigue uniform

For fatigue during winter or on campaign, the above ranks wore a dark blue shell jacket fastened with either 11 or 12 buttons, and trimmed on collar, cuffs, edges, back seams, and shoulder straps with yellow worsted binding. The Dragoons were considered an elite corps, and their fatigue jackets were originally made of finer material than those of other branches of service. The dark blue cloth was of the quality of the dress coat rather than the kersey used by other corps. The dragoon jacket was also fully lined in flannel with quilted padding in the front. Jackets issued later in the war were less well-made, with false external pocket flaps, and minus the two laced 'cushions' at the base of the rear seams, designed to support the weight of the sabre belt. The white summer jacket, not worn in Mexico, was more elaborate than that issued to dismounted troops, with pointed cuffs fastened by a single small button.

Model 1839 forage caps were the same as for other branches of service. According to Sam Chamberlain, a member of the 1st Dragoons, the more flamboyant 2nd Dragoons wore an 'orange band' around their caps when coming to his rescue after escape from Mexican irregulars. The late-war cap worn by James H. Bell, Company D, 2nd Dragoons, was decorated with a yellow band. This regiment was also known for removing the padding from their caps to create a more rakish appearance. By July 1848, an entire command, composed of members of both the 1st and 2nd Dragoons, plus Bragg's battery of light artillery, were described by Sam Chamberlain as being dressed in 'bright red flannel shirts, and black broad brim felt hats; this, with their white belts, burnished arms, gay banners, and dashing horsewomen galloping up and down our flanks made an effect seldom witnessed in the dull routine of Uncle Sam's service.'[26]

Dragoons wore a 2 inch-wide, whitened buff leather waist belt with a brass buckle bearing the letter 'D', from which the Model 1840, brass-hilted heavy cavalry sabre, known as 'old wristbreaker', hung in a shiny iron scabbard by two white straps. The sabre was also supported by a strap of the same colour, running from right shoulder to left hip.

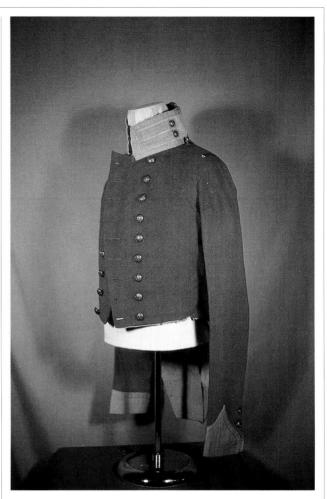

A wide white belt was suspended from the left shoulder to the right hip, with a large brass buckle worn over the square of the back. Suspended from this by an iron clip was the dragoon's carbine, either the breech-loading Model 1843 Hall carbine, or the Model 1847 musketoon, which was little more than a cut-down musket. The .52 calibre Hall carbine was the first percussion firearm adopted by the army, and had been accepted for service in 1819. Dragoons also carried one or two single-shot, muzzle-loading pistols, made both as flintlock and percussion weapons.

Regarding flags, the 1847 'General Regulations for the Army' stated that each dragoon regiment should have 'a silken standard', and each company 'a silken guidon'. The former measured two feet three inches on the lance by two feet five inches on the fly, and bore the arms of the U.S. embroidered in silk on a blue field edged with a yellow silk fringe. The number and name of the regiment was embroidered in a scroll underneath the eagle.

The guidon was made swallow-tailed, measuring three feet five inches from the lance to the end of the swallow-tail; fifteen inches to the fork of the swallow-tail; and two feet three inches on the lance. The top half was red bearing the letters U.S. in white, and the bottom half was white with the letter of the company

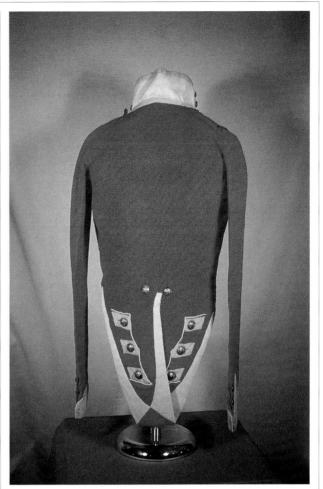

Opposite and top left and right.
Front, side and rear of a 'Ringgold'-pattern dress coat for a musician of the horse artillery. Courtesy Smithsonian Institution/ photos by Ross M. Kimmel.

in red. The regimental number was also unofficially added to the latter shortly after 1836.

CORPS OF ENGINEERS

Organised on a formal basis in 1779, the Corps of Engineers was established at West Point to constitute a military academy during 1802. At the outset of war in 1812 it was made a Staff Corps, and by the beginning of 1846 it was composed of only a small number of engineer officers. The full dress uniform of these officers consisted of a dark-blue coat fastened by a single row of nine buttons placed at equal distances; a standing collar of black velvet, meeting in front, either side of which was a gold embroidered wreath of laurel and palm encircling a five-pointed star; black velvet cuffs; and coat tail turnbacks of the same cloth as the coat, the skirts being embellished with the same insignia as found on the collar, but set in a black velvet lozenge with embroidered edging. Slashed flaps on the sleeves were black velvet, embroidered with gold. Those of field officers were six inches long, with four

coat buttons attached; a captain's were four and a half inches long, with three buttons; whilst a subaltern's were three inches long, with two buttons. Parallel with each button, and running towards the wearer, was a gold embroidered sprig of palm and laurel. Rank was also indicated via epaulettes, based on the same system as employed for other branches of service, with a silver turreted castle set within the crescent.

Winter trousers were dark blue cloth, with a one and a half-inch wide black velvet seam stripe. Summer pants were plain white linen or cotton. Their black cocked hats were essentially the same as worn by general officers, except that the corners were four and a half inches long, instead of six. Hat devices consisted of a plain gold loop with raised embroidered edge, and ornamented with gilt eagle and scroll; cockade and tassel the same as for general officers; and a plume of three black ostrich feathers. The cloak worn by engineer officers was lined with blue.

All buttons were gilt, slightly convex, and of the distinctive Engineer pattern, dating from approximately 1812, with eagle-castle-rising sun design, incorporating the 'Essayons' motto.

The engineer officer's sword, or 'light rapier', was a special model made for the Corps. Very ornate, it was the only official edged weapon with a triangular blade

Top left.
Richard Barnes Mason was promoted to colonel of the 1st U.S. Dragoons in 1846. Taken at that time, this image offers a close view of the gold lace loops and edging on his full- dress coat collar. USAMHI/photo by Jim Enos.

Top right.
The uniform worn by this dragoon poses more questions than it answers. While his cap, trousers, sword belt, and Model 1840 heavy cavalry sabre are all regulation, his coat is single-breasted; his shoulder-knots are worsted, instead of brass; his collar has loops and buttons, rather than being plain yellow; and his pointed yellow cuffs are trimmed with yellow worsted binding, which was prescribed for chief musicians and sergeants only. Courtesy of Herb Peck, Jr.

Bottom left.
Fatigue cap worn by Captain Duncan, 2nd U.S. Artillery. Officers' caps do not seem to have been made with the neck flap found on those of enlisted men. West Point Museum Collections, United States Military Academy.

known to have been manufactured in the United States. Carried in a metal scabbard covered with black leather, it was devoid of a sword knot. For full dress occasions, a black velvet sword belt, with gold

Top left.

Second Lieutenant Bezaleel Wells Armstrong, an 1845 graduate of West Point, served in the 2nd U.S. Dragoons. He wears the dress uniform coat prescribed in 1833, along with a Model 1839 officer's forage cap - a peculiar and very non-regulation combination. Note the star on his cap, orange waist sash, button-up gauntlets, and two yellow trouser stripes. The latter appear to have been edged with gold lace, another non-regulation feature. Courtesy of William J. Schultz, M.D.

Top right.

Lewis Cass, Jr., son of soldier, diplomat, and statesman Lewis Cass, was initially a major of volunteer infantry but, in April 1847, was assigned to the newly formed 3rd U.S. Dragoons. His non-regulation dark blue double-breasted fatigue coat has plain, flat buttons. His gold edged shoulder staps bear a silver oak leaf at either end indicating the rank of lieutenant colonel. His corduroy trousers are also non-regulation, but probably very comfortable! Amon Carter Museum, Fort Worth: accession # 81.65.1.

Bottom right.

Dragoon enlisted man's dress cap, surmounted by a white horsehair plume, and bearing the starburst plate with federal eagle, prescribed by General Orders Number 38 on 2 May 1833. Courtesy Smithsonian Institution/photo by Ross M. Kimmel.

embroidered sprigs or laurel and palms, was permitted. A black patent leather belt was worn for service. Until 1841, the officer's rectangular waist belt plate bore an engineer's turreted castle set between a sprig of laurel and palm. During that year, the castle was replaced with the letters 'U S', although both patterns were probably worn during the war with Mexico.

For service dress, engineer officers were prescribed a dark blue frock coat after the pattern worn by General Staff. Although forage caps were to have a black velvet band, with a gold embroidered wreath of laurel and palm, encircling a silver turreted castle, that worn by Third Lieutenant McClellan was plain dark blue.

Company of Sappers, Miners, and Pontoniers

On 13 May 1846, a Company of Sappers, Miners, and Pontoniers was authorised by Congress as part of the permanent establishment of the Regular Army. This unit became a part of the Corps of Engineers at West Point. Second in command Lieutenant Gustavus W. Smith, recalled:

'Soon after the hostilities with Mexico broke out... an act was passed, providing for an engineer company of one hundred men, to be composed of ten sergeants, ten corporals, thirty-nine artificers, thirty-nine second-class privates, and two musicians; all with higher pay than that of the enlisted men in the line of the army'.[27]

Captain Alexander J. Swift, Instructor of Practical Military Engineering at the Military Academy, was assigned as commanding officer, having been sent to Metz to receive instruction in the French system. Swift's experience clearly influenced the adoption of French-flavoured military nomenclature. The Sappers within his company were the ordinary engineer soldiers; the Miners were elite engineer troops specializing in subterranean siege warfare of mines and countermines; and the Pontoniers handled pontoon bridges.

The third in command of this company was Lieutenant George Brinton McClellan, who would later command the Army of the Potomac during the Civil War.

Considered from the outset to be an elite unit, every effort was made to recruit native-born Americans to its ranks. Most of those who enlisted for the five-year term of service were from New York and other eastern cities. Lieutenant Smith commented:

'...with two exceptions, the enlisted men of the engineer company were native born, and all but four were raw recruits. Each of these four had served with credit during one or more terms of enlistment in the

regular army. Three of them were promptly made sergeants, and the fourth was a musician [bugler].'[28]

This company trained at West Point from June until September 1846, after which it left for Mexico, arriving at Veracruz on 9 March 1847, having been involved in considerable movement via land and sea. Joining Scott's army, one of the unit's major functions was the repair and improvement of roads, particularly for the emplacement of artillery at Cerro Gordo - where a number of engineer soldiers joined the final assault - and during Scott's march south of Lake Chalco to outflank the fortifications blocking the direct route to Mexico City.

The full dress uniform worn by the company was specified in General Orders of 4 June 1846, and slightly amended on 1 September. The dark blue coat was based on the same pattern as that worn by the infantry and artillery, with facing colours and buttons the same as those worn by engineer officers. Hence, the collar, cuffs, and turnbacks, were of black cotton velvet. The collar was trimmed with a single button and loop of one and three-eighths inch-wide yellow 'Prussian binding'. A sergeant's slashed sleeves had three buttons and loops of the same material, conforming in pattern to those worn by a captain; corporals and enlisted men had two buttons and loops.

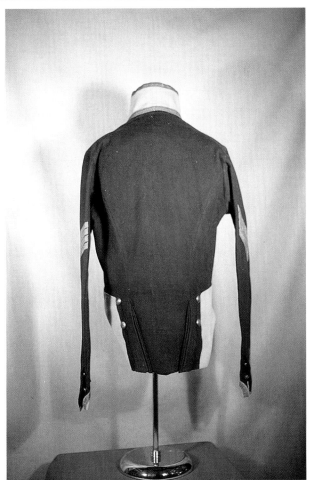

Opposite, top left and right.
Front, side and rear of Dragoon NCO's dress coat. The four chevrons are unexplained. Courtesy Smithsonian Institution/ photos by Ross M. Kimmel.

On the right breast was a small slashed pocket, covered by a flap, for carrying percussion caps. A sergeant's rank was also shown by two yellow silk epaulettes with quarter inch-wide bullion fringe, and solid brass crescent. That of a corporal was indicated by epaulettes of the same material and pattern, with one-eighth inch-wide bullion. Enlisted men wore two yellow silk straps with pad and half fringe. The First Sergeant also wore a red sash.

The dress cap was the same pattern as that worn by the artillery, but with brass insignia consisting of a national eagle over the turreted castle of the Corps of Engineers (which was also shared with the Corps of Cadets at West Point at this time. Sergeants wore a 12 inch-long black upright hackle, while other ranks had a black worsted spherical pompon.

Belt plate worn by Dragoon officers. In this example, the Old English letter 'D' is totally enclosed by a wreath of laurel leaves, which deviates from that prescribed. From artfefacts, drawn by Ron Field.

Trousers were light blue with one and a half inch-wide black cotton velvet seam stripes for sergeants, and a narrower black welt for other ranks. The great coat worn by this unit was patterned after that worn by the artillery, with engineer buttons.

The winter fatigue jacket prescribed for this company was dark blue, with collar trimmed in the same style as the dress coat, and yellow braid around the shoulder straps. This garment was also prescribed a percussion cap pocket on the right breast. Like that issued to engineer officers, the forage cap was to have a black cotton velvet band, but with a yellow metal castle in front. A surviving example is minus the black

Top left.
Lieutenant Cave Johnson Couts of the 1st U.S. Dragoons wears his frock coat unbuttoned to show his gaudy cravat. Note the jutting shoulder straps, minus fringe, prescribed for use with the dragoon frock coat. He proudly sports a riding whip. San Diego Historical Society.

Left.
The Type I forage cap of Private James Bell. This is possibly the only surviving cap with the yellow corps-coloured band. Gift of Mr. James H. Bell, Minnesota Historical Society.

Top right, and opposite: top left, top right and bottom right.
Front and rear of late-war winter fatigue jacket worn by Private James H. Bell, Co. D, 2nd U.S. Dragoons. Made from a coarser, almost black cloth, the ⅜ in. yellow worsted binding was carelessly attached. (*details*) collar and cuff. Note the non-regulation vertical line of binding running up the outside edge of the cuff vent. Gift of Mr. James H. Bell, Minnesota Historical Society.

band. Enlisted men were also allowed to wear 'canvass overalls, to be drawn over the trousers'.[29]

Concerning the fatigue uniform worn in Mexico, one member of the engineer company complained: 'When our clothing came to us we were indeed

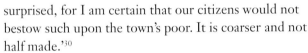

surprised, for I am certain that our citizens would not bestow such upon the town's poor. It is coarser and not half made.'[30]

This company was armed with the U.S. Sappers and Miners Musketoon, Model 1847. This was a .69 calibre percussion smoothbore which was 41 inches in length. The only real difference between this weapon and the artillery musketoon was its brass-handled, Roman-sword bayonet, which was fixed by means of a bayonet stud on the right side of the barrel. The latter was worn on a special model waist belt of black buff leather, fitted with the same two-piece brass plate as worn by the foot artillery. A black buff leather frog held the bayonet scabbard, and it seems probable that the Model 1841 rifle cartridge box was also slid on the belt.

TOPOGRAPHICAL ENGINEERS

After a short-lived earlier history during the War of 1812, the Topographical Engineers were re-established as a corps attached to the General Staff on 24 April 1816. During August 1818, a separate Topographical Bureau was established in the War Department, under the immediate direction of the Secretary of War and the Chief Engineer. On 21 June 1831, an independent Corps of Topographical

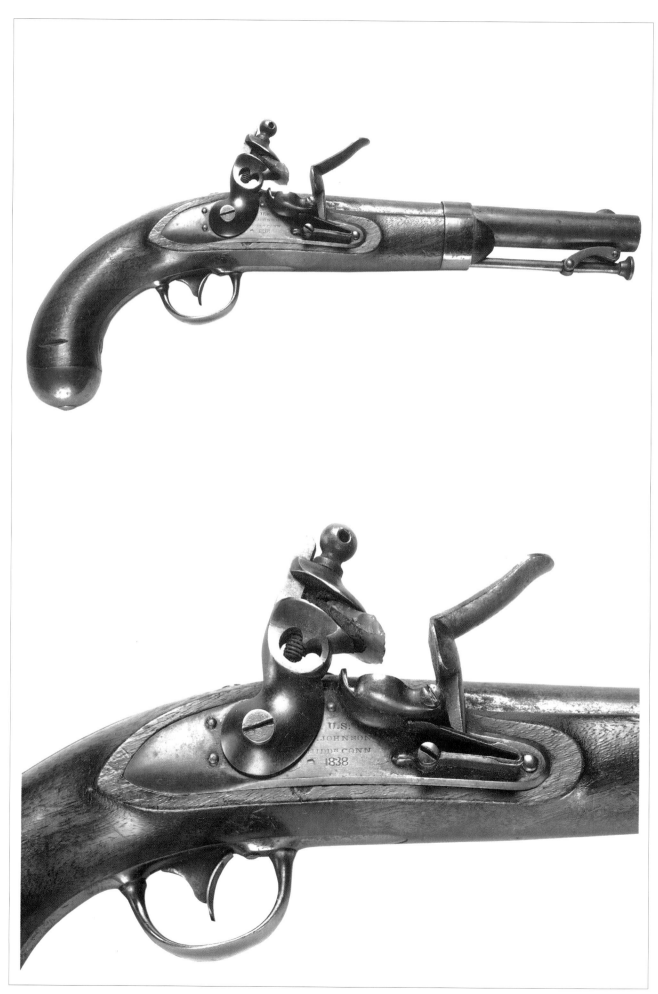

Top left and right.
Winter fatigue jacket, Company of Sappers, Miners, and Pontoniers (*front and side view*). Note the collar trim is identical to that for full dress. This example has two functional welted pockets, rather than the 'pocket for percussion caps, covered by a flap' prescribed in the regulations. Courtesy Smithsonian Institution/photo by Ross M. Kimmel.

Engineers was created.

By 1846, the officers of this small corps wore for full dress a dark blue, double-breasted, tail-coat with two rows of ten buttons. The coat-tails bore a slashed flap on each skirt, of dark blue cloth with three large

Opposite.
Pistols of the type carried by the U.S. Dragoons. (*top*) Model 1838 flintlock pistol of the type used by the U.S. Dragoons. This single-shot weapon was manufactured for the Federal Government by I.N. Johnson at Middleton, Connecticut. (*bottom*) Detail of lock.

Forage cap, Company of Sappers, Miners, and Pontoniers. The 'band of black cotton velvet' required by regulations is missing, although the yellow metal castle is very much in evidence. Courtesy Smithsonian Institution/photo by Ross M. Kimmel.

buttons at each point, plus two at the waist. Collar, square cuffs, and skirt turn-backs, were of dark blue velvet. Collar, cuffs, and slashed skirt-flaps were embroidered in gold, with oak-leaves and acorns. Via General Orders of 11 June 1832, the gilt buttons worn by this corps bore the U.S. shield over the letters 'TE' in Old English characters.

Within the crescent, epaulettes also displayed the U.S. shield embroidered in gold over the Old English characters 'TE'. The latter were silver for all ranks except that of a major, who wore yellow letters to form a contrast with his silver lace epaulette straps. A colonel wore a silver spread eagle on his gold lace

58 U.S. Regular Army

Top left and right.
Front and rear of full dress coat, Corps of Topographical Engineers, worn by Captain George W. Hughes, circa 1846. An open brass strap on the underside of the epaulette straps passed through the cloth loops seen on the shoulders, thus helping to secure the epaulettes in place. Also note the slashed flaps on the coat tails and Topographical Engineer insignia embroidered at the end of the turnbacks. West Point Museum.

straps, whilst those for all other ranks were plain. Rank was also indicated by a crimson silk sash.

The cocked hat worn by this corps was the same as that worn by the General Staff, except for the Topographical Engineer button and black plume. Winter full dress trousers were dark blue with one and three-quarter inch-wide gold seam stripes. Cloaks were the same as for General Staff, with blue lining and corps buttons.

Topographical engineers carried dragoon sabres in

Opposite.
(top) **Model 1839 dragoon pistol converted to percussion. This weapon was made by A. Waters of Milbury, Massachusetts.**
(bottom) **Note the eagle head above the maker's stamp.** North Carolina Museum of History.

polished steel scabbards. The black patent leather waist belt was fastened by a gilt, eliptical plate bearing an eagle and shield, with the designation 'CORPS OF TOPOGRAPHICAL ENGINEERS', in small Roman capitals, around the edge of the plate.

For undress, dark blue frock coats fastened by a single row of ten buttons were prescribed. Undress trousers were dark blue with one and three-quarter inch-wide black silk and worsted lace seam stripes, with gold oak leaf and acorn embroidery. Forage caps were plain dark blue.

ORDNANCE DEPARTMENT
Established by an act of 14 May, 1812, the Ordnance Department consisted of officers, a limited number of enlisted men including the Ordnance Sergeants, who served as caretakers of Ordnance and other stores at army installations, and civilian employees of the various Federal armouries and arsenals. This Department was merged with the Artillery during the general reduction of the Army in 1821. In 1832, its independence was again recognised, and it was fully restored to its earlier status.

Ordnance Department officers occasionally commanded siege artillery during the conflict with Mexico. Ordnance men also manned the Mountain

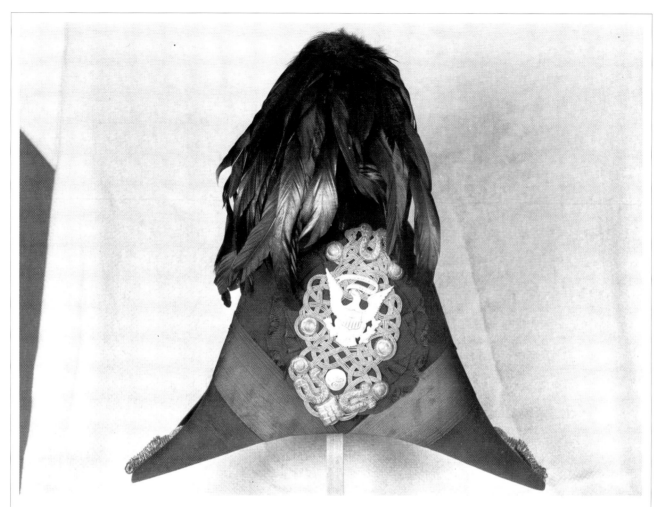

Cocked hat worn by Captain G. W. Hughes, Corps of Topographical Engineers. West Point Museum.

Howitzer and Rocket Company of 100 men formed in 1846 under Major George H. Talcott. Attached to the division commanded by Brigadier General David E. Twiggs, this unit took part in Scott's advance on Mexico City, during which it was involved in the bombardment of Veracruz, became heavily engaged in the action at Cerro Gordo, Contreras and Churubusco, and took part in the momentous attack on Chapultepec. At the end of hostilities, the Howitzer and Rocket Company served in the occupation force that remained in Mexico City for almost nine months, after which it was disbanded at New Orleans in May 1848.

By 1846, officers of the Ordnance Department wore a full dress coat patterned after that of the artillery, minus red facings. Buttons were gilt and convex with a flaming bomb above cross cannon. Epaulettes were the same as for artillery, minus regimental number. The chapeau bras and ornaments were the same as for General Staff, with red plume, as per artillery. Trousers were dark blue with one and a half inch-wide seam stripe of the same colour, welted at the edges. Sword, scabbard, and sword-belt plate,

were the same as that worn by the artillery. The sword-belt was black patent leather, and worn around the waist. Frock coats and cloak were also the same as for artillery.

Ordnance Sergeants wore the same uniform as that for the Sergeant Major of artillery, minus the aiguillette. The one and a half inch-wide trouser seam stripe was dark blue. The uniform of ordnance enlisted men was the same as their artillery counterparts, but with red shoulder straps, pad, and half-fringe.

Ordnance Department fatigue wear for enlisted men and labourers consisted of a dark blue jacket with a scarlet welt around the collar. Trouser, or 'overalls', were also dark blue with a scarlet welt in the outside leg seams. Forage caps were plain dark blue. Waist

**Opposite: top left and right, bottom left and right.
Front, side, rear and interior view of full dress coat of a sergeant, Company of Sappers, Miners, and Pontoniers. Distinctive features include black cotton velvet collar and cuff facings, and wide 'Prussian binding' forming the collar loop. The red piping around collar and slashed flap on sleeves, plus red lining in tails, were described in the regulations as being 'after the pattern of an Artillery Sergeant's' coat.** Courtesy Smithsonian Institution/photos by Ross M. Kimmel.

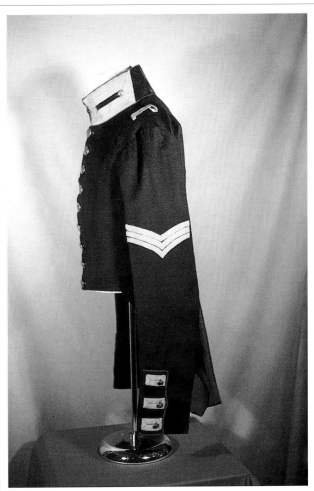

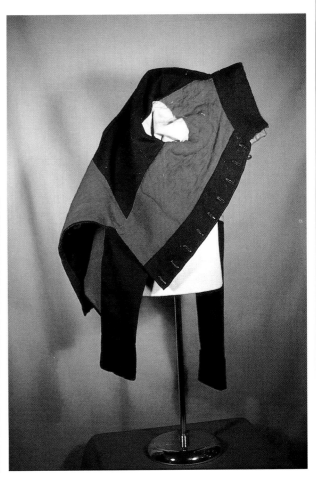

Top left and right.

Front and side view of ordnance man's winter fatigue jacket,

Ordnance Department. Courtesy Smithsonian Institution/photo by Ross M. Kimmel.

belts were white buff with a two-piece brass 'US' buckle. Ordnance Sergeants wore a red worsted sash and carried the Model 1840 NCO's sword. In peace time, Ordnance men were armed and equipped as infantry.

The Hale's rockets used by the 50-man rocket 'division' of this unit during the Mexican War lacked an adequate guidance system and inaccurately dispersed their fire over a very large area. For this reason, they did not prove particularly successful in battle. The 12-pounder mountain howitzer did prove its worth. This short-range, light-weight cannon served well, with its two-wheeled carriage moved by multiple teams of horses, which also pulled the caissons and limbers loaded with ammunition chests. According to Bavarian immigrant Frederick Zeh, who enlisted in the Howitzer and Rocket Company as a labourer, Ordnance men continued to be armed and equipped as infantry with 'rifles', with which they hunted 'half-wild cattle' during their service near Veracruz. Zeh also mentions that his 'saber had been

blasted away from the ragged belt' at Contreras, which suggests that some men in the unit were armed as light artillery with the M1840 sabre.[31]

MEDICAL DEPARTMENT

The personnel of the Medical Department was headed by a Surgeon-General, and comprised the surgeons and assistant surgeons who formed the 'Medical Staff' of the army, civilian physicians hired on contract, and hospital stewards. The latter were soldiers detailed to hospital service from the line, and had no distinctive insignia.

Officers of the Medical Department wore a dark blue coat with two rows of ten gilt buttons bearing the spread eagle and shield surrounded by stars, with a plain border. The collar and cuffs were faced with black velvet, the former being embroidered either side with a five inch-long gold laurel branch, while the outer edges were embellished with a gold vine of laurel leaves. The latter also had similar laurel branch and vine embroidery. Coat tails were plain, lined with blue cloth, and made after 'the fashion of a citizen's coat'.

Epaulettes had a gold crescent, bullion fringe, and strap. The strap was also of gold lace trimmed with silver for all ranks except Surgeon, who wore a silver

Captain Benjamin Stone Roberts, U.S. Regiment of Mounted Riflemen. Roberts was second in command of one of the storming parties during the assault on Chapultepec Castle. He wears an enlisted man's fatigue jacket, and holds a foot officer's sword. USAMHI/photo by Jim Enos.

Second Lieutenant George H. Gordon belonged to Company I, U.S. Regiment of Mounted Riflemen, which was one of the two companies of the unit to see mounted service by May 1847. Rank is indicated by the plain straps on the shoulders of his frock coat, and the gold embroidered spread eagle with letter 'R' in silver on his forage cap. Before the discovery of this daguerreotype, there was no evidence that this insignia had ever been produced. The crimson sash, peculiar to officers of this regiment, is tied around his waist. He holds the officer's model of the 1840 heavy dragoon sabre. Wounded at San Juan Bridge in 1847, Gordon later became a brigadier general in the Union Army during the Civil War. Courtesy of William J. Schultz, M.D.

strap trimmed with gold. A gold laurel wreath surrounding the Old English characters 'MS' was embroidered within the crescent. The Surgeon-General also wore a silver spread eagle on his strap. All officers of the Medical Department wore gold aiguillettes.

Headgear consisted of a black chapeau bras ornamented with a black button and black silk gimp loop, a cockade and gilt spread eagle, and gold tassels.

Winter trousers were dark blue, with one and a half inch-wide black mohair lace down the outer seam, decorated with a laurel vine with satin face.

The Medical Staff sword was adopted in 1840 and worn only on ceremonial occasions. Its hilt was of gilded brass, without knuckle-bow but with gracefully scrolled quillions and two shields, one bearing the letters 'MS' above a group of stars. The sword-knot consisted of a gold lace strap with gold bullion tassels. A decorative scabbard of gilded brass was carried on a black patent leather sword-belt, fastened by a gilt,

rectangular plate with the letters 'US' set within a silver laurel wreath.

For undress, Medical Officers wore forage caps, and a dark blue frock coat with a single row of eight buttons, and shoulder straps according to grade.

U.S. REGIMENT OF MOUNTED RIFLEMEN

Authorised on 19 May 1846 to patrol the Oregon Trail, this regiment was instead ordered to Point Isabel, Texas, to support Taylor's army. Shortly after arrival, it was again onboard ship bound for Vera Cruz to fight under Scott's command. Most of the unit's

64 *U.S. Regular Army*

horses were lost at sea, and only two companies, C and I, were eventually remounted on captured horses by May 1847. These men saw action against Mexican guerillas harrying Scott's lines of communication and supply line. The remainder of the regiment served as foot rifles, and played a valuable part in the storming of Mexico City.

General Order No. 18 of 4 June 1846 stated that: 'The "Undress" of the United States "Regiment of Mounted Riflemen" shall, for the present, be the same as that for the Dragoons', with certain exceptions. Presumably this also referred to officers, who were only ever issued dark blue M1839 forage caps, and frock coats. Officers' cap insignia consisted of an embroidered spread eagle with the letter 'R' in silver on the shield. The sash was crimson silk. Non-commissioned officers and enlisted men wore shell jackets of the same pattern as that issued to Dragoons. Eagle buttons for all ranks bore the letter 'R'. Trousers were dark blue, rather than sky blue, with a seam stripe of black cloth edged with yellow cord. The uniform of this regiment occasionally caused confusion in battle. After Churubusco, a member of the 15th U.S. Infantry recalled: 'As we were halting from the pursuit, we saw troops who looked like Mexicans in their dark blue clothing, right on our lately left battle ground, among our wounded. This, for the moment, was most alarming, but we soon recognised the yells of our own rifle regiment, sent forward too late to help us.'[32]

The Mounted Riflemen were originally armed with Model 1841 ('Mississippi') rifles, Model 1840 sabres, and flintlock pistols. The War Department subsequently purchased 1000 six-shot Whitneyville-Walker Colt revolvers for this unit, 220 of which were delivered shortly after the fall of Mexico City.

The standard of the Regiment of Mounted Riflemen consisted of a yellow silk field measuring 26 inches on the lance by 29 inches on the fly. Edged with a yellow fringe, it bore the national coat of arms, and the name of the unit in yellow on a red scroll underneath.

Opposite.
Reconstruction: Private, U.S. Regiment of Mounted Riflemen, 1847. The Rifles wore the same fatigue jacket as the Dragoons, except for 'R' replacing 'D' on the buttons. Trousers were dark blue with a black seam stripe edged with yellow worsted cord. Our figure is armed with the M1841 'Mississippi' rifle and the M1840 dragoon sabre. His saddle is the Grimsly model, which began to supercede the Ringgold saddle in 1847.
Photo by Ross M. Kimmel; courtesy Don Troiani.

This fifer from the Mexican War period wears distinctive light-coloured trim on his jacket and cap. According to his buttons, he may have belonged to a Vermont unit. Courtesy of John M. Hightower/photo by Dennis A. Waters.

U.S. REGIMENT OF VOLTIGEURS, OR FOOT RIFLEMEN

This regiment was formed via General Order No. 7 of 11 February 1847, and was envisaged as a combined command containing dragoons, infantry, and artillery. Half of the unit were supposed to be mounted on horses, and for rapid deployment, each foot rifleman would climb up behind the saddle of a voltigeur. In practice, the Voltigeur Regiment operated as infantry and artillery only, and gave a good account of itself with the Model 1841 ('Mississippi') rifle, and mountain howitzer. After landing at Veracruz, the Voltigeurs were assigned to Major General Gideon J. Pillow's division and marched under Scott towards Mexico City, where on 19-20 August they were involved in the battles of Contreras and Churubusco. Following the armistice, the regiment was again in action in the assault on Chapultepec, where their flag was the first to wave from the Castle ramparts.[33]

Only undress was ever prescribed for this regiment. Officers were to wear a single-breasted nine-button

frock coat of dark grey cloth, patterned after the dark blue ones worn by other branches of the regular service. Rank was to be indicated via 'Scales-or counter straps' rather than epaulettes, with insignia corresponding to that worn by the rest of the army. Eagle buttons were to be gilt, convex, bearing the letter 'V' in the shield. Winter trousers were also to be grey, with seam stripes of the same colour edged with yellow cord. Summer trousers were to be plain white cotton. Swords and scabbards were the same as for

Top.
This fatigue jacket was made for the U.S. Regiment of Voltigeurs in 1847. Originally grey, but oxidised to brown, with orange/yellow trim on collar and shoulder straps, the regiment never received these jackets, which were lost at sea along with the rest of their original uniforms. Courtesy Smithsonian Institution/photo by Ross M. Kimmel.

Bottom right & left.
Front & rear view of trousers which match the Voltigeur jacket in colour, and may belong with it. Curiously, the army had officially abandoned fall-front trousers in favour of fly fronts in 1845. These trousers are constructed exactly like a number of pre-war summer issue white cotton fall-front trousers in the Smithsonian collection. Note the adjustment belt in the rear band. Courtesy Smithsonian Institution/photo by Ross M. Kimmel.

infantry. Shoulder belts were black patent leather, but in every other respect conforming to that worn by the infantry.

Non-commissioned officers and enlisted men were authorised a jacket and trousers of dark grey cut in the same style as for regular infantry. Several Voltigeur shell jackets survive in the collection of the Smithsonian Institution, which may represent the first uniform this regiment was intended to wear. Made originally of grey cloth, oxidation has changed their colour to brown, while collar and shoulder strap trim remains a strong, orange shade of yellow. Such clothing was made and shipped to Mexico, but was lost at sea. Hence, the Voltigeurs eventually drew ordinary sky blue infantry fatigue jackets and trousers. Forage caps were presumably standard-issue dark blue for all ranks.

At one point, the regimental commander, Colonel Timothy P. Andrews, anxious that his men should wear more distinctive apparel, requested black felt slouch hats and fringed grey hunting shirts. These were approved and the Schuylkill Arsenal was ordered to produce such garments. The hats were made but apparently never shipped. Nothing is known of the hunting shirts. A letter from Colonel Andrews dated 8 January, 1848, reveals that a further uniform issuance, this time of dark blue cloth, had been made during 1847:

'The Uniform of the Regiment should be changed to the color it has so far worn [except the officers] i.e. "*dark blue*" with trimmings, buttons, strap, etc., as at present. The color of cloth prescribed for the Regiment was "dark grey", but none of that color has ever been received by the Regt.'[34]

Further evidence to suggest that the Voltigeurs did eventually acquire a distinctive uniform survives in a letter written on 27 May 1848 by Captain James J. Archer, in which he discusses the resignation of a comrade for cowardice. Archer wrote to his brother that it would be'none too good' for the man to wear 'the uniform of the regiment' upon his return to Baltimore, and that his buttons should be cut off if he did!

BANDS
The 1847 U.S. army regulations stated that a band should wear the uniform of the regiment or corps to which it belonged. However, the commanding officer was permitted, at the expense of the corps, to make 'such additions in ornaments as he may judge proper'. Hence several quite distinctive band uniforms were worn during the Mexican War. The Regimental Band of the 1st Dragoons was authorised in December 1846 'a double stripe (like a Sergeants) on their Wool Overalls and two yellow bands of worsted or cloth around the Cap with the number of the Regiment on a blue ground in front'.[35] On 5 June 1848, the Band of the 10th U.S. Infantry adopted the following uniform: '...a white band, one & a half inches wide, around the forage cap, - a white stripe, half an inch wide, on each side of the outer seams of the pantaloons, half an inch to intervene between the stripes - and a white bugle on each sleeve of the jacket midway between the shoulder and the elbow'. At the same time, field musicians of this regiment were authorised to wear the same additional trim, only in scarlet.[36]

U.S. Navy and Marines

The U.S. Navy performed a significant role on both land, and at sea, during the war with Mexico. Naval operations under Commodore John D. Sloat and Commodore Robert F. Stockton on the West Coast gave significant assistance to the American conquest of California. Operations under Commodore David E. Connor on the east coast of Mexico provided considerable assistance to U.S. action in that sector, especially Scott's landing near Veracruz.

The uniforms worn by the U.S. Navy in 1846 were based on a series of Regulations dating back to 1830. Despite the influence of these regulations, there was considerably more tolerance, even laxity, in their enforcement than in the regular service ashore. Much

depended on the whim of an individual ship commander, especially while at sea. Furthermore, naval uniforms were intended to be worn in a greater variety of temperature and more difficult weather conditions than were normally expected of army clothing.

In 1846 there was no grade in the navy above that of captain, although a captain in command of a squadron was, by courtesy, called 'commodore'. Below

U.S. Navy Captain, full dress (*left*); service dress (*centre*). Passed Midshipman in undress shell jacket with fouled anchor and star on each collar, and unofficial gold lace band around his cap (*right*). After photographs, by Ron Field.

Ron Field

this the two other commissioned grades of sea officer were: master commandant and lieutenant. All naval officers were prescribed three classes of uniform: full dress, undress, and service dress. Each of these in turn had a winter and summer version. The former merely meant a change from dark blue cloth pants to others of white drill. For undress, the officer could wear a light-weight coat and pants in warm weather, or change to white pants and straw hat. The service dress permitted the use of an entire uniform of white drill in warm climates.

For full dress, commissioned officers wore a dark blue coat described as 'double-breasted, with long lapels; the width to be in proportion to the size of the coat, and cut with a swell, to be buttoned back with nine buttons on each lapel...'[37] The standing collar was embroidered in gold around the upper edge with a rope, plus oak leaves interspersed with acorns. Captains had the same style of embroidery on cuffs and pocket flaps; master commandants on collar and cuffs only; lieutenants on collar only. These coats were lined and faced with white cloth. Since 1830, naval buttons had the device of an eagle perched on the stock of a foul anchor.

Captains wore two gold epaulettes with two rows of bullion, and a silver embroidered eagle couched on an anchor on each strap. Those captains entitled to fly the 'broad pennant' of a commodore added a silver star above the eagle. The senior officer of the Navy wore this combination of device at all times. Master's Commandant wore gold epaulettes, with plain straps. Lieutenants - one gold epaulette with plain strap, on the right shoulder.

Only captains and master commandants were permitted to wear gold-laced chapeau bras. Either white pantaloons or breeches were permitted in full dress, but only pantaloons, either blue or white, in undress. The full dress belt under the 1830 order was to be of white webbing, and the undress belt of blue webbing.

Pursers, surgeons, and midshipmen had a narrower border of embroidery on the collar, minus the rope, to allow for the distinctive devices introduced in 1830. The pursers collar displayed the cornucopia of the Purser's Department. The Medical Department had the 'Staff of Esculapius'. The device for a midshipman was a gold foul anchor, with a star behind it for passed midshipman. For full dress, the latter wore the same double-breasted coat as their seniors; but midshipmen were directed to wear a single-breasted coat. These ranks were also prescribed plain black chapeau bras.

In undress, officers had the option of wearing round hats or blue cloth caps. Captains, masters

commandant and lieutenants were permitted to wear gold lace bands around their caps; other officers showed a blue cloth band.

The forward warrant officers - boatswains, gunners, carpenters, and sailmakers - wore a full dress coat similar to that of commissioned officers, but with only eight buttons in each row. Furthermore, this coat was lined with blue, instead of white, cloth. For undress, these officers wore a 'coatee of dark blue cloth lined with the same, rolling collar, double-breasted...', but without the button shown on the full dress collar. The grips of the swords of all commissioned officers of both line and staff, and of midshipmen, were white, while those of warrant officers were black.

The clothing worn by seamen, ordinary seamen, and other enlisted crew members was only generally described in 1846. There were many variations to be found in the patterns worn aboard different ships. Although the Navy Department purchased clothing for enlisted men on contract, some seamen made their own clothes according to time-honoured practice.

Naval officers' full dress rank insignia. (*top left and right*) Captain's collar and cuff. (*middle*) Captain's coat pocket flap. (*bottom left to right*) Collar for Surgeon, Midshipman, and Purser. By Ron Field.

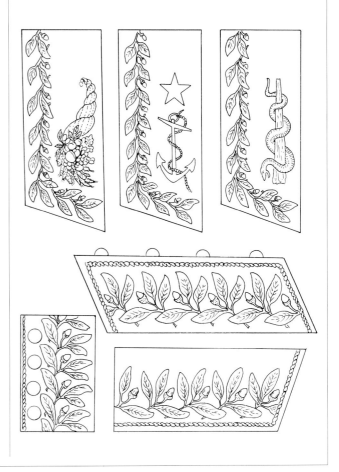

U.S. Seaman wearing dress shell jacket over plain white frock. Note the unofficial anchor device painted on his black varnished hat. Michael F. Bremer collection.

The dress garment of the petty officer and crew was a loose, double-breasted broadcloth shell jacket with wide, long lapels, and two rows of at least nine medium-sized navy buttons. It could be worn unbuttoned, and held together by a loop and two buttons at the base of the lapels. The sleeves were slashed and fastened by three or four small buttons. The first device for petty officers appeared in the 1841 Regulations, and took the form of a spread eagle perched on the stock of a foul anchor.

The traditional garment for service wear consisted of a loose navy blue shirt, or frock, without buttons at the front, open at the neck, and with a wide 'sailor's' collar, six and a half inches deep, hanging down the back. There were at least three different patterns of yoke in use during the period. A small pocket was usually found high on the left breast, while the full sleeves were gathered tightly at the wrist into a cuff fastened by two buttons. It was common to decorate the breasts and collars of these frocks according to individual taste and fancy.

A white linen or duck frock, closely resembling the

blue version, was worn in warm weather. Its collar and cuffs could be white or covered with blue dungaree or nankeen, and could be either plain or trimmed with white edging. Frocks were habitually tucked into the top of the trousers.

Blue woolen or white duck trousers could be worn with the above frocks in any combination. Both had wide bottoms to the legs, and a broad fall front secured by four to seven buttons across the top. It would also appear that fly-front trousers were issued, or acquired, during the period.

The black varnished hat had traditionally been worn since the War of 1812. Made of black glazed, or japanned, straw or tarpaulin, it had a low crown and wide brim. A plain black silk ribbon was fastened around the crown and hung down the back. This was replaced during warm weather, by the white straw, or 'sennit', hat which was also fitted with a black ribbon. A black silk neckerchief, probably three feet square, was worn underneath the collar of the frock. By the 1840s it was traditional wear and surrounded by various myths.

Dress regulations make no mention of foul weather gear for petty officers and seamen, although it is apparent that they were worn in bad weather. Some of the higher ranks possibly wore overcoats of officers' pattern, but the pea jacket was the obvious garment for most. This was a medium-length, double-breasted overcoat made of coarse navy blue woolen cloth.

Boarding parties, and those seamen involved in land actions, during the Mexican War, carried cutlasses, pistols, revolvers, muskets, and breech-loading rifles, and wore cartridge and cap boxes. In 1841 the U.S. Navy had ordered an unknown quantity of Jenks breechloading percussion rifles, which were a calibre .54 weapon with a 'mule-ear' side-hammer and an overall length of 52½ inches. The Jenks had a bayonet stud under the barrel to take a socket bayonet. Both the rifle and bayonet were stamped 'USN'. Experimental orders were placed about the same time with Samuel Colt for rifled repeating carbines as well as for revolvers. The carbines had already been used in the Seminole War and 100 more were ordered in 1845. The Model 1842 musket was also in widespread use by the Navy.

The Navy also purchased a considerable number of smoothbore, percussion, single-shot pistols of the U.S. Model 1842 pattern. Those designed for naval service were stamped with an anchor or 'USN', usually on the barrel. These weapons were designed primarily for use by seamen, and were kept on the arms racks aboard ship. Those made under contract by N. P. Ames were a shorter weapon, and had a 'box-lock', the hammer being inside the lock plate to facilitate handling when carried inside a sailor's belt.

In 1845 the War Department ordered for the Navy '100 boarding pistols, 5-charged each $25.00, including appendages'. These were the first revolvers ordered for naval use, and were Model 1839 Colts of the Paterson model. Apparently only 50 were delivered.

Regarding edged weapons, petty officers and seamen carried the Model 1841 Naval Cutlass which had a 21 inch blade and a brass hilt, with grip and pommel cast in the same mold as the foot artillery sword, pattern of 1813. This was carried in a black bridle leather scabbard which was seamed down the reverse side with 44 copper rivets. Although dirks had not been authorised since 1813, they were probably still carried by many seamen. Most seamen also probably supplied themselves with a clasp knife ostensibly for cutting ropes during rigging.

Seamens' waist belts were usually white buff leather, with standing loop and eyelet holes at one end and brass hook riveted to the other. Where used, the cap pouch was slid onto this belt. Unless fitted with an attached 'frog', the cutlass scabbard was hung on the waist belt by a separate frog of black buff leather with a pocket notched to accept the brass stud on a scabbard. Navy pistols and revolvers were also carried on the waist via similar frogs bearing the navy-yard stamp in an oval. The Navy Musket Cartridge Box, of black bridle leather, with 'USN' embossed on the outer flap, was suspended from a black buff shoulder belt.

Regarding naval flags, every U.S. Navy ship carried in several sizes, and hoisted at different positions, the national ensign - the Stars and Stripes. Also flown was the jack which consisted of the union of the national ensign and which was displayed from the jack staff at the bow of the vessel when moored. Numerous naval signal flags were used for communication between vessels. Certain general purpose flags were also raised to issue an order or to indicate something was happening, or about to happen, i.e. ship taking on powder, under quarantine, or recalling boats.

In addition to the above were designation flags and pennants indicating the rank of the commander of a vessel or a group of vessels, and the vessel, or flag-ship, on which the commander was located. During the 1840s, a long, narrow pennant known as the commission pennant, or 'coach-whip', was the mark of a naval captain, or officer of lower rank when in command of a vessel of war. This was blue with a line of white stars near the staff, while the remainder of the field consisted of two stripes, red over white.

U.S. Seaman in warm weather white frock with plain blue dungaree or nankeen collar and cuffs. His waist belt would appear to be non-regulation. Michael F. Bremer collection.

A captain placed in command of a fleet or squadron, and by courtesy called a commodore, was entitled to fly a 'broad pennant', consisting of a forked flag, or 'burgee', with slightly converging top and bottom. It was normally blue and contained the same number of white stars as the union of the national ensign. Should two or more squadrons come together, only the senior commodore wore this blue pennant; the next in rank hoisted a similar one in red with white stars, while the lowest ranking commodore used a white pennant with blue stars.

U.S. Marine Corps

The first Americans to set foot on Mexican soil after Resaca de la Palma were Marine skirmishers in a naval force, under Captain J. H. Aulick, USN, which occupied Burrita some 15 miles north of the mouth of the Rio Grande. Throughout the remainder of the war, the U.S. Marine Corps played an important role on both coastlines within the landing forces which raided or captured ports of strategic importance, such as Tampico, San Juan Bautista, Yerba Buena, and Los

Second Lieutenant Daniel J. Sutherland, U.S. Marine Corps. Photographed by W. & F. Langenheim of Philadelphia, in 1847, Sutherland wears the M1840 dark blue dress uniform, and holds a mameluke sword across his lap. Courtesy of William J. Schultz, M.D.

Angeles. On 3 March 1847, Marine Commandant Archibald Henderson received permission to raise a Marine regiment, but reluctance on the part of Commodore Matthew C. Perry to relinquish control of the Marines within the Gulf Coast naval brigade prevented the realisation of this project, and only a Marine battalion finally arrived at Veracruz on 1 July 1847. Attached to Scott's army within the division of General John A. Quitman, this unit was initially commanded by Lieutenant Colonel Samuel E. Watson, who was succeeded by Levi Twiggs. The Marine Battalion took part in the assault on Chapultepec Castle, and were subsequently among the first American troops to fight their way into Mexico City on 13 September 1847.[38]

Some of the Marine detachments drawn together from various stations at the beginning of the Mexican War were possibly still wearing the undress uniform adopted in 1834, which consisted of a grass green frock coat fastened by a single row of nine buttons;

light grey trousers with buff seam stripes for officers and NCOs; and dark blue cloth fatigue caps. Due to fading caused by constant exposure to saline air, this uniform had become extremely unpopular, and by 1840 had been officially abandoned. The new uniform adopted on this occasion marked a return to the blue, white, and scarlet colour scheme worn by the Corps during the War of 1812.

For full dress, officers wore a dark blue, double-breasted tail-coat faced and piped with scarlet, having gold lace false button holes on the cuffs and skirts, and larger loops on the collar. Trousers were dark blue with 1¾ inch-wide scarlet seam stripe in winter, and plain white linen drilling in summer. Officers of captain's rank and above wore a chapeau bras with black silk cockade, gold lace loop, and crimson and gold tassels. This was surmounted by a scarlet cock-feathers plume. The plume of the Commandant, Marine Corps, was of 'red and white cock feathers, equally divided from tip to stem'. Subalterns wore a black beaver dress cap with bell crown and brass scale chinstrap, topped with red cocks-feather plume. The shield-shaped brass cap plate bore an eagle and anchor device over which was an arc of stars.

Since the 1820s, Marine officers had carried a distinctive curved sword with a 'mameluke hilt of white ivory', suspended from a two-inch wide white buff leather waist belt fastened by a rectangular eagle plate. Underneath this was a crimson silk sash.

Enlisted Marines wore a similar tail coat which was double-breasted for sergeant majors and quartermaster sergeants and single-breasted for others. Also piped with scarlet, the binding on collar, cuffs, and skirts was yellow worsted. Epaulettes were also yellow worsted. Pants were 'light sky blue' with 1½ inch-wide dark blue, edged scarlet, seam stripe for NCOs, and plain for enlisted Marines. The dress hat was similar to the black beaver cap worn by subalterns except it bore a red pompon and a cut-out brass eagle and foul anchor. Musicians wore a scarlet cloth coat with white linings, collar, and turnbacks, which was double-breasted for drum and fife majors, and single-breasted for other musicians. Marine buttons were described in the 1839 regulations as being 'gilt, convex, with eagle, anchor, and stars, raised border'.

The fatigue uniform for all Marine officers, except subalterns, was a dark blue frock coat with two rows of ten buttons, which closely resembled the navy pattern. That worn by subalterns was single-breasted. Trousers were also dark blue minus seam stripes. Fatigue caps were also plain dark blue, with a foul anchor within a wreath, embroidered in gold. Officers were also authorised a dark blue cloth or kerseymere shell or mess jacket edged with gold lace around collar, down its front, and around its bottom edge. This garment was lined with white shalloon, and had one false row of 16 small Marine buttons, being fastened by hooks and eyes.

Enlisted Marines wore a sky blue kersey fatigue uniform similar to that of the army, but without the trim. Sergeants' rank was indicated by two diagonal stripes of yellow worsted lace below the elbow on each arm. Corporals had single stripes. Forage caps were also dark blue. Enlisted mens' shirts were made of red flannel. Shirts of white cotton were also issued for warm weather.

In general, Marine NCOs and musicians wore the same swords as infantry. Enlisted Marines, except the higher grades of NCO, wore 2¼ inch wide white buff leather cross belts, with a slightly narrower waist belt of the same material. Breast plates were plain and oval. A black leather cartridge box was suspended on the right from one shoulder belt, the bayonet scabbard on the left from another, and the cap pouch was slid on the waist belt. NCOs' and musicians' swords were carried with the bayonet on a double-frogged shoulder belt. The enlisted Marines were armed with the U.S. breech-loading flintlock rifle calibre .52, Model 1819 (Hall's Patent), which were probably manufactured at Harper's Ferry, Virginia.[39]

U.S. Volunteers

On 13 May 1846, President Polk and Congress initially authorised appoximately 45,000 state volunteers to be taken into U.S. service for one year. About 20,000 men were raised among Alabama, Arkansas, Georgia, Illinois, Indiana, Kentucky, Mississippi, Missouri, Ohio, Tennessee, and Texas. Another 25,000 additional infantry were hopefully to

This unidentified sergeant wears an oilskin forage cap, and non-U.S. regulation jacket with unusual collar trim. With the photo frame removed, his trousers were also non-regulation, being made from a striped corduroy material. He is probably a member of a volunteer regiment. David Wynn Vaughan collection.

be enrolled in the northeastern states but not called into service until later.

The governors of these various states, in concert with the state legislatures, put out the calls to arms. Companies were raised in various locales, usually rallying around prominent citizens who expected to receive commissions. These companies subsequently rendezvoused with others and were formed into regiments and battalions. The number of regiments from each state was generally proportionate to both the population of the state, and to its degree of affiliation with the expansionist Democratic Party. Hence the southern and western states ultimately provided the most volunteers, e.g. 20,000 from the South, 40,000 from the West, 8,000 from the Northeast.

During the Fall of 1846 it became apparent that hostilities in Mexico would not end as soon as originally believed. More troops would be required, especially if the contemplated expedition against Veracruz and the Mexican capital was to be carried out successfully. On 16 November a call for nine volunteer regiments to be raised for immediate service, and to serve for the duration of the war, was sent to the governors of Massachusetts, New York, Pennsylvania, Virginia, North Carolina, South Carolina, Mississippi, Louisiana, and Texas.

The federal government initially required state troops to provide their own clothing, whilst weapons and accoutrements came from U.S. arsenals. During the first flush of recruitment, many uniformed volunteer militia companies, in states such as South Carolina and Virginia, volunteered for Federal service as a body, and paraded in their full dress uniforms. As far as is known, all of these units replaced this with fatigue or service clothing as and when they embarked for Mexico.

By law, each volunteer was allowed $3.50 per month for clothing during the time he was in Federal service. To enable the volunteer to provide himself

A uniformed volunteer militia company parading in Exeter, New Hampshire, in 1846. Their bell-crowned caps and frock coats would have been exchanged for plainer wear for Mexican War service. Amon Carter Museum, Fort Worth; accession # 79.33.

with good and sufficient clothing, a commutation allowance of $21 for the first 6 months was advanced each man after he was mustered in. Later in the war volunteers drew clothing from Federal depots. Authorities in some states, such as Virginia and Michigan, used the commutation money to get large contracts so their men would achieve a well-clothed and uniform appearance. Other states, like Missouri and Texas, apparently let volunteers have the money to spend as they saw fit, with the result that their troops went off to war in whatever suited their fancy or, worse still, having squandered the cash, in the clothes on their backs. A number of states, including Illinois and Indiana, allowed each volunteer company to get up its own uniform. The combined result of these various policies was an amazing array of cut, colour, and cloth among the U.S. Volunteers, at least for the early part of their war service.

Alabama

The 1st Regiment of Alabama Volunteers, commanded by Colonel John R. Caffey, was raised by this state as a result of the call of May-July 1846. The Eutaw Volunteers and the Greensboro Volunteers were the only two uniformed companies in this regiment at the outset of service. The former company wore 'cottonade suits made by the ladies, and straw hats'. The latter left home wearing 'a green worsted frock suit'. Much to the annoyance of other companies in the 1st Alabama, the Eutaw Volunteers, on reaching Camango in Mexico, received a new uniform consisting of 'navy blue Suits, with brass buttons, and Caps'.[40]

The 1st Alabama arrived in Mexico on 4 July 1846 and, by March 1847, were involved in Scott's Veracruz expedition as part of the brigade commanded by General John A. Quitman. After the fall of Veracruz, this brigade occupied Alvarado, a coastal town about 60 miles South East of that city. Quitman's brigade subsequently followed Scott's main army towards Mexico City. On reaching Jalapa, the twelve-month term of enlistment of the Alabama regiment expired and, refusing to re-enlist for the war, the unit returned home via New Orleans.

Presumably in desperate need of clothing to replace worn out uniforms prior to leaving Jalapa, the Alabamians were offered captured Mexican uniforms.

Top left and right.

Reconstruction of an enlisted man of Captain Schaeffer's rifle company, District of Columbia and Maryland Regiment of Volunteers. Collar trim is conjectural. He holds a M1841 rifle, whilst his bullet pouch and flask are M1839 pattern. Photo by Ross M. Kimmel.

S. F. Nunnelee recalled:

'They sent down a wagon load of Mexican soldier uniforms for us to "rig" ourselves out in, if we chose[.] I picked out a coat that would button in front but the front button struck me just below my nipples, and the "swallow tail" struck me just below my back suspender buttons. I declined to play "The camp Fool" in that garb, but proposed to auction off the whole lot, free gratis for Uncle Sam. I did not get a bid.'

The 1st Battalion of Alabama Volunteers enlisted for five years, and arrived in Mexico during January 1848 under the command of Major J. J. Seibles. After several months in 'camp of instruction', the Alabama Battalion joined the brigade under Colonel James Bankhead which occupied the cities of Cordova and Orizaba.

Arkansas

A solid Western state, Arkansas provided one regiment

of cavalry, or 'mounted gunmen', and one battalion of infantry, during the summer of 1846. The former was assembled at Washington, Arkansas, and were mustered in on 13 July under the command of the inexperienced Colonel Archibald Yell. Nick-named the 'Mounted Devils', this regiment took part in the Chihuahua Expedition during the Fall of 1846. A particularly ill-disciplined unit, members of Yell's regiment massacred Mexican citizens at Cantana in retaliation for the guerrilla assassination of an American picket. A squadron of two companies, commanded by Captain Albert Pike, was permanently detached from this regiment in January 1847, and served with distinction. Meanwhile, the remainder of Yell's command disgraced itself at Buena Vista by retiring from the battlefield 'almost at the first firing'. Yell was killed during the battle attempting to rally his men.[41]

A battalion of four companies of Arkansas riflemen, commanded by Lieutenant Colonel Roane, also served in the Chihuahua Expedition, with little more distinction than their mounted counterparts. All these Arkansian units were mustered out on 7 June 1847.

District of Columbia

Despite its diminutive size, the District of Columbia

provided a six company infantry unit known as the Battalion of Baltimore and Washington Volunteers, also known as 'The Old Baltimore Battalion', which rendezvoused at Fort Washington, near the federal capital during the summer of 1846 under the command of Lieutenant Colonel William H. Watson. Captain John R. Kenly recalled in 1846 that this battalion '...was dressed in the regular blue uniform and equipments of the regular troops of the line of the army, and was the only command of volunteers thus equipped that I am aware of, at this time.' As a result, the men from this unit often got into fights with other volunteers when they '... were forever wandering about, and frequently came into collision with volunteers from other States, who, being mostly from the rural districts, had some curious-looking uniforms and hats, and would not understand the character or take the fun of these city fellows, particularly as they were dressed in [regular] army uniforms.'[42]

Brigaded with the 1st and 3rd Regiments of U.S. Infantry, under the command of Lieutenant Colonel John Garland, within Twigg's Division of Regulars, the Baltimore Battalion saw hot action in the streets of Monterey in 1846. The flag carried by the Baltimore Battalion was chosen by General Quitman to fly over the State House after his brigade had taken formal possession of Victoria, the capital of the Mexican State of Tamaulipas on 29 December 1846. Subsequently, with their supply lines stretched to the limit, this entire division was reduced to a shabby appearance. By the time his Battalion had moved to Tampico to assist Scott's planned offensive in central Mexico, Kenly noted that his men were 'ragged and nearly barefoot'.[43]

With the end of its one-year service, the Baltimore Battalion was sent home and mustered out. However, John Kenly and other officers recruited a successor unit known as the District of Columbia and Maryland Regiment of Volunteers. This new regiment returned to Mexico where it spent most of its service garrisoning the town of Jalapa on Scott's line of march to the interior. During December 1847, Kenly recalled the arrival of 'a fine company from Washington, recruited and commanded by ... Captain Francis B. Schaeffer; it was a rifle company, handsomely dressed in dark blue jackets and pants', which attracted 'marked attention from our weather-beaten companies from the same city'. This company was permanently attached to the Columbia and Maryland Regiment.[45]

Florida

This state was required to raise a battalion of five companies of 'foot soldiers' for one year's service in

Reconstruction of an Illinois Volunteer, based on a description by Alexander Konse of the Texan Guards, Co. H, 2nd Illinois. He wears a 'glazed' cap of waterproof material, and pale blue jacket and trousers of 'light summer-goods', with red trim on collar and cuffs. Photo by Ross M. Kimmel.

May 1846. Although none of these companies was intended for out of state service, being required to replace regulars withdrawn from the forts at Pensacola and St. Augustine, three of them were sent to Mexico. The first to be raised, during December 1846, was 'Johnson's Company', commanded by Captain Allen G. Johnson, which spent its entire period of duty stationed at Fort Brooke, Tampa, where it 'performed the important service of restraining the Indians in South Florida from hostile activities'. The second was that raised by Captain W.W.J. Kelly, officially known as Company A, Florida Volunteer Battalion. It was mustered into service on 9 April 1847 and, after training at Fort Pickens, finally left for Mexico in September. Assigned to General Patterson's army, this company saw no real action, but performed valuable duty keeping the line of communication open between Veracruz and Scott's forces in Mexico City. The company raised by Captain R.G. Livingston in June 1847 was officially designated Company C, Florida

Top left and right.

These two men, presumably brothers, both volunteered for service in the Cass County Volunteers, Co. G, 1st Indiana Regiment of Infantry, in 1846. **Captain Stanislaus Lasselle (left) wears his officers' frock coat with home-made style shoulder straps indicating his rank. Second Sergeant Jacques M. Lasselle (right) wears the 'tight bodied' coat 'trimmed with silver lace' adopted by this company before they set off for Mexico.** Cass County, Indiana, Historical Society.

Left.

Private William Walters, Co. A, 4th Regiment of Illinois Volunteers, 1846. Walters enlisted in June 1846 at Springfield, Illinois and was appointed Adjutant of his regiment. He died enroute to Mexico on 29 July of the same year. His light blue uniform jacket, typical of that obtained by the 4th Illinois, is similar to the U.S. enlisted man's jacket with high standing collar and shoulder straps. Illinois State Historical Society, Springfield, Illinois.

Volunteer Battalion. This unit also saw service in Mexico where it joined Kelly's company under Patterson's command.

A composite company mostly recruited in Florida in April 1847 became Co. K, 13th U.S. Infantry, whilst Johnson's original company was reorganised 'for the

Flag of 4th Indiana Volunteer Infantry. Smithsonian Institution.

war' under Captain William Fisher in January 1848. It is assumed all these companies were issued regular U.S. Infantry clothing.[45]

Georgia

This state was requisitioned for one regiment of infantry, or riflemen, during May 1846. The ten companies which formed the 1st Regiment of Georgia Volunteers were gathered at Columbus, where they elected Henry Roots Jackson as colonel. Only three of these companies - the Columbus Guards, Sumter Volunteers, and Crawford Guards - appear to have spent at least part of their commutation money on the purchase of fatigue uniforms. The remainder, which included the Irish Jasper Greens and Richmond Blues, either had theirs ready made, or went off to war without a uniform.

This regiment left for Mexico on 20 June 1846. After languishing in Camp Belknap, on the San Juan River, it spent the remainder of its time guarding money trains and supplies at Monterey, Tampico and Veracruz, never once coming within shooting distance of the Mexican army.[46]

Illinois

Though this mid-western state was apportioned three regiments in 1846, its Democratic citizens were so striken with war fever that four full 'twelve months' regiments of infantry coalesced during the summer of 1846. The 1st Regiment of Illinois Volunteers, commanded by Colonel John J. Hardin, arrived in Mexico on 2 October of that year. The 2nd Illinois under Colonel William H. Bissell followed close behind. Both these regiments served with Taylor on the Buena Vista campaign. The 3rd Illinois was commanded by Colonel Ferris Foreman, whilst Colonel Edward D. Baker led the 4th Illinois. Both of these regiments campaigned within Scott's army from Veracruz to Mexico City. The 5th and 6th Illinois regiments, the former being commanded by Colonel E. W. B. Newby, volunteered 'for the war' in 1847 and served in the Veracruz area of New Mexico.

Via General Order No. 2 on 29 May 1846, Governor Thomas Ford of Illinois informed volunteers from his state that they should fit themselves out in a 'blue Jeans or cassinet Jacket or roundabout, standing collar and brass buttons, and blue jeans or cassinet pantaloons and glazed caps'. Officers' uniforms were to be agreed upon 'after the companies shall be organized into Regiments'. He also

The Mormon Battalion, by George Ottinger. This oil painting depicts the unit preparing a ford over a creek for their wagons to cross. Note the officers wear dark blue uniforms. The standard bearer carries a Stars and Stripe topped by a brass eagle. Enlisted men wear a variety of fatigue clothing, some of which may indicate distinctive company dress. Museum of Church History & Art: Church of Jesus Christ of the Latter Day Saints Historical Department.

announced that, as the U.S. government would pay for the clothing, 'any person who will furnish the uniform for the companies... will be secured by a lein on the pay rolls of the companies'.

As a consequence, Illinois volunteers set out for war in a great variety of uniform styles, of various shades of blue, or grey, with different coloured facings, procured from different sources. The Quincy Riflemen, who became Company A, 1st Illinois, outfitted themselves in 'a grey frock coat, trimmed with black, and a forage cap to match, and black pantaloons'. According to the *Alton Telegraph and Democratic Review* of 6 June 1846, the uniform for the remainder of this regiment was 'paid for by the United States', and consisted of 'bluejeans or Cassinet Jacket or Roundabout, with standing collar, and brass buttons; Pantaloons of the same material; and a glazed

Cap'. These uniforms were made up by the 'Patriotic Sewing Society', who also furnished the 1st Illinois with blankets and provisions.

According to Alexander Konze, a German immigrant and private in the Texan Guards, Company H, 2nd Illinois:

'My brothers-in-arms are thus far, at least, no experts in the art of dealing with weapons, and their uniforms mere makeshifts. Colonels wandering about in shabby frocks and in very inadequate trousers of a color no longer distinguishable are no longer a novel sight; many a captain is commanding his company with drawn walking-stick, indeed, I even saw one with his shirt-sleeves rolled up leading his men into the presence of the colonel.....The uniforms, which differ with every company, consist of short jackets or coats, usually blue or gray with red or yellow facings. The cloth is light summer-goods, rarely broadcloth'.[47]

Sam Chamberlain, originally a sergeant in the Alton Guards, Company A of the same regiment, said of the dress of the first three Illinois regiments: 'We were uniformed as each company selected and strange grotesque costumes now filled the Camp.' His company chose 'jackets and pants of blue mixed Kentucky jeans with yellow stripes across the breast like a Dragoon Bugler'. By special permission,

Chamberlain had his uniform made of dark blue cloth, and trimmed only with sergeant's chevrons, which he recalled was 'quite a neat affair'.[48] A coloured drawing he made of himself and men depicts him in plain dark blue, with the others in light blue with yellow stripes.

The 4th Illinois left their home state without uniforms on 27 June 1846. On reaching Missouri, they were temporarily quartered at Jefferson Barracks near St. Louis, from which city they had uniforms cut and made before their departure via steamboat for New Orleans on 24 July. In a letter from Jefferson Barracks to his brother, Private B. F. Perry, of Co. G, wrote: 'The officers have ordered their uniforms[.] it will be blew cloth frock coats[,] a buff stripe on the pantaloons, white ovel buttons with the eagle on.' The latter was possibly a description of the 1821 pattern, white metal, general service button. Headgear was to consist of 'white caps if they can get them[,] if not, cloth[.] According to Perry, the rank of captain was indicated by two 'strerilins', or federal-style straps with an eagle, on each shoulder. The rank of first through third lieutenants were signified by the numerals one to three consecutively. Swords were to be 'strate with brass mountings and brass scabbard'.[49]

Non-commissioned officers were to wear 'the sheretin', or chevron, inverted and on the left arm only. The first sergeant wore two inverted chevrons, underneath which was sewn the numeral '1'. The second through fourth sergeant wore a single inverted chevron over the numerals '2' through '4' respectively. N.C.O.s were to carry a 'sord, but have to carry a musket two [sic]'. They were also to wear 'the uniform of the company [and presumably the regiment] which will be blue cloth roundabouts and pant [with a] buff stripe and glazed cap and boots'.

The *Missouri Republican* described the 4th Illinois as follows as they left St. Louis: 'The regiment is handsomely uniformed in blue roundabout and pantaloons, with glazed oil cloth caps and in the equipment of the United States Infantry they make as handsome display as has at any time been seen in our streets.'

Regarding arms and equipage, Alexander Konze of the 2nd Illinois recalled: 'I have seen practically nothing but muskets...a few companies are fitted out with fairly long rifles and daggers that would not look out of place in a museum of curiousities. To every six men there is a tent which looks pretty at a distance, but which could gain a great deal of attractiveness if were roomier and cooler.'

After landing at Brazos Island on 12 August 1846, the 4th Illinois took up line of march along the banks of the Rio Grande. In a letter to the *Illinois State Register*, an anonymous member of the regiment described the regiment's accoutrements thus: '...For the first time we were marched fully equipped, with knapsacks, haversacks, cartridge boxes, muskets and canteens with water. We were strapped and harnessed in style.' In a letter home dated 22 August, Private John Nevin King, Co. D, added further detail: 'We are all provided with tin canteens which hold only three pints'.

During September, 1846 Colonel Baker, who was still a member of the House of Representatives, returned to Washington where he concluded a speech in Congress offering resolutions that the volunteers be supplied with clothing the same as regulars, at the prices paid by the government. Returning to Mexico during in February 1847, he brought new uniforms for the 4th Illinois, which were subsequently described by Private King as consisting of 'Blue pants, Blue Cloth Caps and white coats [possibly undress jackets]'. Clad in their new garb, this regiment accompanied General Scott's army south and participated in the battles of Veracruz and Cerro Gordo.

Indiana

Three full regiments of infantry were provided by Indiana in 1846. These were the 1st Indiana, commanded by Colonel James P. Drake; the 2nd Indiana, led by Colonel William H. Bissell; and the 3rd Indiana, under Colonel James H. Lane. Two further regiments had been raised by 1847.

Via General Order No. 1, the Adjutant General of Indiana, David Reynolds, advised the companies being raised in his state for Mexican service that they could adopt such uniforms as they chose, but that officers were requested to pattern their uniforms on those of the Regular Army. Subsequently, on 5 June, he issued General Order No. 2 which stated:

'A dress or parade uniform is never required in actual service and will not be used in this campaign by either officer or private. To purchase such would, therefore, be a useless expense. For uniforms for service, a cloth or forage cap and a gray mixed or sky blue jeans, hunters frock coat and pantaloons without stripes is suggested (not required) for neatness and comfort. The coat reaching half way down the thigh, double-breasted, double-row of white military buttons, eagle stamped, or black mould buttons, made to button close around the throat. For non-commissioned officers, same as above, only the Sergeants are to wear white worsted epaulettes on each shoulder and the pants to have a white worsted stripe one and one-half inches wide down the sides. Corporals to wear epaulettes but not stripes. The

Top left.

Reconstruction of an enlisted man of the 1st Regiment of Mississippi Rifles in the red shirt and white duck trousers which Sam Chamberlain described seeing this unit wearing at Buena Vista. Hats seem to have varied between straws and wide-brimmed black slouches. He carries a Bowie knife in lieu of a bayonet, and a M1841 rifle, which became better known as the 'Mississippi' rifle because of the fame it won in the hands of this regiment in Mexico. His bullet pouch and flask are U.S. M1839 pattern; the haversack and canteen are federal issue types. Photo by Ross M. Kimmel.

Top right.

Peter Ott enlisted in Captain Walter Biscoe's Company, Mounted Battalion of Louisiana Volunteers, on 4 August 1847. In this image, taken shortly before his departure for Mexico, Ott holds a M1841 'Mississippi' rifle, and wears a brand new jacket trimmed on collar, shoulder straps, and cuffs. Photo courtesy of his great grandson Albert J. Ott.

Left.

This young volunteer is typical of the Mounted volunteers from Missouri who followed Doniphan and Price in New Mexico and Chihuahua. He wears a 'Model A' glazed forage cap, cotton overshirt and woollen pants of either grey or light blue cloth. Herb Peck collection.

This engraving, which accompanied the journal of William H. Richardson published in 1850, depicts Missourians under Doniphan's command wearing the fatigue dress they purchased themselves, which was described as being similar to that worn by the Regulars.

orderly Sergeant is distinguished by a red worsted sash on duty. Each soldier is to have a blanket.'[50]

General Order No. 3, issued three days later, provided further instructions for officers' uniforms:

'When a uniform is adopted by a company, the same material will answer for the commissioned officers making the usual variations in the trimmings. For instance: in case of the adoption of gray mixed or blue jeans frock coat mentioned in Section X of General Order No. 2, the officer might wear a similar coat with a single instead of a double row of buttons in front.'[51]

An engraving of a Missouri volunteer of Doniphan's command, based on an original drawing of J. W. Patton, made after the battle of Brazito. Note he wears a poncho over his fatigue clothing, and appears to be armed with a M1841 rifle and dragoon sabre. From John Taylor Hughes, *Doniphan's expedition; containing an account of the conquest of New Mexico,* Cincinnati, 1850.

This eye-witness painting by Sam Chamberlain depicts the Mississippi Rifles' defeat of the Mexican cavalry brigade, commanded by General Julián Juverna, at Buena Vista on 23 February, 1847. Note that the Mississippians have the black leather cartridge box for the M1841 rifle slid on to their white buff waist belts. San Jacinto Museum of History Association.

General Order No. 6 authorised the captain of each company to contract for clothing:

'not exceeding two uniform suits, two pairs stout shoes with broad and thick soles, suitable hat or cap, in addition to ordinary forage cap, two cotton shirts, two flannel shirts, two pairs of drawers, stockings, and one good blanket for each man'.[52]

Such a relaxed series of orders gave the Indiana volunteers considerable leeway in their choice of uniform. In a letter dated 19 June 1846 and published in the *Democratic Pharos* of Logansport, Indiana on 8 July, a member of the Cass County Volunteers, Company G, 1st Indiana, reported:

'We are getting our uniforms made and are to have blue cloth tight bodied coats trimmed with silver lace and three rows of buttons on the breast - pants of blue satinet, also trimmed with silver lace - no vest - caps of cloth with glazed tops, all of which will cost about $18.00.'

Sergeant Jacquis M. Lasselle was photographed in the final version of uniform chosen by this company. His blue coat was fastened by a single row of nine buttons, with blind silver, or white, braid running across the breast through each button. His standing collar was edged with one-inch wide braid of the same colour. Rank was indicated by a single strip of silver, or white, lace sewn on each shoulder along the seam with the sleeve. Presumably the white worsted epaulettes recommended by the Adjutant General were difficult to acquire in rural Indiana.

His brother, Captain Stanilaus Lasselle, who commanded the Cass County Volunteers, was photographed in a plain nine-button frock coat with square-cut standing collar edged with half-inch wide silver, or white, lace, with rank indicated by narrow silver-edged straps on each shoulder, also sewn along the seam with the sleeve.

The Monroe Guards, who became Company A of the 3rd Indiana, acquired a uniform from New Albany which consisted of 'a gray cashmere [cassimere] sack coat with black velvet stripes up the front, pants of the same material with black velvet stripes up the legs, broad brim, gray hat with brim turned up at the side'. They were armed at Baton Rouge with Model 1822 Flint Muskets, and 'hand made cartridges consisting of

one large ball and three buck shot'.[53]

When Company E of the 3rd Indiana left for their appointed regimental rendezous on 14 June 1846, they were reported to have 'purchased uniforms of bright blue jeans and had styled themselves "Brown County Blues," a name by which they were known all through the war'.[54]

Although considerable modifications were made in the uniform recommended by Adjutant General Reynolds, it is apparent that its basic model remained popular with Indiana volunteers. Thus when their state clothing began to quickly wear out on active service, they resented attempts to re-clothe them in regular Army fatigue uniforms. One Indiana soldier said: Let 'em go to Hell with their sky blue, I'll be blowed if they make a regular out of me.[55] The popularity of Reynold's basic uniform recommendations became evident in 1847 when the federal government called upon the state for a fourth regiment of volunteers. On this occasion the Adjutant General repeated his 1846 instructions almost verbatim in prescribing the uniforms for the new

Captain George Ellis Pugh, 4th Ohio Volunteer Infantry, had this image taken at Veracruz on 16 September, 1847. Courtesy of Michael F. Bremer.

volunteers.

Only after the government had requested a fifth regiment from returned veterans of the first three did Reynolds adapt his recommendations to incorporate some of the experience acquired by these men in Mexico. Hence, General Order No. 14, issued on 31 August 1847, stated in paragraph XV:

'In relation to clothing .... A service uniform only is necessary. It is recommended that for neatness and comfort, it consist, as in the regular service, of a blue cloth roundabout to be double breasted with a double row of white metal buttons, eagle stamped and made to button tight at the throat. The commissioned officers are to wear blue cloth frock coats and a single row of buttons and pantaloons with white worsted stripes one and one half inches wide down the sides.'

Although the uniform of the 5th Indiana conformed more closely to the cut and style of the Regulars, the sky blue colour was not adopted. Some years after the war, Pyrrhus Woodward, who served as a sergeant in Company H, 5th Indiana, recalled:

'We remained at Camp Madison about three weeks where we received our uniforms which were of dark blue cloth something like those worn in the late [Civil] War, and we wore caps. The light blue overcoats worn during the late war, were very similar to those issued

Top.
The 1st Ohio Volunteer Infantry on parade in front of the Cathedral at Monterey in 1847. Amon Carter Museum, Fort Worth: accession # 78.87.

Bottom.
Private William Hall enlisted in the Alexandria Volunteers, Company B, 1st Virginia Volunteer Regiment, on 1 December 1846. An illiterate 22-year-old shoemaker, he served with his unit until it returned home in August 1848. He wears a dark blue uniform partially conforming to that supplied to his regiment by the state of Virginia during December 1846. Dale S. Snair collection.

to the regiment.'

The 4th Indiana, raised in 1847, was presented a silk regimental flag bearing thirteen red and white stripes, and a white union painted on which is an eagle perched on the top third of a globe, over which is arrayed 29 red stars.

Iowa

Newly admitted to the Union, this state responded to the call for volunteers issued in May 1846 by organising the Mormon Battalion, composed almost entirely of members of the Church of Jesus Christ of

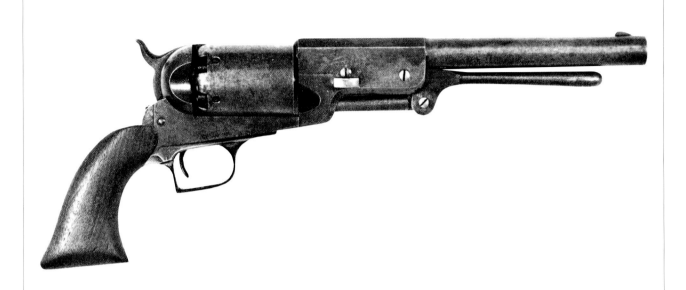

Top.
Colt Walker .44 calibre percussion revolver, dated 1847. One of a pair (serial numbers 1009 and 1010) specifically made for Captain Samuel Walker of the Texas Rangers, who was instrumental in designing the weapon. Peter Newark's Western Americana.

Bottom.
Colonel Robert Treat Paine, colonel of the 1st Regiment North Carolina Volunteers, acquired a reputation as a very strict disciplinarian. Encamped near Buena Vista within Cushing's brigade during June 1847, his regiment suffered heavily from sickness and developed a reputation for unruliness. Their subsequent mutinous behaviour was treated very harshly by their commanding officer, who shot and mortally wounded one of his men. Paine's regulation double-breasted coat is fastened by U.S. infantry eagle-'I' buttons, whilst his sword belt clasp bears the state seal of North Carolina, featuring the figures of Liberty and Plenty. His sword has a pommel with a Phrygian helmet pattern, and a four-sided knuckle-bow that curves below the grip and terminates in a quillion with a disc finial bearing what appears to be a rosette. Amon Carter Museum, Fort Worth: accession # 81.65/17.

Latter Day Saints. A large number of Mormons, recently driven from Nauvoo, Illinois, had gathered at Council Bluffs, and were planning to settle in California. In order to dispel feelings of hostility towards the U.S., and to enlist some reliable fighting material, Colonel Stephen W. Kearny was authorised to accept a body of these immigrants not larger than a quarter of his entire force. Enlisting on the understanding that they would be discharged in California following a year's service, four companies, and part of a fifth, amounting to about 500 men, had been mustered in at Council Bluffs, Iowa, under Captain James Allen, of the 1st Dragoons, by 16 July 1846. Accompanied by 'twenty-seven women, for laundresses', this unit took part in the Sante Fe expedition under Kearny, before finally ending up being mustered out after further service in California.[56]

Volunteers received into the Mormon Battalion were promised that they could keep their arms and equipage once their twelve month's term of service had expired. At Fort Leavenworth they received 'tents, arms and all the accoutrements necessary for the campaign'. According to Henry W. Bigler, who enlisted in Company B, each man was issued 'guns and knap sacks and cartridge boxes in each of which were 36 rounds of ammunition'.[57] Robert S. Bliss of the same unit recalled: 'we are cheerful and happy notwithstanding we have to carry our Guns, accoutrements, Napsacks [sic], Canteen, haversacks, and Push our Waggons all day over hills which are not few nor far between'.[58]

Whilst at Fort Leavenworth in August 1846, the Mormon Battalion drew their commutation, or clothing money, most of which, according to Henry Bigler, was sent back to Iowa to help their brethren. Hence this unit appears to have embarked on the march to Sante Fe mostly wearing civilian attire, or fatigue shirts of various colours, with slouch hats and white accoutrement straps and belts.

By 27 June 1847, having reached the Platte River, John Steele of the Mormon Battalion recorded:

'Our men that looked natural enough when they left Council Bluffs, now look like mountaineers, sun-burned and weather beaten, mostly dressed in buckskin with fringes and porcupine quills, mocassins, Spanish saddles and spurs, Spanish bridles and jinglers at them, and long beards, so that if I looked in a glass for the young man who left the Bluffs a year ago, I would not have known myself. Went away afoot, came home riding a fine horse...'

After their twelve month period of enlistment had expired, enough Mormons re-enlisted to form one

Colonel John Francis Hamtramck, 1st Virginia Regiment of Volunteers. As a youth, Hamtramck had served as a sergeant with Major Zachary Taylor's expedition up the Mississippi River, and his gallantry in action at the mouth of the Rock River in Illinois, 19 July, 1814, was apparently responsible for his appointment to the U.S. Military Academy in 1815. After resigning from the army as a second lieutenant in 1822, Hamtramck worked as an Indian agent until 1831, when he settled down as a planter near Shepherdstown, in Jefferson County. In 1835 he was commissioned as a captain in the Virginia state militia. He wears a single-breasted dark blue frock coat, instead of the double-breasted version normally prescribed for field-grade officers. His rank is indicated by the eagle in his shoulder strap. A single digit or letter, probably a Roman numeral 'I' for 1st Virginia Volunteers or a letter 'I' for Infantry, appears inside the looped horn on his wide-crowned forage cap. He grips a sword or sabre with an elaborate hilt that includes an eagle head pommel. The Virginia state seal can clearly be seen on his sword belt clasp and buttons. Amon Carter Museum, Fort Worth: accession # 81.65.3.

company of infantry, which served until 14 March 1848.

Kentucky

The Commonwealth of Kentucky sent three volunteer

John Turner Hambrick, a Caswell County merchant, enlisted in January or February 1847 in the 1st North Carolina Regiment. He wears the pale blue, or grey, Federal-style fatigue uniform acquired by his regiment. This consisted of a nine-button shell jacket, with shoulder straps and slash sleeves fastened by two buttons. Although the unhooked standing collar is devoid of the lace found on Regular Army jackets, it still has the two small buttons either side, normally found at the end of lace loops. His breast pocket is set at an angle and is fastened by a small button from which is hung a pick-and-brush tool for use with a flintlock musket. His waist belt, fastened with an oval 'US' buckle, and cartridge box sling, with 'eagle' breast plate, are of buff leather, after US regulations for the 1840s. North Carolina Archives, N 67.7.1.

Lieutenant Michael R. Clark, of the Richland Company of the Palmetto Regiment, wore this dark blue frock coat and pants when he posed for this quarter-plate daguerreotype by J. T. Zealy of Columbia. His dark blue forage cap rests on the table by his elbow. South Caroliniana Library.

regiments to fight in the Mexican War in response to the call issued in 1846. These consisted of the 1st Kentucky Volunteer Cavalry, the 1st Kentucky Infantry, and the 2nd Kentucky Infantry. All three units served with Taylor in northern Mexico.

The 1st Kentucky Cavalry, also known as 'The Hunters of Kentucky' after the title of a popular song which lauded the Kentucky Rifles who stood with Jackson at the Battle of New Orleans, was organised in May 1846 under Colonel Humphrey Marshall. Raised from the ranks of the 3rd Regiment of Kentucky

Militia, which claimed a pre-Revolutionary War heritage, this regiment served at Buena Vista on 22-23 February 1847, and was mustered out on 7 June 1847 at New Orleans. The 1st Kentucky Cavalry were described as 'generally athletic men, riding splendid horses, and their picturesque dress imparts to them a romantic appearance. The hat particularly is very fanciful. It is drab beaver with a broad brim, ornamented with several gold stars, and looped up with gold lace in the three cornered fashion of the Revolution. They all wear their beards unshorn with boots over the legs of their trousers, reaching above the knee, armed with huge spurs on the heel and faced with red morocco.'[59] This uniform did not last long for, on 23 September, 1846, a correspondent of the Kentucky *Observer* reported of Colonel Marshall's regiment: 'They are barefooted, and some of them literally without breeches, many without hats and coats.'[60]

The 1st Kentucky Infantry, otherwise known as the

Major William H. Polk, brother of President Polk, served in the 1st North Carolina Regiment, later transferring to the short-lived 3rd U.S. Dragoons, during the Mexican War. His frock coat was single-breasted, with lapels, and front held together by hooks and eyes. (*Detail*) Originally tailored to accommodate epaulettes during his service with the Tar Heel Regiment, the shoulders were subsequently altered and patched to display a Dragoon major's straps. The surviving yellow metal buttons bear the eagle-'D' device. North Carolina Museum of History: photos courtesy of Alan McBrayer.

This unidentified daguerreotype of a young American volunteer was found in Massachusetts, and may depict a member of the regiment from that state. His jacket has unusual trim on the cuffs, and elaborate scales on each shoulder, whilst his oval breast plate appears to display the crest of the State seal - an arm, the hand of which grasps a broadsword. He holds a M1839 Type 1 forage cap with oil-skin cover. Note the prick-and-brush tool attached to his jacket breast. Helder Costa collection.

Louisville Legion, was constituted on 21 January 1839, and was mustered into Federal service on 17 May 1846 under Colonel Stephen Ormsby, with nine companies of infantry and one of artillery. It served at the battle of Monterey on 10-23 September 1846, where it was brigaded with the 1st Ohio Infantry in the 1st Brigade, Field Division. The 1st Kentucky was not involved at Buena Vista, and was withdrawn from Taylor's army on 14 April 1847. This regiment was mustered out at New Orleans on 17 May 1847.

The 2nd Kentucky Infantry was organised in May 1846 under Colonel William R. McKee, and was mustered into service on 9 June 1846 at Louisville. This regiment served at Buena Vista where it helped to hold back a fierce Mexican attack. The 2nd Kentucky was mustered out at New Orleans on 9 June

1847. A single Kentucky company, raised by John S. Williams, excluded from these commands, and accordingly mustered in the 6th U.S. Infantry for one year.

With the second requisition for troops from Kentucky, the 3rd Infantry was raised under Colonel Manlius V. Thompson, whilst the 4th Kentucky Infantry was commanded by Colonel John Stuart Williams, who had finished his twelve month's service with the Regulars. A further twelve independent companies were raised in Kentucky during 1847, four of which enlisted into the regular army.

A uniform for the enrolled militia of Kentucky had existed in the statute books unchanged since 1815, although it is not known to what extent this influenced the dress of volunteers from this state. The first two Kentucky infantry regiments wore a dark blue uniform with glazed caps or slouch hats. Unable to acquire dark blue cloth, the 3rd Kentucky adopted brown jackets and pants.[61] At least one Kentucky regiment was armed with the U.S. Model 1842 Rifle.

Mississippi

This state provided the 1st Regiment of Mississippi Rifles, the 2nd Regiment of Mississippi Rifles, and the Battalion of Riflemen. Several individual companies of Mississippians were also raised, and saw service in units from other states. The Sparrow Volunteers, commanded by Captain James D. Galbraith, volunteered as Co. E, 4th Regiment Louisiana Volunteers in May 1846. The Claiborne Volunteers, also organised in May 1846 under Captain W. H. Jacobs, failed to join the 1st Mississippi, and took passage to Mexico where they were assigned to the 1st Texas Regiment.

The 1st Mississippi Rifles, named after the U.S. Model 1842 Rifle it used so effectively, was commanded by Colonel Jefferson Davis, who in 1861 became President of the Confederacy. Raised in May 1846 for twelve months service, this regiment served under Taylor in northern Mexico, and took part in the Monterey Campaign and the battle of Buena Vista. It was mustered out at New Orleans in June 1847.

The 2nd Mississippi was raised for the period of the war on 27 November 1846, and commanded by Colonel Reuben Davis, arrived in northern Mexico the day after Buena Vista, and saw little war experience before its return home in July 1848.[62]

The Battalion of Riflemen, raised during the summer of 1847 partially from the veterans of the disbanded 1st Mississippi, was commanded by Lieutenant Colonel James P. Anderson. Arriving on the Mexican coast too late to take part in active service, this battalion was used to preserve order at the war's end.

Joseph Davis Howell, of the 1st Mississippi, wrote to his mother on 25 September 1846 that General Taylor referred to his unit as 'the striped tigers from our uniforms being all striped.'[63] This may indicate that Mississippi volunteers were initially outfitted in uniforms made of striped mattress ticking, in lieu of more suitable jeans or woollen cloth. Later, in February 1847, Sam Chamberlain witnessed this regiment going into action at Buena Vista and recalled:

'This gallant regiment passed by us with the light swinging step peculiar to Indians and hunters, their uniform a red shirt worn outside of their white duck pants, and black slouch hats, armed with Windsor [M1842] Rifles, and eighteen-inch Bowie Knives.'[64]

Headgear of this unit may have varied, as a Mississippi soldier's letter describing the aftermath of the battle said of a fallen comrade: 'But for the straw hat... I should have failed to recognise the body of young Eggleston.'[65]

Regarding the arm carried by the 1st Mississippi, Jefferson Davis recalled later in life:

'General Scott endeavoured to persuade me not to take more rifles than enough for four companies, and objected particularly to percussion arms as not having been sufficiently tested for the use of troops in the field. Knowing that the Mississippians would have no confidence in the old flint lock muskets, I insisted on their being armed with the kind of rifle then recently made at New Haven, Conn., the Whitney rifle.'

The arms were duly sent to the regiment via ship to New Orleans, but were without bayonets, there being no time to make them.

According to regimental surgeon Dr. Thomas N. Love, the 2nd Mississippi left home without providing themselves with sufficient clothing. When they rendezvoused at Vicksburg in January 1847, a few were supplied with 'wollen [sic] clothes and hardly one in ten with flannel'.[66]

Louisiana

New Orleans had long been active in recruiting military companies for service against Mexico, and several had been openly assembled there for departure to the Texas War of Independence in 1836. When it became apparent that the small regular army under Taylor was without artillery when it occupied Fort Jesup in Western Louisiana during the summer of 1845, General Edmund P. Gaines, commanding the Department of the South at New Orleans, called for volunteer artillery to serve a three month's tour of duty with Taylor's army. In response, the Washington Battalion and the Bataillon d'Artillerie d'Orleans offered their services. Gaines selected the Native American Artillery, led by Captain Henry Forno, from the former unit; and Captain Eusebe Bercier's Company from the latter. These two batteries were placed under Major Louis B. Gally, veteran commander of the Orleans Artillery, who had served under Napoleon. Gally's battalion arrived at Corpus Christi in Texas on 30 August 1845 with a battery consisting of two twelve-pounders and six six-pounders. Towards the end of a three-month spell of camp life, during which the discipline and ability of the unit was praised by General Taylor, mounted batteries of the regular army arrived, and the Louisianians returned home.

The uniform of the Native American Artillery, later designated the Washington Artillery of New Orleans, comprised a dark blue coat with red collar and cuffs, with gold epaulettes for officers and red worsted for enlisted men. Trousers were sky blue with red seam stripes. Headgear consisted of a 'high military cap of white canvas... faced with the crossed guns of the artillery and topped by a tall red plume'. This company was presented a flag on 21 June 1845, which was described as bearing 'a cannon surmounted by a spread eagle holding in its beak a scroll, on which is the inscription of "Liberty"; a drum, a pile of cannon balls, the whole, ornamented with flags in graceful folds is on a beautiful bank of green. The ground of the flag is a rich yellow, trimmed with silver fringe tassels.' The Native American Artillery carried this flag with them to Texas.[67]

With the outbreak of hostilities in 1846, General Gaines again issued a call for Louisiana troops to serve for three months against Mexico. Colonel Persifor F. Smith was promoted to brigadier general in command of four Louisiana volunteer regiments, and James B. Walton was appointed colonel of the Washington Regiment, the whole of which volunteered to take the field. This included the Native American Artillery, which became Co. A and agreed to serve as infantry. Designated the 1st Louisiana Volunteers, this regiment joined Taylor's army in Texas, and were part of the first American forces to cross the Rio Grande.

After advancing on Matamoras, Taylor refused to accept the re-enlistment for twelve months' service of most of the Louisiana Brigade, and they were discharged in late July 1846. The handful of men who remained formed a unit under Captain Albert C. Blanchard called the Phoenix Company, since it had arisen from the ashes of the brigade. This unit served through the Monterey Campaign, and took part in the action at Veracruz and Cerro Gordo. The Phoenix Company dressed in 'every sort of clothes and carried every sort of weapon' during the Monterey Campaign.[68]

The Mounted Battalion of Louisiana Volunteers arrived in Mexico during August 1847, and were involved in various actions against guerillas under Brigadier General Joseph Lane.

Missouri

This state provided the St. Louis Legion; three mounted regiments, namely the 1st, 2nd, and 3rd Regiments of Missouri Mounted Volunteers, or Riflemen; and a battalion of light artillery and infantry respectively. The St. Louis Legion, commanded by Colonel Alton R. Easton, was a hastily organised regiment of foot which served in northern Mexico only until 25 August 1846. A unit variously known as the 'Separate Battalion of Missouri Volunteers', the 'Indian Battalion' and the 'Oregon Battalion', under Lieutenant Colonel William Gilpin, was formed in July 1847 to protect the Santa Fe Trail.

The 1st Regiment of Missouri Mounted Volunteers was commanded by Colonel Alexander W. Doniphan; the 2nd Regiment was led by Colonel Sterling Price.

Doniphan's Regiment numbered some 700 men recruited from Jackson, Lafayette, Clay, Saline, Franklin, Cole, Howard, and Calloway counties. This force was later supplemented by the Chihuahua Rangers, a company of about 100 men organised at Santa Fe. One of the original companies (Company E) of this regiment was armed with the Hall Rifle and bayonet, and was dismounted and attached to Captain William Z. Angney's battalion of Missouri Infantry.[69]

The Light Artillery Battalion, Missouri Volunteers, commanded by West Pointer Major Meriwether Lewis Clark, included nearly 250 men consisting of 'Battery A' of St. Louis under Captain Richard H. Weightman, a company under Captain Waldemar Fischer, a graduate of the Prussian artillery service, and a company led by Captain Thomas B. Hudson. This battalion was armed with twelve 6-pounders and four 12-pounder howitzers, and served in Kearny's Army of the West, as did the battalion of Missouri infantry under Captain William B. Angney.

Missourians appear to have been reasonably well uniformed at the outset of their one year term of service. Frank S. Edwards, who enlisted in Weightman's battery, recalled:

'Each soldier was to furnish himself with a good horse, saddle and clothing—in short everything except arms. Although we were not absolutely required to

A half-plate daguerreotype of Mexican War veterans at Chester, South Carolina. The man in the centre holding the colour is Nathaniel R. Eaves. There is no sign of Santa Anna's ears in his waist coat pocket! South Caroliniana Library.

uniform ourselves, it was recommended that a suitable uniform would be desirable, so we provided a neat dress, somewhat similar to the fatigue dress of the regulars.'[70]

Upon enlistment William H. Richardson, who joined Captain William's Company, Doniphan's Regiment, recorded in his journal: 'I immediately set about preparing - bought my regimentals, canteen, saddlebags'. An engraving accompanying Richardson's journal published in 1850, entitled 'A Camp Washing

Day', depicts men dressed in dark-coloured (possibly dark blue) M1839 fatigue caps, shell jackets with 'wings', and pants with narrow seam stripes.[71] Before departure from Fort Leavenworth, Company C of this regiment, from Clay County, and commanded by Captain O. P. Moss, was presented with a national flag bearing the motto 'THE LOVE OF COUNTRY IS THE LOVE OF GOD'.[72]

Regarding arms and equipage, Frank Richards recalled:

'An important part of our equipment was a stout leather waist belt, supporting a good butcher-knife, to which many of us added a revolving pistol - a weapon

This sword was presented to Michael Clark by the Governor's Guards of Columbia, South Carolina, when he was elected a second lieutenant in the Palmetto Regiment in 1846. During the assault on Chapultepec Castle, a Mexican bullet smashed into Clark's hand. One can see where the pearl grip of his sword was splintered by the blow directly below the pommel. The 'U' on the accompanying sword belt plate was converted to a 'C' during Clark's service in the Confederate army. S. C. Confederate Relic Room & Museum, Columbia; courtesy of John Bigham.

The second flag of the Palmetto Regiment. Measuring 61½"
on the staff by 69" on the fly, the eagle was worked in gold
thread, the streamers red with 'E PLURIBUS UNUM' above the
eagle, and 'PALMETTO/REG^T S.C./VOLUNTEERS' below. S. C.
Confederate Relic Room & Museum, Columbia; courtesy of John
Bigham.

we found very useful. And knowing that we should be
obliged to go over long distances without finding
water, we all provided ourselves with tin canteens
holding half a gallon:—these covered with a piece of
blanket, kept wet to cool the water, are a very
necessary article.'

Concerning saddles, Richards recorded:

'We also got our Spanish saddles all made of one
pattern. The common but good article we procured
could hardly, strictly, be called a saddle, as it consisted
of nothing but the skeleton or tree of one, with the
girth and stirrups attached. The object of this
simplicity was to render it as light and cool as possible
to the horse; and by putting a good Mackinaw blanket
above as well as beneath, it made a comfortable seat—
the blankets forming our beds at night.'[73]

By the end of its war service, during which
Doniphan's Regiment went without pay, clothing
issue, and frequently food for men and horses, its

military appearance had deteriorated dramatically. An
anonymous observer recorded the following
description of the unit in the Matamoras (Texas)
American Flag on 7 June 1847:

'The unshorn beards and goat and deer skin
clothes of many of them reminded us of descriptions
we have read of the inhabitants of some countries of
the Russian empire'. Another account stated that when
their civilian clothing had worn out 'and there being
no opportunity of obtaining more, they bought many
skins, and dressed themselves with them, true Indian
fashion'.

An English traveller who visited the camp of the
Missouri Mounted Riflemen during their incredible
3,000-mile trek from Fort Leavenworth through the
desert of northern Mexico described the scene as
follows:

'From appearance no one would have imagined
this to be a military campment. The tents were in a
line, but there all uniformity ceased. There were no
regulations in force with regards to cleanliness. The
camp was strewed with the bones and offal of the
cattle slaughtered for its supply, and not the slightest
attention was paid to keeping it clear from the
accumulations of filth. The men, unwashed and
unshaven, were ragged and dirty, without uniforms,
and dressed as, and how, they pleased. They wandered
about, listless and sickly-looking, or were sitting in
groups playing at cards, and swearing and cursing,
even at the officers... Sentries... were voted
unnecessary.'

The most detailed description of Doniphan's
command was provided by a young man in New
Orleans as the unit was being moved back to Missouri
after its long and eventful odyssey.:

'The greatest attraction in the city at present is
Col. Doniphan and his Regiment... who are called
"Lions" here, but in my opinion look more like Rocky
Mountain *Bears*... If you can imagine a man about six
feet two or four and a half inches high, and well
proportioned, with a deer skin (hair on) hunting shirt
and pantaloons, the seams fringed with the same
material cut into strings, and a bear skin stretched over
his face with nothing but eyeholes cut in it, you can
see a large portion of Doniphan's Regiment. They are
swaggering about the verandah and St. Charles with
an air of the most perfect *non chalance* of any set of
fellows you ever saw.'

Private Richardson's journal provides a less
romantic view of his appearance on arrival at New
Orleans on 17 June 1847:

'Upon my head there was no hat, having lost my
last remnant overboard in the Gulf. My pants I had

thrown away three days before, because (being composed of deerskin, worn into tatters), I despaired of making them look decent. A pair of drawers, rather the worse for wear, and an old overcoat, constituted my dress.'[74]

When some of Doniphan's men were challenged by a recalcitrant Mexican *alcalde* who demanded their passports to travel through his district, their officer 'pointed to his thirteen men, dressed in skins, with long beards... every one of his party having, in addition to his gun, holster pistols, sword, and revolving pistols...', and suggested that these were all the passport they required! A veteran of Doniphan's regiment recorded that their principal weapon was the Mississippi Rifle (U.S. M1842). Their holster pistols would most likely have been the U.S. M1836 flintlock or possibly the M1842 percussion. Their revolvers could have been Colt's patent 1836 original or perhaps, pepperboxes. The swords mentioned were most likely the M1840 dragoon sabre.

Ohio

This state contributed five infantry regiments, fifteen independent companies of infantry, five companies for the 15th U.S. Infantry, and one company of the United States Riflemen to the Mexican War. The 1st through 3rd regiments were raised during June 1846. The general rendezvous for Ohio volunteers was Camp Washington, near Cincinnati. The 1st Ohio Volunteer Infantry was organised at that place on 23 June 1846, under command of Colonel Alexander M. Mitchell. This regiment served under Taylor at Monterey in September 1846, where it was brigaded together with the Louisville Legion, of Kentucky. It also took part in the action at Ceralvo during March 1847, and was mustered out on the 15th of June of that year.

The 1st Ohio was congratulated by General Wool for its 'good disipline, orderly conduct, and fine military appearance' at the end of its Mexican War service. A member of this unit sketched his regiment drawn up on parade in the Main Plaza at Monterey during 1847, and depicted officers wearing frock coats, probably dark blue in colour, whilst enlisted men wore either light blue, or grey, jackets and trousers, with white cross belts and waist belts.

The 2nd Ohio Volunteer Infantry was raised on 22 June 1846, and was led to Mexico by Colonel George W. Morgan. It garrisoned at Camargo prior to taking part in the battles of Aqua Fria and Buena Vista. It was mustered out at New Orleans on 23 June 1847. The 3rd Ohio was commanded by the Adjutant General of Ohio, and commandant of Camp Washington, Samuel

Captain James Miller, Company K, 2nd Pennsylvania Volunteer Infantry, wears a dark blue frock coat identical to those worn by regular infantry officers. However, he has violated regulations by unfastening his collar and turning it down. The brave Miller assumed command of the storming party furnished by Twigg's division during the assault on Chapultepec Castle in 1847. He later died in the Civil War while leading the 81st Pennsylvania Volunteer Infantry at Fair Oaks in Virginia on 1 June 1862. USAMHI: photo by Jim Enos.

R. Curtis. This regiment was involved in many skirmishes as part of Taylor's 'Army of the Rio Grande', and did much in the way of protecting wagon trains and escort duty, before being mustered out on 24 June 1847. The 4th Ohio was organised at Cincinnati in June 1847 under Colonel Charles H. Brough, and saw active service at Puebla and Atlexco.

The 2nd Ohio was officially reorganised into the 5th Ohio, but clung on to its original designation as the 'Second Ohio Volunteer Infantry', after the expiration of its original term of twelve month's service, and took part in numerous skirmishes with guerrillas near Puebla during the winter of 1847/48.

An additional 15 independent companies from Ohio also served in Mexico. The first of these was the Independent Company of Mounted Volunteers, commanded by Captain John R. Ducan. The last two were known consecutively as the 'First Foot', under Captain William Kenneally, and the 'Second Foot' led by Captain Robert R. Riddle.[75]

Tennessee

The 'Volunteer State' raised three regiments of infantry, and one mounted regiment in 1846. The 1st Tennessee Volunteer Infantry, later nick-named the 'Bloody First', was led by Colonel William B. Campbell. Recruited in Middle Tennessee, it was composed of twelve companies, as opposed to the usual ten. This regiment carried off to war a beautiful flag made by 'the young ladies of the Nashville Female Academy, which bore a motto composed by 'their headmaster Elliot': 'Weeping in solitude for the fallen brave is better than the presence of men too timid to strike for their country.'[76] Commanded by Colonel William T. Haskell, the 2nd Tennessee was a 691-man regiment composed of only eight companies. As part of Quitman's brigade, the 1st Tennessee took part in the siege of Monterey, and the battle of Cerro Gordo. The 2nd Tennessee, also at Cerro Gordo, lost nearly 80 men as Pillow's brigade advanced against Mexican batteries.

The volunteers from Tennessee probably set off for Mexico in 1846 wearing uniforms influenced by the Militia Law of 28 January, 1840. This Law stipulated that general, field and staff officers should wear the same uniform as that of officers of 'the same grade in the United States' army'. Captains, subaltern officers, and staff officers, could wear U.S.-pattern uniforms, or those of their own choice. Light infantry were prescribed long blue hunting shirts, blue pantaloons, and round black hat and red plumes; riflemen wore long black hunting shirts, black pantaloons, and hats as for infantry, with white plumes.[77]

Texas

In response to a call for four Texas regiments issued in 1846, the 'Lone Star' state supplied two mounted regiments, and one battalion of infantry. The first of the mounted units was the Regiment of Texas Mounted Volunteers, commanded by Colonel Jack Hays. The second, led by Colonel George T. Wood, was subsequently known as the East Texas Rangers.

According to S. Compton Smith, an 'Acting Surgeon' with Taylor's army, the Texas Rangers were 'the genuine, brave, and hardy pioneers of that young and rising State. They were the men of Goliad and San Jacinto [during the war of Texan Independence in 1836]—men whose greatest sport was an open prairie-fight with the untamable Camanches. They had measured arms with the Mexicans, and had a just appreciation of them. They knew their weakness, and how to take advantage of it.'[78]

Armed with this experience, the Texas Rangers formed themselves into regular squadrons in 1841. Prior to the outbreak of war, they were described as wearing dragoon caps, and dragoon jackets fastened with buttons upon which were a single star and the word 'TEXAS'. The latter is probably a reference to the grey fatigue jackets prescribed the 'Army of the Republic of Texas' in 1839. Some Texans who rallied under the 'Stars and Stripes' in 1846 may have worn remnants of this uniform at the outset of their Mexican War service.[79]

Colonel Hays' regiment did not come to the Rio Grande in a body, but by companies and as individuals. Hays was described as wearing 'a round jacket, Mexican hat, and no badge of rank other than a silk sash tied around his waist after the fashion of the Mexicans...'. Among the companies commanded by Hays was that led by Ben McCullogh, which reached Matamoros by 23 May 1846. Raised among the Indian and Mexican fighters on the banks of the Guadalupe River, it was exceptional. A member of the unit wrote:

'This company was perhaps the best mounted, armed, equipped and appointed corps that was out in the ranging service; and from the time of its arrival at headquarters until after its disbandment at Monterey, enjoyed more of the trust and confidence of the commanding general than any other volunteer company of the invading army.'[80]

Advancing ahead of the pioneers as Taylor's army approached Monterey during September 1846, McCullogh's 'strange-looking company' was described as follows:

'Mounted on quick, tough horses and marching at will, the men were dressed as they pleased; but they agreed substantially on leggings, trousers belted round the waist, coarse red or blue shirts, and either a buckskin cap or a soft felt hat. Each carried a heavy rifle, a pouch of bullets, a large powderhorn and a bowie knife, and some had Colt revolvers. At every saddle-bow hung a braided lariat for a tether; and a bag of parched and pounded corn, together with whatever else the rider thought he needed, was bound to the saddle with thongs.'[81]

Colonel Hays had put Samuel Colt's bankrupt firearms business back on its feet in 1846 with an order for 1,000 revolvers - two for each of his 500 men.

Towards the end of 1847, Scott required additional cavalry to maintain communications with Veracruz once Mexico City had been captured. One of the units he secured was Hay's Texas Mounted Volunteers, which reached the Mexican capital on the 7th of December of that year. Observing the Texans enroute, an American officer recorded:

'About the middle of November, five companies of Texas rangers [sic], under command of Colonel Jack Hays, arrived in Pueblo... certainly an odd set of fellows, and it seemed to be their aim to dress as outlandishly as possible. Bob-tailed coats and "long-tailed blues," low and high-crowned hats, some slouched and others Panama, with a sprinkling of black leather caps, constituted their uniforms, and a thorough coating of dust over all their huge beards, gave them a savage appearance. Their horses ranged from little mustangs to large American full-bloods and were of every shade and color. Each man carried a rifle, a pair of pistols, and one or two of Colt's revolvers, or 'five shooter's.' A hundred of them could discharge a thousand shots in two minutes... I watched them closely as they passed silently by me, and could distinguish no difference between officers and men. They carried no sabers.'[82]

These men were not 'rangers', many probably being recent arrivals in Texas, and would have been more at home in a buggy than on a horse. The same officer was impressed by the appearance of Colonel Hays, whom he described as:

'...wiry looking...very modest...very plainly dressed, and wore a blue roundabout, black leather cap, and black pants, and had nothing about him to denote that he belonged to the army, or held any military rank in it...dark hair and dark eyes...no beard or moustache...small size—he being only about five feet eight—made him appear more like a boy than a man.'

New York
Colonel Jonathan D. Stevenson's 1st New York Regiment, also known as the New York Legion, or 'New York California Volunteers', was raised in 1846 specifically to provide a force to occupy California. A large number of this unit, which numbered about 800 men who wished to be discharged on the West Coast, were mechanics who carried with them 'saw and grist mills, mechanic's tools, &c.'.

Colonel Stevenson, with 250 volunteers, belatedly sailed from New York onboard the ship *T. H. Perkins* on 26 September 1846, and finally arrived in San Francisco on 6 March 1847. The residue arrived shortly thereafter. Four companies under Stevenson were ordered to occupy Monterey, whilst three companies led by Lieutenant Colonel Burton were stationed at Santa Barbara. By 22 June, the regiment was very much scattered, being distributed among different posts, from Sutter's Fort on the Sacramento River to La Paz in Lower California, a distance of 1500 miles.[83]

On 3 August, 1846, the New York *Herald* reported that the uniform of the California Regiment would soon be completed. Designed by the unit's third in command, Major James A. Hardie, it was described as 'very neat and serviceable; pantaloons of dark, mixed grey, with scarlet strip or cord up the seam of the leg, blue coats with scarlet trimmings, [and] a new style of French cap, very becoming ...'. A self-portrait of Lieutenant J. M. Hollingsworth of the regiment indicates that the cap chosen was based on the shako adopted by the French army in 1837, and appears to have been black piped with yellow cord.

Colonel Stevenson was photograped in an undress uniform consisting of a double-breasted dark blue coat and trousers. His M1839 forage cap bore an embroidered spread eagle surrounded by an elaborate wreath. This regiment was armed with 'percussion muskets, and flint muskets, with 200 rifles, and six pieces of artillery'.[84]

For the campaign in Mexico, New York was initially called upon to raise seven regiments which were to be enrolled, but not called into service until further notice. In November 1846, this order was changed to one regiment of volunteers to service 'for the war'. The resulting 1st New York Volunteer Regiment, commanded by Colonel Ward B. Burnett, was slow to fill its ranks. Composed of approximately 800 men, only about 300 were Americans, the remainder being Dutch, Irish, French, English, Poles, Swedes, Chinese, and Indians. This regiment took part in Scott's campaign in central Mexico within the volunteer brigade of General James Shields. One of its officers accepted the surrender of General Nicolás Bravo after the fall of Chapultepec Castle in September 1847. During the battle of Churubusco, General James Shields rallied the faltering ranks of the 1st New York shouting: 'Come on, boys, and form line; if you don't do so right away, then better pull off your blue jackets and don't call yourselves any longer Americans!', which suggests this regiment was dressed in regular infantry uniform.[85]

Throughout much of its service in Mexico, Burnett's regiment bore a flag measuring 52" on the staff by 60" on the fly, with a blue field embroidered with the U.S. coat of arms and eagle, and the designation '1st REGIMENT / NEW YORK / VOLUNTEERS' in a red scroll. This flag was carried over the walls of Chapultepec Castle by Sergeant Hippolyte Dardonville and others during September 1847.[86]

Virginia

On 19 May 1846 Virginia was called upon to raise, and hold in readiness, three regiments of infantry for Mexican War service. Five days later, William Smith, Governor of Virginia, announced that he would receive the tender of thirty companies of infantry. In response to the lack of opportunity for 'immediate action', only thirteen companies of infantry, five of riflemen, and three of artillery, totalling 1,800 men, had volunteered by the 11th of July of that year. Shortly thereafter Smith was informed by the War Department that existing circumstances did not justify calling any portion of these volunteers into active service. None-the-less volunteer companies continued to be raised, with talk of organising what was to be known as the 'Virginia Legion'.

By the Fall of 1846, circumstances had changed again, and Virginia was requested to provide a regiment of ten companies for immediate service, and for the duration of the war. The Governor's proclamation was issued on 18 November, with preference being given to the companies formed as a result of the previous call, provided they accepted service under the new terms and re-elected their officers.

Initially the Virginia Regiment was to be mustered in at Guyandotte, on the Ohio River, in Cabell County. From there it was to be transported down the Ohio and Mississippi to New Orleans. In consequence of the snow, and the wretched conditions of the western roads, the state capitol was eventually chosen as the mustering in point, and six companies of the regiment had arrived there by the end of December 1846, with the remainder following shortly thereafter. Colonel John Francis Hamtramck was commissioned to command this regiment on 22nd of that month. Arriving in Mexico after the battle of Buena Vista, and too late to take an active part in the campaign in the north, the Virginia Regiment spent its time digging defence works and guarding wagon trains, being re-organised into the volunteer brigade of General Caleb Cushing during June 1847.

In order to outfit the Virginia Regiment in high quality clothing, Governor Smith undertook to have their uniforms made of good materials purchased at reasonable prices and supplied through the agency of the state. As a result, the commutation allowance due to the volunteers was diverted to the state in reimbursement for the clothing. An itemized estimate of costs showed that the whole uniform could be purchased for $16.95 per volunteer, which was well under the six-month commutation allowance of $21.00.

Agents were duly sent to Philadelphia, where they purchased goods from the contractors who supplied Schuylkill Arsenal, which included grey blankets, dark blue 'Dragoon cloth' for jackets, pantaloons, and caps, and light blue cloth for overcoats. These were sent to Richmond, where contracts were let for making up the finished articles. Via General Orders published by the state adjutant general on 15 December 1846, each volunteer of the Virginia Regiment was to receive: one navy blue cloth cap, one navy blue jacket and pair of pantaloons, two pair of bootees, two flannel shirts, one overcoat, and one leather stock. Volunteers were also urged to supply their own shoes, socks, and shirts.[87]

Based on evidence gleaned from bills of cost, contract documents, and the surviving daguerreotype of Private William Hall, Co. B, Virginia Regiment, the cloth actually used for these uniforms was 'lighter than the dragoon jacket, but next in quality to it'. The jackets were to be wadded, and were fully lined, with cotton in the sleeves and black cambric in the body. Twenty buttons, two hooks and eyes for the collar, and one and a half yards of worsted lace (colour not specified), were apportioned for each jacket. The trousers had interior trim of black cambric, with six large and six small buttons allowed, presumably for suspenders and fly enclosure respectively. One buckle was also specified, no doubt for a small belted closure at the back of the waist.

Private Hall was photographed wearing a uniform which roughly corresponds with these specifications. His headgear was similar in shape to the M1839 Type 1 cap used by the U.S. Army, although the crown and visor were smaller. Nine buttons, which appear under magnification to bear the Virginia state seal of Liberty vanquishing a tyrant and the motto 'Sic Semper Tyrannis', are visible down the front, and four smaller buttons are attached to each cuff. As Hall's collar appears to be plain, the remaining three buttons were presumably kept as spares. There is no sign of the specified worsted lace, presumably for collar loops and trim, on his jacket, which may indicate that Hall's clothing was not the official Virginia Regiment uniform. His vest, which is possibly of military cut, was clearly a private purchase as no record of vests exists in the official papers. Furthermore, Captain E. C. Carrington, commander of the Company G, noted that 'the men, many of them, prefer getting articles for themselves...'.[88]

The fact that the state acquired light blue cloth for overcoats for the Virginia Regiment would indicate that this garment was probably cut in similar, if not the same style, as that worn by the Regulars. Correspondence regarding the cotton shirts acquired specifies 'an excellent twilled goods, with indigo stripe', which was similar to the 'hickory' shirts described above by Regular Army Lieutenant Dana.

Despite the efforts of the Virginia state authorities to make the best use of the commutation system money, it is evident that it did not suffice, and that uniforms supplied were inadequate to the purpose. On 15 January 1847, and before the regiment had embarked for Mexico, Major Jubal A. Early noted: 'The Commutation for clothing for Six months, is not Sufficient to Clothe the men'. During the following April, after arrival in Mexico, Colonel Hamtramck requested clothing or commutation from the U.S. Secretary of War. In May the Virginia adjutant general informed Hamtramck that the state legislature had failed to take steps to relieve the men's needs, offering the following limp consolation: 'If the War continues however, I trust you will have better fortune...'. By June, with the unit's first six months' service up and the period covered by commutation expired, the Virginians began to draw federal clothing. On the 10th of that month, Lieutenant R. H. Kinney of Company C wrote from Buena Vista to Hamtramck in Monterey: 'Most of our companies here are drawing their new clothing, and some of them... would scarcely be recognized...'.[89]

Nonetheless, clothing shortages continued to cause problems. On 4 April 1848, Captain Kenton Harper, commanding the Light Infantry Company, wrote from Parras to Colonel Hamtramck complaining: 'Many of the men are destitute of clothing. I had *nineteen barefooted* a few days ago, but I made an arrangement to supply them. Pantaloons are the most needed.'[90] When the regiment was repatriated at the end of its war service during the summer of 1848, visitors to its last encampment found the bearded men in worn and tattered clothing, with skin darkened by the Mexican sun. A Petersburg reporter noted that they were 'anything *but parlor* looking boys, and their appearance clearly showed that, though they had never been in battle, they had experienced pretty rough service'.[91]

North Carolina

During the summer of 1846, more than three times the requisite number of volunteers were raised, mainly in the western part of the state, for the 'regiment of volunteer infantry' required of North Carolina for one year's service. When in November the terms of enlistment 'for the war' were announced, the majority of these volunteers were unwilling to muster, and another call for a new North Carolina Regiment of Volunteers was issued on 7 December 1846. Volunteering for this regiment was much slower, but

Abraham Schell was a 22 year old farmer in Bedford County, Pennsylvania, when he joined Company L, 2nd Pennsylvania Volunteer Infantry, on 6 May 1847. Due to difficulties filling its ranks, this company did not finally catch up with its regiment until the following August, by which time Scott's army had occupied the city of Puebla. During November, Schell was promoted to second sergeant, and then to second lieutenant the following month. Sometime thereafter he had this photo taken wearing his new shoulder straps, which appear to have been sewn to his dark blue fatigue jacket. Note the unusual tiny trefoil loops embroidered at the end of his rather high breast pockets. Photo courtesy of Jeff Patrick.

by 19 January 1847 all but one company had been mustered in. Colonel Robert Treat Paine, appointed to command on 18 January, accepted a regimental flag presented by State Adjutant General Haywood on 13 February, and two days later the first elements of this unit left for Mexico. But the North Carolina regiment was not destined a share in the battle honors earned by others at Cerro Gordo, Churubusco, and Chapultepec. Assigned the less colourful role of escorting wagon trains of supplies, illness and discontent would evolve into mutiny by August 1847.[92]

On 1 July 1846 the North Carolina *Standard* published the following list of required clothing for volunteers for the one year term of enlistment: one dress cap, one forage cap, one uniform coat, one woolen jacket, two pairs of woolen overalls, one cotton jacket, three pairs of cotton overalls, two flannel shirts, two pairs of drawers, four pairs of bootees (shoes), four pairs of socks, one linen fatigue frock, one neck stock, and one blanket. Earlier, on 27 May, O.L. Burch & Co. of Raleigh was offering 'the finest and most fashionable BOOTS, to the Volunteers for the Rio Grande.'[93]

When the regiment 'for the war' was finally raised it appears to have been clothed in a simpler uniform based on the sky blue fatigue dress issued to the Regular Army, with minor differences, whilst officers wore dark blue frock coats and pants.

South Carolina

The Palmetto State was required to raise a regiment for twelve months service in June 1846 but, like North Carolina, they were not called for immediately, instead being ordered 'to hold themselves in readiness, and await the exigencies of war.' The call thus created little excitement among 'the military spirits of the state', but was formerly responded to by ten of its numerous volunteer militia companies. With the reissued call for a regiment of ten companies of volunteers 'for the war' in December 1846, the 1st South Carolina Volunteers, or 'Palmetto Regiment', was born. With renewed enthusiasm, the ranks of this regiment were quickly filled. Nathaniel R. Eaves, who became the colour bearer of Company B, from Chester, even promised to bring home 'the ears of Santa Anna in his waistcoat pocket'![94]

The Palmetto Regiment rendezvoused at Charleston on 20 December 1846 under the field officers originally elected to command in June of that year - Colonel Pierce M. Butler, Lieutenant Colonel James P. Dickenson, and Major A. H. Gladden. The right wing of this regiment was composed of volunteers from Districts of Sumter, DeKalb, Fairfield, Charleston and Lancaster. The left, those from Chester, Abbeville, Edgefield, Richland, and Barnwell.

The 1st South Carolina did not adopt a regimental uniform at the outset. According to Private Ben Lane Posey, of the Abbeville Company, some companies of 'the Palmettoes presented in their costume a ludicrous, and some a ferocious aspect.' An anonymous member of the Abbeville Volunteers reported from Mobile on 23 January 1847: 'Our own Company is second to none, we are now in uniform and look quite military—a blue round coat and pants of the same material...'[95] With the arrival of the regiment in Mexico, Posey recalled:

'At Lobos all of them had bought from the sutler, coarse heavy shirts. Some wore blue striped cotton, and some flannel of bloody red color. These shirts reached nearly to the knees, and worn over the pants, made a very showy frock coat. They looked so handsomely that they were adopted as a uniform, worn over the pants and fastened at the waist by a girdle and a buckle. This fantastic costume highly amused the Mexicans.'[96]

A member of the regiment signing himself 'Dan' wrote from the Island of San Antonio de Lizardo on 9 March 1847:

'Imagine some seven hundred men, composing ten companies, each company with the exception of the Charleston and Richland, adorned with red, blue, green, check, and white, shirts over their unmentionables, Kilmarnock caps, or white cotton skull hats, of the old Grimes cut, protecting their seats of knowledge from the pelting of the pitiless storm; while their lower extremities are encased in every variety of boot, shoe and stocking.'[97]

The Palmetto Regiment served with distinction within the ranks of Patterson's division throughout Scott's campaign, and claimed the fame of being the first unit to plant its state flag above the Garita de Belén outside Mexico City on 15 September 1847. This flag had been presented to the regiment by T. Leger Hutchinson, Mayor of Charleston, prior to departure for the war. It was described as follows by Private Posey: 'Upon our flag gleamed not the stars of the union, and the stripes for foes, but upon its folds stood out a single tree—the sad, desolate and solitary palmetto—a speaking, historical memorial of ancient history.'[98]

Company flags were also carried by this regiment. That of the Fairfield Company was described as being 'made of green silk and embroidered with yellow floss.– On one side is the inscription *Love of Country* and on the other the name of the company'. Presented by the ladies of Winnsboro, this small flag was carried throughout the Mexican War.[99]

The 1st South Carolina was the recipient of a second regimental flag after the capture of the Mexican capital. Presented by General Scott, it was made either in Mexico City, or New Orleans, and was one of 31 such flags produced for presentation to the victorious American army on this occasion. All these flags were embroidered, rather than painted, on a poorly-dyed silk field which later faded to a light shade of blue or yellow.

Both flags carried by the Palmetto Regiment were kept under glass in a place of honour in the State

Top left and right.
Surviving fatigue jacket worn by Private Richard Coulter of the
2nd Pennsylvania. (*front & interior*) **Note the fancy padded**
lining which, combined with the absence of trim and shoulder
straps, sets it apart from regulation issue. Westmoreland County
Historical Society courtesy of Richard Brown.

House in Columbia following the Mexican War. As
Federal forces under Sherman approached the city in
1865, they were removed for safekeeping to Chester,
South Carolina. In the confusion of the times the state
flag, by then riddled with bullet holes, was lost.

Massachusetts

Despite the unpopularity of the Mexican War in New
England, enough men in Massachusetts responded in
less than a month during June 1846 to fill its one
required regiment. Most of those who volunteered for
service in the 1st Massachusetts Regiment of
Volunteers, commanded by Colonel Caleb Cushing,
were Irish. Despite government orders that only
undress uniforms were to be worn in Mexico, the
officers of this regiment requested authorisation to
wear a dress uniform consisting of a single-breasted
grey coat, white collar, white sleeve cuffs two and a
half inches deep, and skirts trimmed with white. They

also hoped to obtain swords and epaulettes of the
regular army pattern.[100]

It is possible that the entire regiment acquired a
uniform different from that worn by the Regulars and
eventually supplied to most volunteer units. Indeed,
according to Private S. F. Nunelee of the 1st Alabama,
a 'finely uniformed Massachusetts Company' followed
his regiment into action during the siege of Veracruz
during March 1847. During the following November,
an entire company of this regiment refused to accept a
new issue of uniforms, and were imprisoned for
mutiny by Caleb Cushing, by then a general. Accounts
vary as to the details of this event. Ohio volunteer
John W. Lowe reported that the New Englanders
resented being forced to pay for more clothing when
the uniforms they had were still serviceable. A regular
army officer suggested that they wanted to retain
distinctive clothing which set them apart from other
troops. 'This was entirely unnecessary,' he continued,
'as they were easily to be distinguished from all
others...by their "General rowdy appearance," and
ignorance of a *Soldier's duty*.'[101]

Michigan

The governor of Michigan was first instructed during
May, 1846 to enroll a regiment of twelve months'

volunteers, to be held in readiness for service whenever demanded. In response, the state volunteer militia immediately provided eleven companies of infantry and two of cavalry. Not being required immediately, these companies were soon stood down, and it was not until the following October that orders were finally received to raise the 1st Regiment Michigan Volunteers, to serve for the duration of the war. Commanded by Colonel Thomas B. W. Stockton, the ten companies of this regiment were mustered in at various dates during the months of October, November, and December, 1847, and January and February, 1848.

The first elements of this regiment left for the seat of war on 24 December 1847, with the balance following shortly after. Arriving in Mexico after the main battles had been fought, the Michigan regiment performed garrison duty at Cordova and Veracruz until July, 1848, when they returned home.

The uniform worn by the 1st Michigan Volunteers was provided by the state from the commutation money due the regiment for the first six months' service. Via General Orders No. 20, issued by State Adjutant and Quartermaster General J. E. Schwarz on 18 October, 1847, each company was to wear 'the U.S. Infantry undress uniform, as to style, and as near the color as may be practicable, with the exception of the button. The button to be worn by the Regiment, whether by the officers, non-commissioned officers, musicians or privates, to be silver plated, and of the shape of the present staff buttons, with the arms of the State of Michigan embossed on the same'.[102]

Pennsylvania

The 1st Pennsylvania Volunteer Infantry, commanded by Colonel Francis A. Wynkoop, was accepted into service for 'three years or the war' on 16 July 1847, having been organised at Carlisle sometime earlier. The 2nd Pennsylvania Infantry, under Colonel William Roberts, joined them several days later. Both these regiments were assigned to the Veracruz Expedition, and saw service under General Scott from the siege of Veracruz through to the fall of Mexico City. The 2nd Pennsylvania was at first detailed to guard supply wagons for the army during the early battles around Mexico City, but took an active part in the final stages of war within Quitman's division. On 13 September 1847, both Keystone regiments participated in the storming and capture of Chapultepec Castle and the Garita Belen.

According to Private Richard Coulter of the Westmoreland Guards, who became Company E, 2nd Pennsylvania Volunteers, it was more lucrative for many men in his regiment to take the $21 bounty money paid on enlistment and buy their own clothing, rather than receive the government uniform when they joined. Consequently, the Westmoreland Guards contracted with a military supplier or tailor named Digby to provide the whole company with 'jackets and pants for $7'.[103] A jacket which Coulter left among 'extra clothing' in a box at Veracruz while involved in the campaign to Mexico City, survives today in the collection of the Westmoreland County Historical Society. Possibly one of the garments supplied by Digby, it is made of light blue twill wool cloth, with nine molded pewter copies of the standard U.S. infantry button of the period. The collar appears originally to have been trimmed in a manner consistent with the standard U.S. infantry fatigue jacket. However, according to the fancy lining and wadding mark, this is a non-regulation garment.[104]

As the Pennsylvania regiments embarked for Mexico without a 'stand of colors', Captain William F. Small, of Company C, 1st Regiment, 'caused to be made from such material as was found on board the ship', a 'crude representation' of the State flag, which the unit is reputed to have carried with it in all its battles. Its present disposition is unknown.[105] Several other company flags were carried by the regiment during its war service. Before their departure for Philadelphia, Company B, the Washington Artillery of Pottsville, were presented with a silk national flag, measuring 54" on the staff by 72" on the fly, which had embroidered on its dark blue canton, 'Presented by the Ladies of Pottsville.' Company I, the Wyoming Artillerists, carried a cotton national flag measuring 78" on the staff by 93" on the fly, with 29 stars in its canton.[106] After the fall of Mexico City, the Pennsylvanians were presented by General Scott with two regimental flags of the standard federal design, with the appropriate regimental designation embroidered on the red scroll beneath the national eagle. These were part of the 31 banners presented on that occasion.

Mexican Spy Company, U.S. Army

This uniqe unit was created among unpatriotic Mexicans to provide scouts, guides, spies, couriers, escorts and interpreters for the U.S. Army. Known as the *contra guerrillos*, or the Spy Company, it was organised and controlled by Winfield Scott's inspector general, Lieutenant Colonel Ethan Allen Hitchcock, about 1 August, 1847. The Spy Company was led by Manuel Dominguez, a retired bandit leader who entered American service as a dispatch rider shortly after the occupation of Puebla. According to 'Colonel' Dominguez, his unit was formed among highway robbers in response to the fact that Mexican guerillas had broken up, or rather monopolised, their trade on the Veracruz road.[107]

The Spy Company consisted of about 150 men who were actually organised into two companies, each with a captain, two lieutenants and the usual number of NCOs. A small third company was later organised as part of the garrison Scott left at Puebla during his advance on Mexico City. These units were disbanded at Veracruz in June, 1848, but about half their number, including Dominquez, felt it safer to accompany the departing Americans.

The Spy Company was armed with lance, carbine, and sabre. Several of James Walker's paintings of Scott's campaign depict members of the unit, always wrapped in multi-coloured *jorongos*, or ponchos. They are also identifiable by big red scarfs around their hats, possibly bearing the legend 'Spy Company', and by their red lance pennons. Otto Zirckel, a German immigrant who served in the U.S. Army, described their dress as follows: 'The soldiers wore round felt hats encircled with a red scarf and grey jackets. The officers and non-coms wore the insignia of our army. Later their uniform was changed and they wore parrot green coatees with a red collar and cuffs.'[108]

Often members of the Spy Company operated in disguise as ranchers, peddlers, or loyal Mexican guerillas, in which case they appear to have worn the Mexican rancher's *charro* rig of leather and heavy cloth, usually grey or brown. The 'parrot' green jackets adopted later were probably captured Mexican cavalry uniforms. Those embers of the unit who took up asylum in the United States after the war were issued the grey U.S. Regiment of Voltigeurs uniform.

Mexican Army

An engraving by Smyth published in the *Illustrated London News* in 1846 depicting elements of the Mexican army. The central figure in the group portays an auxiliary, or *Ranchero*, who often fought alongside the Regulars and militia. To his left is a mounted standard bearer, whilst to his right is a cavalry officer. Both the latter may have belonged to the Hussars of the Guard of the Supreme Powers. In advance of the mounted group is an infantryman in elements of full dress. Note his accoutrements are suspended from broad white shoulder belts. His bare feet typifies the poor state of supply in the Mexican army. An Indian guide is seen on the extreme left, whilst a Field Chaplain brings up the rear.

Mexico entered the fray in 1846 confident of victory, and full of doubt that the United States had either the will or the way to win a war. There were at that time about 24,550 soldiers in the Mexican Army, which was about three times larger than that of their northern neighbours. It had also gained considerable battle experience during the preceding decade, commencing with the Texan War of Independence in 1835. A *London Times* correspondent in 1845 even reported that Mexican soldiers were 'superior to those of the United States'.[109]

In truth the odds were clearly stacked against the Mexicans, whose population of about 7,250,000 was

less than half that of the United States. The Mexican nation was ruled by a rather unstable government on the eve of war. On 4 January 1846, Mariano Paredes y Arrillaga became president, to be replaced by Nicholás Bravo on 28 July 1846. Bravo was replaced on 5 August by José Mariano Salas, who was removed from office that Christmas by Valentin Gómez Farías. Farías was replaced by the self-styled 'Napoleon of the West', Antonio López de Santa Anna, on 22 March 1847. Santa Anna lasted until 1 April when Pedro Mariá Anaya was proclaimed president. Anaya remained in office only until 20 May, when Santa Anna returned to remain president until 22

Mexican headgear. (*left*) A cavalry officer's 'stove-pipe'-pattern cap about 8 inches tall with blue-grey woven lace cinch bands and triple loop over tricolour cockade. *(top middle)* A fine quality cap modelled on the French army pattern of 1837. A dark green pompon is mounted on a gold thread stem, while a silver double loop surmounts the cockade. The top cinch band is of golden/yellow woven lace. The oval brass plate with bugle device and 'VICTORIA' designation indicates that this cap was probably worn by a rifle company officer of the wealthy Victoria Battalion of National Guard. (*right*) A slightly 'bell-crown' dress cap with red pompon and top cinch band; chinstrap of yellow metal scales mounted on black velvet, attached at the sides by large yellow metal buttons to a gold-coloured woven lace cinch band. The flaming grenade devices on this cap indicate it was probably worn by a grenadier company officer. (*bottom middle*) Mexican cap plates bearing the national coat of arms - a spread eagle with serpent under a phrygian cap surrounded by bursting rays, 'REPÚBLICA MEXICANA' in ribbon over wreath of laurel and oak leaves.

Based on artefacts in the Museo Nacional de Historia, by Ron Field.

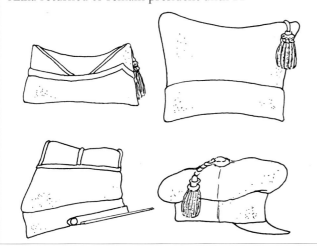

Mexican barrack or forage caps, including – a French/Spanish *bonnet de police* (*top right*), and conventional French-style kepi (*bottom left*).

September. Manuel de la Péna y Péna became temporary president until Anaya again took up office on 14 November 1847.

The army was invariably involved in these rapid changes in power, with units supporting one or other faction. This had a tremendous effect on discipline which was, at the best of times, rather lax. Not until 1847 were enlisted men in the Mexican Army ordered to salute or remove their hat in the presence of an officer. A good majority of Mexican officers were, in any case, unsuitable for command, being in the army for social and political reasons rather than military. A German visitor to Mexico in 1838 stated there were 160 generals for an army of 30,000, but out of all these, 'every one of whom could issue a glowing proclamation, probably not a single "Excellency" could properly handle a small division, while few out of thousands of colonels could lead a regiment on the field, and some were not qualified to command a patrol'.[110] The most damning criticism came from the British Minister to Mexico, Charles Bankhead, who wrote home in April 1846: 'The Officers...are, as a Corps, the worst perhaps to be found in any part of the world. They are totally ignorant of their duty...'.[111]

The other ranks of the Mexican Army were filled by conscription, lots being drawn on the last Sunday of every October. Those chosen entered the army on 15 December for six years. All single males or childless widowers from 18 to 40 years of age, married men not living with their wives, and childless married men at least 60 Mexican inches tall were subject to compulsory military service. A number of categories, including attorneys with offices, chaplaincy aspirants, and men engaged to be married, were exempt from service. Wealth also bought exemption, and those who ended up in the ranks were usually the peóns, or poor, who worked the land. The end result, according to

Ulysses S. Grant, was that:

'...the Mexican army of that day was hardly an organization. The private soldier was picked up from the lower class... his consent was not asked; he was poorly clothed, worse fed, and seldom paid. He was turned adrift when no longer wanted. With all this I have seen as brave stands made by some of these men as I have ever seen made by soldiers.'[112]

Future Confederate General P.G.T. Beauregard, serving as an aide to chief of engineers, Colonel Joseph Totten, commented: 'The Mexicans stood artillery and infantry fire "fully as well as our own troops"'.[113] According to Roswell Sabine Ripley, who entered the war as a second lieutenant in the 2nd U.S. Artillery:

'...the Mexican army was characterized by many of the necessary qualities of a good soldiery. Patient under suffering, requiring but little subsistence, with extraordinary capacity for enduring fatigue, and with quite enough of physical courage to enable them to encounter danger without fear, the Mexican troops might, if properly led, compare well with the troops of other nations.'[114]

The Mexican Army was reasonably well paid until January 1847, after which time many units were expected to fight for little or no recompense. The supply of uniforms, arms and equipage varied tremendously. The mixed force under Brigadier General José A. Heredia lying near Chihuahua, in the path of Doniphan's advance during February 1847, was unusual, being well clothed and armed by the local population. Others were less fortunate. As early as September 1846, some recruits and auxiliaries at San Luis Potosi were dramatically described as being 'nearly naked', whilst in June 1847 units in the Army of the North were more realistically reckoned to be 'poorly dressed'.[115]

A British Tower flintlock musket, also known the 'Brown Bess'. This weapon was picked up off the battle field at Buena Vista by an American soldier. According to Scots volunteer George Ballentine, thousands of these were collected and destroyed. West Point Museum.

Mexico had less uniform-producing facilities than the United States. Uniforms supplied to the Regular Army were manufactured by private concerns under Government contract, and were generally made of what was known as 'Querétaro' cloth of various colours. The contract uniform issued to the Mexican

Regular soldier in 1846 was based on detailed regulations published on 10 July 1839. Since 1835, the general issue per infantryman in theory consisted of a cloth tail-coat; two white canvas jackets; a pair each of gala (full dress), cloth and canvas trousers; a shako with cords and ornaments; a barracks cap; an overcoat; a necktie; three shirts; one pair of shoes; a blanket with carrier; knapsack with straps; a tool set; canteen; crossbelt with cartridge box, crossbelt with frog, scabbard and bayonet; musket; satchel of trimmings and towel.

The Mexican tail-coat was a mixture of the French 1806 pattern coat and 1815 pattern *habit-veste*, with important differences. The square cuff had straight cuff flaps with three buttons, all piped in the distinctive trim colour of the regiment. The coat-tails were generally longer than the French style, and the turnback ornaments and collar insignia were distinctly Mexican.

Shakos, or dress caps, were produced in a variety of patterns representing several decades of military

Left and below.
A cal. .76 flintlock carbine of Mexican manufacture. (*detail*)
Close-up of lockplate showing the eagle and serpent under the Phrygian cap and sunburst mark. West Point Museum.

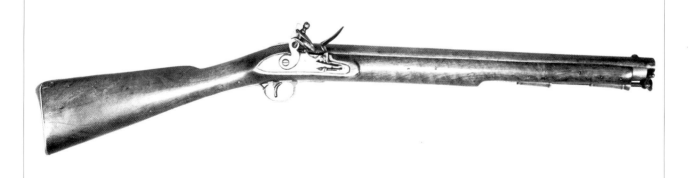

Top and bottom.

Two Mexican cavalry pistols. (*top*) A cal. .67 flintlock converted to percussion with the mark 'ESTADO DE GUANAJUATO' on the lockplate, indicating that this weapon was made at an arsenal in the State of Guanajuato. (*bottom*) A cal. .56 percussion pistol. The mark on the lockplate indicates that this piece was a product of the arsenal in Mexico City. West Point Museum.

fashion. These ranged from the 'bell-crown' style with wide crown, after the type worn by the U.S. army until 1831; the 'stove-pipe' model with parallel sides, similar to those worn for full dress by U.S. infantry and artillery until 1851; to those based on the dress cap introduced to the French army in 1837, which tapered towards the top, and had a crown tilted somewhat forward, being about six inches high in front and seven inches tall at the back. Mexican shakos were generally embellished around top and bottom with wide cinch-bands of woven lace in a variety of colours, dependent on the unit, and were decorated at the front with a cord loop over a creased tricolour cockade, a pompon, and a brass cap plate. The latter varied greatly from oval plates with the regimental name and number, sometimes accompanied by an eagle, or bugle (or both) in the centre, to those with the Mexican eagle

and serpent emblem, surrounded by a laurel and palm wreath over which were flowing ribbons bearing the legend 'Republica Mexicana', the whole being surmounted by a sun ray in the middle of which was a cap of liberty.

Four different styles of barrack caps were in use off duty or inside quarters, but were often worn in action. The first resembled the French/Spanish tasseled cap, or *bonnet de police*; a second was similar with a lower top; a third was a soft crowned, visored cap, not unlike the U.S. Model 1839 fatigue cap, but with cinch band, piping and tassel; the fourth was a conventional French-style kepi. The former two were issued to all ranks, being red at the top, medium blue at the bottom, with a separating band of cord trim, and tassel, of branch designation colour, e.g. red for artillery and cadets, blue for infantry, and black for engineers. These often bore yellow metal branch service insignia on the front of the lower band, e.g. crossed cannon for artillery, flaming bomb for grenadiers. The kepi was introduced to the Mexican army in 1845, and was already being worn by some officers at the beginning of full-scale hostilities with the U.S. The supply of these ceased once the war had started.

Likewise, the Louis Philippe-style French frock

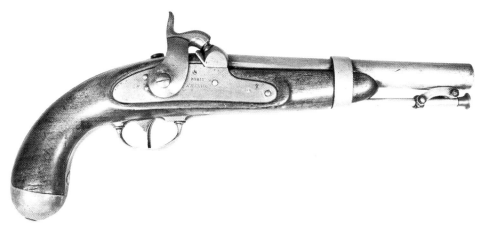

Above.

Mexican flags. *(top)* **Flag of the Batallón Libres de Puebla, National Guard;** *(middle)* **Flag of the 2nd Batallón Móvil, 1847** Museo Nacional de Historia, Mexico City; *(bottom)* **An unidentified variant of the Mexican national tricolour, captured in 1847.** North Carolina Museum of History.

coat was in widespread use as campaign wear by Mexican forces. In many cases those worn by regular line infantry units were dark blue with solid red collar and cuffs, thus abandoning regimental facing colours.

Alternatively, they only had red piping around collar, cuffs, and pockets, and were minus cuff flaps. Frock coats worn by the militia and national guard battalions, plus regular light infantry, were generally grey and mostly had only red piping on collar and cuffs.

The white canvas jackets and trousers issued for fatigue wear, were also permitted for service duty in excessively hot regions. That worn by some units, like the National Guard of the garrison of Mexico City, had solid red collars and cuffs, piped with yellow.

The supply situation remained uneven throughout the war. Frequent requests and complaints of field officers were received by the War Office, and furnish proof that dress and equipment of Mexican field armies seldom conformed to regulations. On 7 February 1842, General Ciriaco Vázquez reported from his field quarters at Jalapa to the Departmental Treasury in Veracruz that:

'...black velveteen had to be used because Querétaro cloth can absolutely not be found in the city, and they could not be made of sailcloth either which is still short...all that was available of good quality was taken for the manufacture of another thousand uniforms for units of this garrison...'

On 15 February of the same year, General Vázquez said that:

'...the greater part of the rank-and-file of the 2nd Active Battalion, 7th Regular Regiment are short of overcoats, blankets or any heavier garment that could serve them as cover on rainy and cold nights or when asleep in their quarters, it being necessary for them to go to sleep dressed, with the result that the only uniform issue they possess is quickly destroyed. To avoid this damage and to provide them with an indispensable garment that will make their service more bearable ... have the kindness to inform His Excellency the President about the great necessity of providing them at least with one burlap blanket each.'[116]

And again on the 7th and 10th May 1842, Vázquez charged every unit under his command to immediately submit an estimate for a canvas uniform, including a shirt, jacket, necktie, pants and barracks cap, in view of the fact that it was impossible to obtain the regulation issue of one cloth and two canvas uniforms, overcoats, blankets, shakos, cloth caps and leather or canvas knapsacks, warning the Treasury that '... His Excellency desires that the units of his command shine not only by their discipline and training, but also by their equipment.'[117] On 14 August 1842, complete canvas uniforms, including burlap blankets and visored caps, were supplied to the Mexican government via a contract with a European dealer named O'Sullivan, of which nothing else is known.

To cover all eventualities prior to the battle of Buena Vista, Santa Anna ordered the 'Liberating Army of the North', setting out on 26 January 1847 from San Luis de Potosí, to 'wear their dress of Russia duck, and over this their suit of cloth; they shall only take two shirts, four rounds of cartridges, and two flints, including the one in their guns...'[118]

The armament situation in Mexico was also poor on the eve of war with the United States. On hand at the end of 1845 in the arsenal at Mexico City were 635 cannon, 25,789 muskets, 8,155 swords, 100,000 artillery projectiles, and 400,000 musket balls.[119] Before independence from Spain, Mexico had a factory producing muskets and pistols of superior quality. The machinery still existed as late as 1834, but was no longer in use. Thus, the Mexican army was mainly equipped with guns and accoutrements imported from Europe, most of which were obsolescent discards. After the battle of Cerro Gordo, Scotsman George Ballentine, serving as a light infantryman in the 1st U.S. Artillery, recorded that he:

'...found the road strewed with the muskets and bayonets which the Mexicans had thrown away in their hasty retreat. These muskets were all of British manufacture, and had the *Tower* mark on their locks; but they were old and worn out, having evidently been condemned as unserviceable in the British army, and then sold to the Mexicans at a low price.'[120]

These weapons were part of a huge number of British weapons purchased by the Mexican government between 1830 and 1843. Included in a consignment received during the latter year were 5,000 muskets, 3,000 carbines or tercercoles, 3,000 cavalry swords, 5,800 sabre bayonets, and 200 musicians' side arms. Many of the former were indeed of the British Tower-type 'Brown Bess' smoothbore muzzle-loading flintlock muskets, condemned as unserviceable by the British government. This weapon had a range of less than 100 yards, and a 0.753 calibre.

British rifles in use by the Mexican army were made by Ezekiel Baker. Three feet 9½ inches in length, and weighing 9.5 lbs without bayonet, with a barrel length of 30 inches, they had a .615 calibre, and an adjustable sight effective up to 200 yards. Earlier Baker models carried an odd bayonet with 17 inch triangular blade fitted into a brass handle. This was replaced later by a 23 inch long broad sword bayonet with brass handle and guard bow.

The Baker carbine of the same calibre and gauge weighed 6.5 lbs, and was 36 inches overall in length, with a 20 inch barrel, and pronounced pistol grip. The

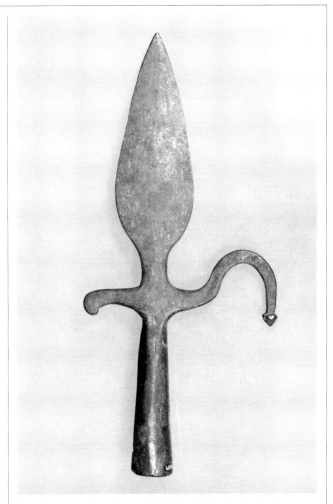

American war booty from 1847, this relic indicates that some Mexican infantry, possibly militia, were armed with pikes in lieu of firearms. The crook on the cross piece was designed to hook on to enemy horse furniture, thereby unseating the rider. West Point Museum.

muzzle had a deep funnel to hold ball and patch while ramrod was being drawn by the mounted cavalryman, the ramrod being attached by a swivel and topped by a large head. Earlier models had barrels of stub twist, browned to show grain of metal. A later contract model of 1806-08 had the Baker mark on the lockplate, plain iron barrel, swan neck cock and fixed backsight, brass mountings, with a bayonet attachment frame brazed on at the side. The ramrod was heavy with a large head. The butt was placed between the feet for loading in order to force the ramrod down with both hands, a procedure at variance with Mexican rifle drill practice. The ball was slightly smaller than bore, requiring a greased leather patch to pad the gap.

The Mexican government also imported Prussian M1839 muskets and Jaeger Short Rifles. The latter had the *tige*, or pin, invented by Colonel Thouvein of the French artillery, projecting from the bottom of the breech, causing the bullet to expand when it was rammed home.

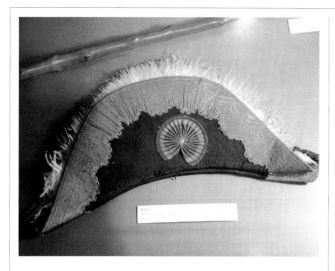

Top.
Fore-and-aft hat said to have been worn by Santa Anna, and captured by Major William H. Polk. (*detail*) Tricolour cockade from the same. North Carolina Museum of History: photos courtesy of Alan McBrayer, and James K. Polk Memorial State Historic State.

Finds in Texas of brass snake-device belt buckles matching those issued to British rifle regiments indicate that the Mexican government purchased British black leather accoutrements, including waist belt and cap pouch, cartridge box and belt. British powder horns are also believed to have seen Mexican service.[121]

There were old-fashioned powder-mills near Sante Fe and at Zacatecas. The latter blew up early in 1845 and, though repaired, worked at a disadvantage. During 1842, these mills had on hand 35,650 lbs of superfine powder for riflemen, 84,150 lbs fine rifle powder, 34,050 lbs of medium fine cannon powder, and 166,450 lbs of coarse miner's powder.

Mexican powder was usually of an inferior quality, and those using it attempted to overcome this by adding extra powder to each cartridge. The excessive recoil produced often caused the Mexican soldier to fire 'from the hip', and to generally aim too high. Private Barna Upton of the 3rd U.S. Infantry noted at

Palo Alto: 'Though they loaded and fired very fast, they did not take good aim, or they would have killed every man of us.'[122]

Infantry accoutrements consisted of a hide or canvas knapsack with buckskin straps and metal buckles; a cartridge box of tin, although black leather ones of British pattern also seem to have seen service by 1836; a buckskin waistbelt, slings and shoulderbelt with frog; a blanket with carrying straps; and a wooden drum canteen with iron bands, suspended from a leather sling, which held about a quart. The latter was often discarded for a gourd, which kept its contents much cooler.

Mexican regimental and battalion colours generally consisted of the national flag, which was a green, white and red tricolour with the eagle and serpent plus unit designation in the centre. Sometimes these flags had red silk streamers with gold lace tasseled ends attached. Guide, marker, and company flags were also carried by many units. The Mexican soldier proved he was prepared to die rather than surrender his flag on a number of occasions. At Palo Alto, not a single colour bearer remained alive; the 4th Light Infantry Battalion alone lost three colour bearers in a row. After the battle of Buena Vista in 1847, South Carolinian B. Lane Posey of the South Carolina Regiment recalled:

'The Tampico battalion [of Active Militia] was the Palmetto Regiment of the Mexican army. Half of them fell upon the field, and it was only when every other corps had fled that they retired in sullen mood from the field. Their flag bearer tore their flag from its staff, and wrapping it around him, sought to save it from falling as a trophy to their victors, but he was shot down with that proud flag as his winding sheet.'[123]

On 13 September 1847, the San Blas Battalion left nearly all officers and men as casualties on Chapultepec Hill but its commander, Lieutenant Colonel Felipe Santiago Xicoténcatl, with a deadly wound, managed to salvage the battalion colour before he died. Subaltern Suazo of the Mina Battalion dying under fire, attempted to save the flag by wrapping it around himself before it fell, bloodstained, into American hands.

Organisation of the Mexican Army
The Mexican armed forces in 1845 consisted of the regular army, or *ejercito permanente*, divided into infantry, cavalry, artillery, and engineers; and the territorial militia (*milicia activa*), or national guard (*guardia nacional*), which, since gaining veteran status for their involvement in the Federalist-Centralist wars of 1832-34, were considered to be the same organisation. The regular army and territorial militia/

national guard were under the direct control of the chief of staff of the army, while the directors of the corps of artillery and of engineers controlled their own respective arms. Also under the control of the chief of staff were the medical corps, and the local general staff detachments or *cuerpos del detall de las plazas*, who performed administrative duties in the major fortresses, seaports, and garrison towns.

General Staff

The army general staff, or *plana mayor general del ejercito*, consisted of all the general officers, the general staff corps, or *plana mayor*, under the chief of staff, and of such auxiliary officers as were considered necessary.

There were two grades of general officers - generals of division, and generals of brigade. Both grades wore a gala, or full dress, uniform consisting of a turkish blue tail-coat with bright red piping, lapels, collar, cuffs, shoulder straps, and turn-backs; half-inch wide gold embroidered design of interlaced palm, laurel and olive branches around collar, cuffs, and lapels - two rows of this embroidery on a division general's cuffs, and one row on a brigade general; horizontal pockets with gold embroidered flaps and three eagle buttons; and coat tail clasps in the form of large eagles with four inch wide wingspan. Epaulettes were of heavy gold with three inch long bullion fringes, the strap in raised leaf work and a white eagle in the centre of each strap.

A sky blue sash with five inch gold fringes and knots with two rows of embroidery, signified a division general, and a green sash with the same fringes, but one row of embroidery on the knots, a brigade general.

Trousers were also turkish blue with one inch-wide gold seam stripes. A black fore-and-aft bicorne described as a three-point hat, displaying a two inch-wide undulated lace garnished around the edges with white plumery, had a loop and tassels of gold bullion, and was topped with three 9 inch-long plumes in the national colours - red, white and green, in addition to a three inch-diameter tricolour cockade under the gold loop. It seems, however, that a loose tuft of roosters feathers in the three colours was used more frequently.

A straight sword in a black frog was suspended from a waist belt under the tail coat, with a metallic gold tassel tied to the guard. A cane with black silk tassels and chamois colored gloves completed the gala dress. Overcoats and capes for generals were not specified, and appear to have been left to individual taste.

A surviving hat, said to have been worn by Santa

Gala dress coat and sword belt worn by Brigadier General Juan Morales, who commanded the defence of Veracruz in March 1847. Morales was imprisoned by Santa Anna in the Fort outside Perote for allowing Veracruz to fall, and several months later was captured by the advanced guard of Worth's division. San Jacinto Museum of History Association.

Anna, follows the basic pattern described above, minus plumes and gold bullion. Texas Ranger John S. Ford recalled of the capture of Santa Anna's apartment at Tehuacan on 22 January 1848: 'A coat of Santa Anna's, by actual test, weighed fifteen pounds, so much was it embroidered and embossed with solid gold. This was given to the State of Texas. There was a resplendent gold bullion sash of immense proportions and weight. This was sent to some other state...'[124]

The service half-uniform for generals consisted of a turkish blue tail-coat with cuffs of the same colour, and minus piping, but with the regulation embroidery on collar and cuffs. Buttons and clasps were the same as for gala dress, but without pocket flaps. This coat could be worn with or without epaulettes. Trousers were plain turkish blue, without seam stripes or piping. The gala sash was permitted with this uniform, whilst the hat was worn without tricolour plumes. Generals could also appear in civilian clothing

combined with their sash with gold embroidered insignia, under tail-coat or frock coat.

The saddle used by generals was a mixed ranch-type and military model, all leather parts being black with gilt ornaments. Precious stones set in saddles were prohibited. The gala saddle blanket and triple holster covers were of scarlet cloth edged with 2 rows of gold lace, the outer one 2½ inches and the inner one 1 inch wide. A gold embroidered rising eagle with 5 inch wing span decorated the hind corners of the blanket. With service half-uniform, the saddle blanket and holster covers were turkish blue with a single 2 inch-wide gold lace edging.

For mounted wear with either uniform, turkish blue pants without stripe, high boots with white boot-hose, and spurs with straight bar and strap were prescribed. The gold lace trouser seam stripe, gold sword knot, and gilt eagle button, were specific insignia for generals, and no other rank was permitted to use them.

Both the general staff corps and the local general staff detachments wore blue uniforms until 1842. The general staff corps wore a dark blue coat with light

This lithograph by Ferdinand Bastin was published in 1850, and depicts the defense of the Belen Gate outside Mexico City on 13 September 1847. Mexican forces involved in this action were commanded by General Andrés Terrés, and included two eight-pounder field guns, and one six-pounder. Terrés may be the officer wearing the cocked hat to the left of centre, whilst his second in command, Colonel Guadalupe Perdigon Garay, sits a horse next to him. The infantrymen advancing either side wear typical Regular Infantry uniform. Several presidial, or auxiliaries, may also be seen assisting with the removal of the wounded. DeGolyer Library.

blue facings, and the local general staff detachments a light blue coat with dark blue facings. The uniform of the local general staff detachments was changed, in July 1842, to a red coat with black velvet facings and gold trim and buttons, dark blue trousers with gold piping, and a cocked hat with gold binding. The use of this uniform was extended to the general staff corps in August 1842. The general staff corps changed the facings on its red uniform to white in September 1844, while the local general staff continued to wear black velvet facings.

Mexican Regular Army

The Mexican Regular Army in early 1845 consisted of fifteen infantry regiments. These were the 1st - 4th and 6th - 12th Line Infantry Regiments; the 1st - 3rd Light, or *Ligero*, Infantry Regiments; and the Grenadier Guards of the Supreme Powers. There were also two Standing, or *Fijo*, battalions - that of Mexico, and that of the Californias; the Mexico Invalid Unit; the Puebla Invalid Battalion; and seven independent garrison companies, or *companias fixas*.

The Regular Cavalry consisted of the 1st - 9th Regiments; the Light Mounted Regiment of Mexico; the Hussars of the Guard of the Supreme Powers; the Tulancingo Cuirassiers; the Puebla Light Cavalry; the Yucatan Squadron; four squadrons; the Tabasco Company: and 34 Presidial Companies.

Mexican Regular infantry and cavalry regiments were woefully understrength in 1846. Compared with a paper strength of 784 and 316 respectively, the average infantry battalion fielded about 184 men, whilst the average cavalry battalion strength was 145.

The Corps of Artillery consisted of three battalions of foot artillery, each consisting of six companies of six pieces each; one brigade of horse artillery, with eight batteries of six pieces each; nine garrison companies of foot artillery; three companies of artificers; and two train companies.[125] By 1846 the Artillery had an authorised strength of 266 officers and 4,989 men, but its actual strength on 10 November 1846 was 166 officers and 1,957 men. Not only was the artillery lacking in personnel, but it was woefully short of saddle and draft horses.[126] The Medical Health Corps was incorporated into the regular army in February 1846.

Line Infantry

Line infantry regimental headquarters staff was composed of a Colonel, Lieutenent Colonel, a Commandant, two Second Adjutants, two Lieutenants, two Ensign-Sublieutenants, two Surgeons, two Chaplains, a Drum Major and a Bugle Corporal, two Pioneer Corporals with 16 pioneers and two armourers. There were also a second sergeant as a tailor, and corporals as a blacksmith, mason, and baker.

A line infantry regiment consisted of two battalions of eight companies each. Each battalion contained six fusileer companies, one rifle company, and one grenadier company. Each company consisted of a captain, a lieutenant, two sub-lieutenants, a first and four second sergeants, nine corporals, and eighty privates. The fusileer and grenadier companies had a drummer, a bugler, and a fifer. Rifle companies had four buglers.

By the law of 8 July 1839, the regimental numbers of these units, reorganised during March of the same year, were distributed by seniority and location as follows:

Regimental Number	1st Regular Battalion Formed from:		2nd Battalion Replacement Cadre:
1	Morelas	Active Militia of Guadalajara	Guanajuato
2	Hidalgo	Tres Villas	Veracruz
3	Allende	Active Militia of Querétaro	Jalisco
4	Guerrero	Active Militia of San Luis Potosí	San Luis
5	Aldama	Active Militia of Mexico	Mexico
6	Jimenez	Public Security Force Mexico	Mexico
7	Matamoros	Active Militia of Puebla	Puebla
8	Landero	Yucatán Auxiliary	Veracruz
9	Abasolo	Active Militia of Chiapas	Oaxaca-Chiapas
10	Galeana	Active Militia of Yucatán	Yucatán
11		Active Militia Toluca	
		Active Militia of Mextitlán	
			Mexico-Querétaro
12		Active Militia Tlaxcala	
		Active Militia of Mexico	Puebla-Tlaxcala

The 5th Line Regiment was extinguished for rebellion on 20 July 1839. Most of the remaining regiments fought through all the main battles and campaigns of 1846-47. After making a brave stand the day before,

Top left and right.
Reconstruction: Enlisted man of 2nd Line Regiment with deep red lapels and cuffs, and sky blue collar. (*rear view*)
Accoutrements are suspended from buckskin shoulder belts and slings. Note numerals on wooden drum canteen, which indicate 2nd Regiment, 4th Company, and the natural leather cartridge box. Photos courtesy of Marco Gonzalez.

the 3rd, 4th and 6th Regiments lost almost their entire force, including officers, at Cerro Gordo on 18 April 1847. Remnants of these regiments were subsequently re-organised into the Mixed Battalion of Santa Anna. The 1st Regiment was destroyed at Molino del Rey, whilst the 10th Regiment suffered the same fate at Chapultepec.

Officially, line infantrymen were to receive one woollen dress uniform, and two white canvas uniforms, per year. The dress uniform, originally decreed on 18 March 1839, consisted of a tail-coat and trousers of turkish blue with cloth facings in a combination of distinctive colours which were different for every unit. Unless otherwise noted, the varying colours were displayed on collars, lapels, cuffs, cuff flaps, and piping according to the following scheme:

1st Regiment - Yellow lapels and piping; deep red collar, cuffs and flaps; blue or white vest.

2nd Regiment - Deep red lapels, cuffs and flaps, and piping on pants; sky blue collar.

3rd Regiment - Crimson lapels, cuffs and flaps; sky blue collar and piping.

4th Regiment - Deep red lapels and cuff flaps; sky blue collar and cuffs; white piping.

5th Regiment - Deep red lapels, collar and cuff flaps; sky blue cuffs and piping.

6th Regiment - White lapels; crimson collar, cuffs and flaps; piping in opposite colours.

7th Regiment - Gold embroidered buttonholes instead of lapels; green collar and cuffs; crimson cuff flaps and piping.

8th Regiment - Sky blue lapels and cuff flaps; deep red collar and cuffs; piping in opposite colours.

9th Regiment - Purple lapels and cuffs; buff collar and cuff flaps; piping in opposite colours.

10th Regiment - Purple lapels and cuffs; deep red collar and cuff flaps; buff piping.

11th Regiment - Green lapels; deep red collar, cuffs and flaps.

12th Regiment - Buff lapels, collar and cuffs; deep red cuff flaps; piping in opposite colours.

On 22 December 1841, the uniform of the 11th Regiment was changed to a white tail-coat , with sky blue lapels, collar and cuffs; deep red cuff flaps and piping; and sky blue pants with deep red seam stripes. On 30 June 1842, the pants were changed again to crimson with white seam stripes.

Plain white canvas pants were worn in summer by all regiments. Some contemporary prints depict infantry wearing white gaiters over the shoes, although none of the uniform regulations, clothing contracts, or inventories list this item.

All uniform accessories for regular infantry, e.g. buttons and embroidery - was yellow. The regimental number was stamped on all buttons and embroidered on the collar. It was prohibited to place any extra embroidery on collar or sleeves. An eagle device with two-inch wingspan was attached to all coat-tails.

A comment is necessary on the prevalent uniform colour specified as *turkish blue*. This colour met with a variety of interpretations by government agencies and clothing contractors in Mexico, fluctuating from a blue-black through varying shades of dark and medium blue. Etymologically, turkish blue is a greyish pale blue. In colloquial use in Spanish-speaking regions it frequently designates medium or dark blue.

Shakos worn by the line infantry regiments differed in shape and composition, varying from dull to shiny black leather, and from the 'stove-pipe' pattern with parallel sides, to shakos with wider, 'bell-crown' tops, to those which tapered towards the top with the crown tilted somewhat forward. Similar to the cap introduced in the French Army in 1837, the latter pattern was most popular, being shiny black leather about seven inches tall, with an almost horizontal, square black leather visor, and two small yellow metal buttons either side of the band, to which a scale chin strap was attached. All had a front plate bearing the national coat of arms which consisted of a spread eagle holding a serpent in its beak, and the regimental number set within a wreath of laurel and palm leaves. Above this was a double loop of $^3/16$ thick gold cord under which was a tricolour cockade with green centre and red outer band. Pompons varied from a round wool pattern of either red or green, to a deep red velvet pattern about six inches tall by one inch in diameter.

All line regiment officers wore shakos of similar pattern to other ranks. (For full dress, the officers' turkish blue tail-coat appears to have been embellished with eight bars of gold braid across the breast for subalterns.) Officers' full dress rank insignia was designated by the following epaulette system: - Colonels, two heavy gold lace straps, with 'dead and

bright' gold bullion fringe, with a large eight-pointed silver metal star in each crescent; Lieutenant Colonels, the same minus stars. Both wore bright red silk sashes around their waist. The Battalion Commandant, wore the same plain strap on each shoulder, with a four gold strand, and four silver strand, bullion fringe. Captains wore two plain straps, with five-strand gold bullion fringe. Lieutenants and second-adjutants had a single gold epaulette on the right shoulder; Sub-lieutenants, Sub-adjutants, and Ensigns, a single gold epaulette on the left shoulder. For half-uniform, fringeless epaulettes were worn by all except the Colonel and Lieutenant Colonel. Field grade officers also wore a gorget which bore the national eagle and serpent emblem in the centre, and sometimes a branch service device at either end.

All line infantry officers carried sword-sabres on waist belts under the tail-coat in the field. The sword was suspended from a crossbelt with frog when on garrison duty. Sword knots were deep red without metallic strands. Senior officers carried canes with silk cords, but junior officers temporarily in senior posts

A Mexican lancer carried this grim guidon at Sacramento, where it was captured. In Spanish on its reverse side is the motto 'Liberty or Death'. From an artefact, by Ron Field.

Reconstruction of a trooper of the 1st Cavalry Regiment wearing the new uniform received by this regiment in September, 1845. Photo courtesy of Marco Gonzalez.

were not entitled to canes. When mounted, infantry officers used a mixed model black saddle and reins with brass buckles. Saddle blankets and holster covers were of turkish blue cloth, the former being edged with a two inch-wide deep red cloth band.

First Sergeants and cornet majors had two crimson silk epaulettes. Second Sergeants wore one such epaulette on the right shoulder. Corporals had a ½ inch-wide red diagonal stripe, or half chevron, running from cuff to elbow on both sleeves. Corporals also carried crude wooden sticks, with which to beat privates at their whim.

Preference companies of grenadiers or rifle companies within line regiments were permitted to wear a small vertical yellow flash, or 'sardinete', on their cuffs. In 1836, the Commerce Battalion of Mexico, followed by other regular and militia infantry units, had abused this privilege by allowing every member of the regiment to wear this mark of distinction. Consequently, an order was circulated to restrict this practice to a single flash for grenadier or rifle companies of ordinary line regiments, and a

double flash for elite troops, or columns made up entirely of these preference companies.

Officially, line infantry regiments were only permitted to wear their white canvas fatigue jackets and pants in excessively hot regions. However, due to clothing shortages they often found themselves with nothing else to wear but canvas fatigue clothing. In May 1842, the 2nd Battalion of the 7th Regiment, stationed at Jalapa, received only canvas uniforms including a jacket, trousers, shirt, stock, and barracks cap. None-the-less, regiments appear to have worn full dress on campaign. An Illinois volunteer described the attacking Mexican infantrymen 'in long tall hats, bedecked with tinsel, & what was more their Blue over coats streaming in the wind...'[127]

Light Infantry

Light infantry regiments were composed of eight companies each, one of them being a sharpshooter company, and the remainder line companies. Commands were relayed via bugle calls. In March 1841 a new set of Light Infantry tactics were issued which stated: 'When in closed order in depth be prepared to deploy into an extended or mixed order by three's instantly'. Once deployed, the first man of the small group would open fire, and when he had finished priming, the second would fire, and as he finished priming his rifle, the third man fired, and so on. Thus at any one time there should have been a loaded rifle.

The Light Infantry uniform was introduced by paragraph 8 of the decree of 31 August 1840, as a result of which all three light infantry regiments wore a turkish blue tail-coat with deep red piping on collar, cuffs, and shoulder straps. This garment was fastened by yellow metal ball buttons. The collar was embroidered in the following plain yellow initials - an 'L' on the right side, and a 'P' on the left side, representing *Ligero Permanente*. Trousers and overcoats were a grey mixture of black and white, with deep red seam stripes. The shako was smaller than for line infantry, with a top band at the crown, chinstrap, and loop for tricolour, all of black patent leather. This was embellished with a green pompon and a brass bugle insignia in front. The crossbelts were of dull black leather without a plate. Great coats were grey.

For daily and field service, a grey shell jacket with red piping and trim was worn instead of the tail-coat. The shako was replaced by a grey visored barrack cap with red band, with a yellow metal bugle insignia in front.

A 4th Light Infantry Battalion was authorised by the decree of 30 March 1846. This unit was a reorganisation of the 3rd Infantry Regiment, and was given a considerably different uniform from the other three Light Infantry regiments. This consisted of a dark blue tail-coat with green collar, piping and arabesques; crimson lapels, cuffs and cuff bars; gilt eagle inginia on coat-tail turnbacks; medium blue trousers with crimson seam stripes; and white canvas pants for summer wear. Shakos appear to have been the same as for Light Infantry regiments.

At Resaca de la Palma, the 2nd Light Infantry, commanded by Lieutenant Colonel Mariano Fernandez, provided invaluable service as an advance guard. The sharpshooter companies of this regiment under Captains José Barragan and José Maria Moreno held back a large part of the American forces until all their officers were either killed, captured or wounded. At Buena Vista, the 1st, 2nd, and 3rd Light Infantry regiments, commanded by General Pedro de Ampudia, captured the first ridge in pouring rain, held it all night without camp fires or food, rifles loaded, protecting the powder pans with their bodies; at dawn the next day they again boldly joined battle, still without sustenance, and occupied several more ridges at bayonet point, capturing flags and cannon. The commander of the 1st Light Infantry, Colonel Gayoso, was killed at Churubusco. Lieutenant Colonel Miguel María Echeagaray, commanding the 3rd Light Infantry, led his regiment in a spirited but isolated counter-attack at Molino del Rey.

Although the tail-coat was standard issue for all infantry units, there were occasions during the war, especially on campaign, when frock coats were issued with standard red trim, regardless of regimental colours. They were in some cases dark blue with red collar, cuffs and flaps, and shoulder knots. Sometimes they were issued with only red piping around the collar, cuffs and pockets, and minus cuff flaps. Those worn by militia and national guard units, and by Light Infantry in the field, were grey and mostly had only red piping on collar and cuffs, and were minus cuff flaps.

Grenadier Guards of the Supreme Powers

Organised as an active militia battalion in Mexico City on 7 December 1841, the Grenadier Guards of the Supreme Powers contained 1,200 men in eight companies, each with a Captain, four Lieutenants, five Sergeants, two drummers, one bugler, twelve Corporals, and 125 Privates. Headquarters staff consisted of a Colonel, a Lieutenant Colonel, three Adjutants, an Armourer, a Surgeon, Chaplain, a Drum Major and a Bugle Corporal.

The Guards were originally dressed in 20 inch tall black bearskin caps with brass plate and scale chinstrap; finely made turkish blue tail-coats with sky blue collars trimmed with black arabesques, black cuffs with two vertical loops of yellow braid, and yellow lace trimmed button holes; yellow fringeless epaulettes; plain dark blue pants; black patent leather cross belts with a square brass plate bearing the unit designation.

Half of the officer corps of this elite unit was drained from the regular army, whilst the rank-and-file were contributed by eight Departments at 150 men each '...all of the same height of 5½ ft. Mexican and not a sixteenth of an inch less..' During the summer of 1842, the Guards were incorporated in the Regular Army, and on 9 September of that year were re-uniformed in a deep red tail-coat with sky blue collar, cuffs and flaps; white piping; white lapels with eight yellow lace trimmed buttonholes; two *sardinetas* on the sleeves; yellow fringeless epaulettes; vertical pocket flaps with three tassels in lieu of buttons, and a yellow embroidered grenade device on each coat-tail; sky blue pants with yellow seam stripes; and a bearskin cap with a brass grenade insignia.

Five hundred men from this unit were present at Cerro Gordo under Santa Anna's command, and formed part of the brigade of General Joaquin Rangel in the Army of the North during August 1847. It subsequently took part in the defense of the gates of Mexico City during September of that year.

Standing Battalions of Mexico and the Californias

The Mexico Standing Battalion, or *Fijo de Mexico*, was originally organised as the Replacement Deposit Battalion of Mexico in March 1843. It was renamed and given its distinctive uniform on 27 September of that year. Consisting of eight companies, it fought through the war within the ranks of the Army of the North. At Molino del Rey in 1847 it formed part of the Mexican centre as part of the brigade of General Simeon Ramirez.

This unit wore a white tail-coat without lapels; plain brass buttons; a green collar with two-inch high gold embroidered unit initials either side; and green fringeless epaulettes, cuffs and flaps - all piped in red. Coat-tails had vertical three-pointed pocket flaps with a button on each point; turnbacks had gold embroidered crossed quivers with four arrows in each. Pants were sky blue with deep red seam stripes.

The shako had a cinch band, cockade loop and scaled chinstrap of yellow metal, with a two inch round tricolour cockade over a yellow metal cap plate with national coat of arms and unit initials. The pompon was green for the six fusilier companies, with

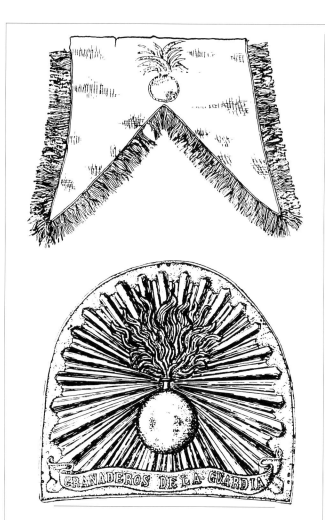

Top and right.

The Grenadier Guards of the Supreme Powers: (*right*) - 1842 uniform; (*top left*) trumpet banner carried by the Grenadiers of the Guard; (*bottom left*) – cap plates worn by the Grenadiers of the Guard. From drawings and descriptions, by Ron Field.

a red top for the grenadier and white top for the rifle company. Each fusilier company had a drummer, bugler, and fifer; the grenadier company had four drummers, buglers, and fifers; whilst the rifle company only had four buglers.

The Standing Battalion of the Californias was established on 19 January 1842, and served until 1 December 1847. Two hundred men from this unit formed part of the garrison at the port of Mazatlan in Baja California when it was occupied by Dupont's naval expedition in November 1846. Its uniform consisted a dark blue tail-coat with red collar, cuffs and flaps, with piping in opposite colours, and the initials 'FC' embroidered on the collar. Buttons and belt plates were yellow metal. Pants were dark blue with red seam stripes, and shakos had a red pompon, and brass chinstraps and cinch band.

In addition to the regular regiments and battalions described above, a number of smaller units performed field and garrison duty. The Battalion of Invalids of

Mexico was given its uniform on 3 October 1839, which consisted of a dark blue tail-coat with sky blue cuffs and cuff flaps and lapels, all of which was piped in red, as were the pockets. Each side of the collar had had the letter 'Y', signifying invalids, embroidered in yellow. Trousers were dark blue with red seam stripes. The shako was black with brass plate and fittings, and red pompon. This unit was involved in the defense of the gates of Mexico City.

The eight independent standing companies of Mexico were established in 1826. In December 1835, these were re-organised into the Acapulco, San Blas,

Tampico, 1st and 2nd Bacalar, Carmen Island, and 1st and 2nd Tabasco. By 1847, they had been reduced to two. In September 1842 these units were given a uniform composed of a dark blue single-breasted coat, with collar, cuffs and flaps, and turnbacks of the same colour cloth piped with red, and company abbreviations embroidered on the collar in red. Shoulder knots were also dark blue, whilst trousers were white.

Line Cavalry

A Mexican regular cavalry regiment consisted of four squadrons with two companies each. Regimental Headquarters staff comprised a Colonel, a Lieutenant Colonel, two Squadron Commandants, four Adjutant Lieutenants, four Guidonbearer Ensigns, a Chaplain, a Surgeon, a First Segeant Marshal, three grooms, one Cornet Major and a Cornet Corporal, two Second Sergeants as saddler and armourer, two Corporals as tailor and carpenter, and three troopers as shoemaker, mason, and baker, all mounted.

A cavalry company contained a Captain, a Lieutenant, two Ensigns, one First and three Second Sergeants, nine Corporals, two trumpeters, 52 mounted and eight dismounted troopers.

On 11 April 1837, after some suggestions to abolish firearms in the cavalry altogether, it was decreed that '...the 1st company of all cavalry regiments shall be of lancers, made up of individuals with the aptitude and other requisites to perform this service...' Independent companies, and those within independent squadrons, were to have a squad of eight lancers led by a corporal. An Ensign and Second Sergeant commanded all lancer squads within a squadron.

The eight Mexican regular cavalry regiments were organised as follows via the law of 8 July 1839:

Regimental
| *1st Regular Battalion* | | *2nd Battalion* |
Number	*Formed from:*	*Replacement Cadre:*
1 Tampico	Active Militia of San Luis Potosí	
		San Luis
2 Veracruz	Active Militia of Zacatecas	
		Zacatecas
3 Dolores	Active Squadron of Durango	
		Durango
4 Iguala	Auxiliaries of the Cold Country	
		Querétaro
5 Palmar	1st & 2nd Active Militia of Jalisco	
		Jalisco
6 Cuautla	Active Militia of Morelia	

		Guanajuato
7 Mexico	Cuernavaca Squadron, Auxiliaries of Ayotla, Chalco, Texcoco & Tulancingo	Mexico
8 Active Militia of Puebla	Active Squadron & Auxiliaries of Tlaxcala	Yucatán

The dress of the Mexican Regular cavalry was more colourful and varied than that of the infantry, and consisted of a tail-coat; a shako with pompon of the same basic patterns as those worn by foot soldiers; and pantaloons with re-inforced inner leg section and 'false boots', or leg endings, of black antelope skin. The individual regiments were uniformed as follows:

1st Regiment - Yellow tail-coat with deep red lapels, collar, cuffs and flaps; piping in opposite colours; medium blue pants.

2nd Regiment - Yellow tail-coat with sky blue lapels, collar, cuffs, cuff flaps, and piping; turkish blue pants and saddle blanket.

3rd Regiment - Turkish blue tail-coat, and pants, with white lapels, green collar and cuffs; piping in opposite colours; green saddle blanket.

4th Regiment - Sky blue tail-coat with deep red lapels, collar, cuffs and flaps; piping in opposite colours; turkish blue pants; green saddle blanket.

5th Regiment - Turkish blue tail-coat with deep red lapels, collar, cuffs and flaps; piping in opposite colours; turkish blue pants; deep red saddle blanket.

6th Regiment - Green tail-coat with white lapels, collar and cuffs, deep red cuff flaps; green pants; deep red saddle blanket.

7th Regiment - White tail-coat with sky blue lapels, collar, cuffs and flaps; turkish blue pants; green saddle blanket.

8th Regiment - Turkish blue tail-coat, and pants, with deep red lapels and cuffs, white collar and cuff flaps; green saddle blanket.

On 10 September 1839, the uniform of the 7th Cavalry Regiment was changed to a crimson tail-coat with green collar, lapels, epaulettes, cuffs and flaps; eight white lace-trimmed button holes; piping in opposite colours; green pants with crimson seam stripe and black leather re-inforcement; black shako with white metal band around top and bottom, with red pompon over a tricolour cockade and white metal cap plate; and sky blue saddle blanket with a white band.

The 9th Cavalry Regiment was created on 22 December 1841, and received a green tail-coat with crimson lapels, collar, cuffs and flaps; white piping; dark blue pants with crimson seam stripes, and green saddle blankets.

On 7 September 1845, the 1st Cavalry Regiment was assigned a new uniform consisting of a short green jacket with collar and cuffs of the same colour, cuff flaps, lapels, and piping yellow, dark green epaulettes with deep red fringe; a black leather dragoon helmet with brass trim and chinstrap, horse-mane tail and deep red plume at left side; grey pants with red seam stripes and black leather re-inforcement; leather half-boots; saddle blanket and holster covers of deep red with white band around; green saddle roll with deep red cover, white band and circular sides with unit number; and a dark blue cape with green collar.

All cavalry buttons and belt plates were white metal. Waist and shoulder belts were generally white buff leather. The regimental number was stamped on buttons, and embroidered on the collar. All ranks wore buckskin gloves or white gauntlets. Officers wore the same uniform as the troopers in each regiment, but made of finer cloth, with a cartouche box, shoulder belt, and waist belt of finer white leather.

In theory, training, drill, and equipment of the Mexican cavalry followed the Spanish cavalry tactics reprinted in Mexico by Galván in 1824. According to these, the standard line cavalry and dragoon saddle had a wooden frame with iron plates covered with leather, and stuffed with horsehair in canvas cushions. Stirrups were iron and pistol holsters were leather. The carbine rested in a cylindrical leather boot at the right of the saddle, with muzzle and ramrod pointing down. Dragoons had a leather quiver in which to insert the rifle butt and a sling nailed to the saddle front to hold the firearm in place. Hussar and light cavalry saddles had a pointed knob with a hole to attach the shabraque, pelt or cloak.

Cavalry arms were the sword or sabre, carbine, pistols, and lance. The sword usually hung from the waist belt, whilst the carbine could be carried attached to the swivel hook on a shoulder belt. The lance was an important weapon, being nine feet in length, including iron point and socket. The point, or blade, was about nine inches long, with three or four cutting edges separated by concave bayonet-like gutters. Underneath this was a socket, and sometimes an iron crosspiece with two 3 feet-long straps, as protection against sabre cuts which could lop off the point. The shaft was about an inch thick and preferably made of beech or nut wood. Under the blade hung a two-pointed pennon a foot in length, sometimes in regimental-facing colours, which was designed both as an ornament and to scare enemy horses by fluttering in front of their eyes.

At a convenient height, a leather sling was nailed to the shaft with a triple loop to suspend the lance from the right arm, or to act as a support in swinging or thrusting. A leather socket, or boot attached to the right stirrup aided in resting the lance, and a loop at the cinch assured that it did not fall out while manoeuvring.

Regulations expected line cavalry and dragoons to carry a blanket 83 inches long by 64 inches wide, and a cape or overcoat, folded into a rectangle, rolled up and strapped under the cloth or leather saddle roll 22 inches long by 10 inches wide and 5 inches deep. Hussars and light cavalry were prescribed a cylindrical roll 20 inches long and 6 inches in diameter containing cloth, canvas or leather pants, a shirt, socks, cloth and shoe brushes, a satchel with comb, scissors, pins, accessories and boot grease. An 18 inch-wide canvas sack with two pockets contained apron and sponge; spare horseshoes were carried in a saddle pocket and fatigue jacket and raincoat folded under the saddle roll. Although Mexican military authorities copied such detail freely from Spanish tactical manuals, they applied them in practice only sporadically.

Light Mounted Regiment of Mexico

This regiment was originally raised in 1835, and was dressed in a sky blue tail-coat with scarlet collar, epaulettes, cuffs and flaps; dark blue cavalry pants with deep red seam stripes; leather half-boots; shako with red pompon; a sky blue cloak, saddle blanket, holster covers and saddle roll, all edged with a scarlet cloth band. Operating mainly in northern Mexico, two squadrons of this regiment fought at Palo Alto and Resaca de la Palma in 1846. It also saw action at Monterey and Vera Cruz.

The Puebla Light Cavalry, the Yucatan Squadron, and the Tabasco Company, all adopted the uniform of the Light Mounted Regiment of Mexico.

The Hussars of the Guard of the Supreme Powers

This regiment was originally a Light Cavalry squadron transformed on 3 December 1841 from a Public Security squadron. On 1 September 1843 it was designated an élite unit and rode at the head of all cavalry formations. During the summer of that year it was incorporated into the Regular Army. It was designated the Hussars of the Guard of the Supreme Powers on 27 July 1846, although it had been allowed to wear a hussar uniform since 19 December 1843. This consisted of a black busby with a brass plate bearing the regimental title, and a red bag with white piping, tassel and flounders. The jacket, or dolman, was deep red with ice blue collar and cuffs edged in white, with twelve double rows of white cord on the breast, and four rows of white metal ball buttons. This was graced by an ice blue pelisse trimmed with black fur collar, cuffs and edging, white cord trim on the breast, as on the dolman, and double white suspension cords with a slide button and two flounders on the left side. Trousers were ice blue with black antelope skin re-inforcement, and white seam stripes. A black sabretache trimmed with white lace was suspended on two black slings from a white waist belt. All other leather work was also white. Horse furniture consisted of a red cloth saddle blanket with white band around, red holster covers with double white band, and an ice blue saddle roll with white piping.

During the war the Hussars served as the presidential bodyguard, and carried lances with long red-over-blue or red pennons. By November 1846, they numbered 41 officers and 422 men, commanded by Lieutenant Colonel Don Miguel Andrade, and were at San Luis Potosi with Santa Anna as part of the Army of the North. They also took an active part in the battles of Buena Vista, Cerro Gordo, and Churubusco in 1847, and subsequently formed part of the force which defended the gates of Mexico City in September of that year.

The Tulancingo Cuirassiers

This heavy cavalry unit was originally established as an Imperial Escort of four companies in 1823. It was re-organised as a regiment on 15 January 1842. Officers and troopers of the Tulancingo Cuirassiers had two changes of uniform. When mounted, officers wore a brass helmet with silver ornaments, jaguar-skin band, and black horse hair *criniere*; a sky blue jacket with crimson collar and cuffs trimmed with white lace; silver epaulettes; crimson pants with sky blue seam stripes; a brass cuirass with national coat of arms in silver; silver belt buckle and cartouche, and black knee length boots with silver spurs. Troopers wore the same helmets and cuirasses; a sky blue coat with crimson collar, cuffs and cuff flaps, piped in white; silver epaulettes; crimson pants with sky blue seam stripes, and black leather re-inforcement. Horse furniture for officers included a sky blue shabraque edged with silver lace, and a bridle trimmed with silver. A trooper's shabraque was also sky blue with a white band around.

When dismounted and off duty, officers wore a black bicorne hat; sky blue, single breasted tail-coat with crimson collar and pointed cuffs edged with silver

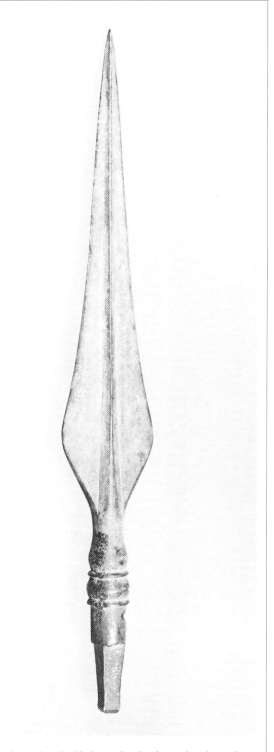

A Mexican lance head with four-edged point and male socket, captured in 1847. West Point Museum.

lace; sky blue pants with crimson seam stripes; silver epaulettes; silver cartridge box; and black boots with silver spurs. Troopers wore a sky blue coat with crimson collar, cuffs, cuff flaps, and turnbacks, all trimmed with white lace; white epaulettes; sky blue pants with crimson seam stripes; and black boots with steel spurs.

The Tulancingo Cuirassers were armed with straight sword with brass grip especially designed for

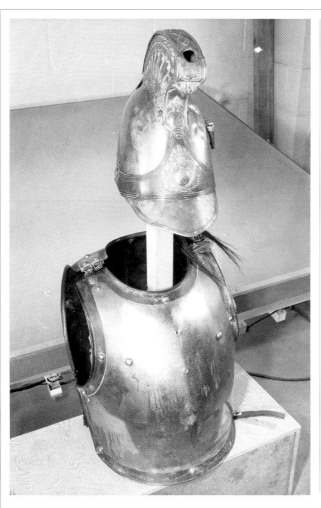

the unit, and musketoons. This regiment took part in the battles of Buena Vista, Cerro Gordo, and Churubusco. At Cerro Gordo, the first adjutant of the regiment, Velasco, was killed leading a party of cuirassers manning a battery whose gun crews had already been devastated by American rifle fire. The unit also formed part of the force which guarded the gates of Mexico City in September 1847.

Top and bottom.
Full dress armour worn by the Tulancingo Cuirassiers. Three different types of helmet, and two types of cuirass, are known to exist. (*top*) This elaborate helmet bearing the flaming grenade devices, and solid brass comb, may have been worn by an officer. An elongated tricolour pompon protruded almost vertically from the socket in the tip of the comb. A plume of unknown colour was inserted in the socket sweated on the left, whilst a long black horsetail was attached to the back base of the comb. A band of jaguar skin encircled the base of the helmet, over which was a scaled brass chinstrap attached by large buttons bearing the eagle and serpent device. (*bottom*) This less elaborate helmet with smaller comb, was possibly imported from France, and worn by enlisted men of the Tulancingo Cuirassiers. The detachable plate has long since disappeared. The holes in the front of both sets of cuirass indicate they once had the national coat of arms attached. West Point Museum.

The Presidial

The Presidial Companies evolved from the Spanish colonial gendarmerie who manned a line of fortified outposts called *presidios* built north of Mexico City around 1570. Two hundred and seventy-five years later, the line of *presidios* had moved up to the present American southwest and extended from Texas to California.

Of the 34 Presidial Companies attached to the Mexican Regular Army by 1846, eight were stationed in Coahuila, three in New Mexico, six in California, and the rest in Mexico. The uniform was the same for

Mexican cavalry. *(left)* Jalisco Lancer, active militia; *(middle)* Mounted Rifles, active militia; *(right)* Tulancingo Cuirassier officer. By Ron Field.

all except the California companies, and was largely still based on that adopted by the Spanish in 1772. It consisted of a coatee of shag or medium blue cloth with deep red facings on collar, cuffs, and coat-tails; blue pants and blue cloth cape; black brimmed hat with white band; and black stock. Although the uniform regulations of 1821 stipulated that a unit number be embroidered on the collar, by the 1840s

Mexican infantry prior to the Battle of Churubusco, 1847

Mexican forces under Major General Manuel Rincón put up a truly inspired defense of the Franciscan Convent of San Mateo at Churubusco on 20 August 1847. A combined garrison of Regular and National Guard units beat off numerous American assaults before finally surrendering to a white flag offered by Captain James M. Smith, 3rd U.S. Infantry. The plate opposite depicts Mexican infantry prior to this battle. (right) The colour bearer of the 11th Line Infantry wears the uniform adopted by his unit between 1841-42. As Mexican colour bearers were given officers' rank designation privileges, he wears a yellow metal gorget bearing an eagle and serpent around his neck. Two diagonal stripes on his lower sleeves denote the rank of second sergeant.

Mexican regimental and battalion colours generally consisted of the national flag emblazoned with the eagle and serpent, plus unit designation. Sometimes these flags had red silk streamers with yellow tasselled ends attached. A brass Napoleonic-style eagle tops the staff.

The private of the San Patricio Battalion (left) wears the uniform prescribed for the Mexican National Guard in 1842. His unit was largely made up of American Catholic deserters from the U.S. Army – hence his ruddy complexion and auburn-coloured hair. He is armed with a British Tower-type 'Brown Bess' smoothbore flintlock musket, thousands of which were condemned as unserviceable by the British government and sold to Mexico during the period 1830 to 1840. Of eighty-seven members of the Battalion captured at Churubusco, at least 30 were tried by U.S. court-martial, found guilty of desertion, and hanged on a hill top overlooking Chapultepec at the moment the Stars and Stripes replaced the Eagle and Serpent flag above the Castle!

The kneeling member of the 4th Light Infantry wears the field dress of his regiment. Embroidered on the collar of his jacket are the letters 'L' (Ligero) and 'P' (Permanente). Note his hide knapsack with buckskin straps, and gourd water carrier.

Painting by Richard Hook.

the initial letters of the province, or *presidio*, name seem to have been used. Accoutrements consisted of a natural leather cartridge box and bandoleer with the *presidio* name often embroidered on the latter.

One such unit under the command of Colonel Velasco was encountered in 1841 by the Santa Fé Expedition of the Texas Republican Army. Designated the Frontier Guard of Durango, their uniform and equipment was described by George Wilkins Kendall as consisting of:

'a blue woollen coatee or jacket trimmed with red, with velvet trousers of the same colour, and instead of a common cavalry cap they all wear a coarse, wide-brimmed wool hat, with a plate of tin some two inches in width entirely circling the crown. Their arms consisted of a carbine, slung to their saddles on the right and with the breech up; on the left side of the saddle is fixed a lance, to the end of which a strip of red flannel or woollen stuff is attached, which flutters gayly as they ride along; a heavy cavalry sword, which clatters at every movement of their horses, completes their equipment, for although a pair of holsters were attached to the pommels of their saddles, I never could see that they contained pistols.'

Colonel Velasco was described as wearing:

'a light blue roundabout or short jacket, with a small red cord along the seams and three rows of small silver-plated buttons in front, while his pantaloons were of cloth of the same colour, foxed with green morocco, to prevent his saddle from chafing and wearing them. He wore a... pair of huge, grizzly, coarse mustaches, which stuck out in almost every direction but the right one. His head was covered with a profusion of long, iron-gray hair but partially covered by a small, rakish cap, drawn over his eyes as if to conceal any sinister expression they might have.'[128]

Mexican cavalry wearing a similar uniform were encountered by Kearny's 'Army of the West' on 14 August 1846. A detail sent from Santa Fe by General Armijo to negotiate with the Americans were described as follows by Lieutenant William H. Emory, Kearny's topographical engineer:

'They were dragoons, dressed in roundabout and pants of light, blue cloth, similar to our own dragoons, with a red stripe down the outer seam of the pants. They all wore large Mexican hats; there was a lieutenant, sergeant and two privates. They rode small horses. The lieutenant had a sabre; the others were armed with carbines and lances.'[129]

The presidial companies of California had two uniforms - a garrison dress with dark blue tail-coat, green collar with the initials 'AC' or 'BC' embroidered both sides; green cuffs, deep red lapels and cuff flaps; white piping; dark blue pants with deep red seam stripes; an ornamented cavalry shako; a shabraque of unspecified colour with a white band all around. Their campaign uniform consisted of a dark blue round jacket with deep red collar and cuffs, grey side-buttoned chaparral pants over boots; a round black hat with white band; a dark blue cape; and a cowman's saddle and shabraque. Presidial troops were armed with the sabre, carbine, and lance.

Artillery

The Mexican National Artillery Corps dated back to 14 Febrary 1824. It had its own general staff, composed of the senior artillery officers, plus its own quartermaster corps, a company of artillery artificers, and its own judiciary, which was shared with the Corps of Engineers.

A Mexican foot artillery brigade was commanded by a headquarters staff consisting of five senior officers, six junior officers, one captain paymaster, one chaplain, one surgeon, one first brigade sergeant, one drum major, one bugle major, one armourer, eight pioneers with one corporal, 12 musicians and two bandmasters. In peacetime a battalion of Mexican foot artillery was composed of six companies, each company consisting of three officers, 20 non-commissioned officers, two drummers, two buglers, and 66 artillerists. A wartime company consisted of five officers, 22 non-commissioned officers, two drummers, two buglers, and 86 artillerists.

The uniform worn by the foot artillery dated back to the decree of 31 August 1840, and consisted of a tail-coat of turkish blue, with crimson collar bearing a 2½-inch flaming bomb embroidered in yellow silk together with the number of the brigade or company. Cuffs, cuff flaps, lining and turnbacks were all crimson. The lapels were black with two sets of seven gilt buttons bearing the grenade device, and trimmed with yellow lace false buttonholes. Coat skirts had four loops and buttons, with a 2 inch-long yellow embroidered flaming grenade at the bottom of each skirt. Fringeless yellow epaulettes decorated each shoulder. Trousers were also turkish blue, possibly with crimson seam stripes. Shakos were black leather with a gold lace band around top and bottom, with two more on the sides at an angle going towards the back. This was adorned with a tricolour cockade, crimson pompon, and brass plate. Overcoats were turkish blue.

Foot artillery officers wore a turkish blue frock coat with crimson collar bearing a gold embroidered flaming grenade, and cuffs, cuffs flaps, and pockets of turkish blue piped with crimson. Lapels were to be of black velvet, but a surviving example of an artillery lieutenant's coat in the Smithsonian has blue lapels, which suggests that this rule was not necessarily followed. Pants were turkish blue with crimson seam stripes. A surviving artillery officer's shako of straight stovepipe-pattern is preserved in the collection of the National Museum of History, Mexico City. Decorated with a deep red, six inch-high cylindrical velvet pompon with a tuft of thin red silk cords hanging from the top, it has a top band of gold lace, and a lower cinch band of black velvet. Underneath the pompon is a tricolour cockade and a brass plate bearing the National Arms above a crossed cannon and flaming grenade device. A scale metal chinstrap is secured either side by large gilt 'flaming grenade' buttons.

When dismounted, officers carried a straight sword on a waistbelt. When mounted they were authorised a sabre suspended from black slings, with brass furnishings, and with a crimson silk sword knot at the grip.

Regimental staff in the Mounted Brigade was the same as for foot, with the addition of a trumpet major, a groom marshall, two saddlers, an armourer, and eight pioneers with a corporal. This Brigade consisted of six companies, each with four officers, two trumpeters, 20 non-commissioned officers, 60 gunners, 88 saddle horses and 50 draft horses.

The uniform worn by the mounted artillery comprised a turkish blue coatee with crimson collar, pointed cuffs, piping, lining and turnbacks; 1½ inch-wide white lace trim following edge of cuffs; and 3½ inch-wide diagonal white lace half chevrons on each forearm. Pants were also turkish blue with black antelope skin seat lining and 'false boots'. The shako was the same as for foot artillery. Gauntlets were buff, with white cuffs. The cape was turkish blue.

Their saddle was similar to that used by cavalry, with saddle blanket and double holster covers of turkish blue cloth with 2 inch-wide crimson border. The saddle roll was also turkish blue with crimson edging.

The artificer and train companies wore foot artillery items, with a turkish blue short roundabout jacket instead of a tail-coat; a round black hat with narrow brim, bearing the corps emblem; and plain turkish blue trousers. Arsenal officers used the same uniform pattern of foot artillery officers.

Artillery accounting employees wore a turkish blue tail-coat cut straight with wide coat-tails; gilt flaming grenade buttons and gold embroidered grenade on collar; and with collar and cuffs edged with indented braid for First, Second and Third Officer. Trousers were turkish blue. Commissioners wore a similar uniform with collar embroidery of laurel leaves mixed with a geometric pattern of gold lace, decreed on 4 December 1822; a black bicorne hat without lace or plume; and straight sword on a black belt.

The nine garrison artillery units were composed of the companies of Tampico, Matamoros, Sante Fe in New Mexico, Alta California, Guaymas, Mazatlán, San Blas, and Acapulco. These companies were presumably uniformed the same as for foot artillery.

Corps of Engineers and Sappers

The Corps of Engineers was founded on 30 June 1838, and consisted of a director general, who in 1846 was General Mora y Villamil; about 50 field and company grade officers; the Battalion of Sappers, or *Zapadores*; the Cadets of the Military Academy; and a small detachment of topographical engineers attached to the army general staff.

The engineers and sappers had the task of clearing obstacles from the path of the army, repairing or opening up roads, constructing bridges, laying mines, building fortifications and conducting siege operations. In the field, senior engineer officers served on the commanding general's staff, and helped to lead columns into battle position. They also established strong points, reconnoitered the terrain, and directed the defence of garrisons. A lack of proper equipment, such as a pontoon train, limited the capabilities of these troops. The main contribution of the Mexican Engineer Corps was in preparing and constructing numerous forts and defence works. Notably, they laid mines at El Penal Pass and at Chapultepec but did not have the opportunity to explode them.[130] The chief of the section of engineers at Chapultepec was Don Juan Cano. Alcaraz records: 'The mines did not happen to be sprung [at Chapultepec] by Lieutenant Aleman; for when he went to the place where the slow matches were, he found it occupied by the Americans.'

Engineer officers dressed in a turkish blue tail-coat with black collar and lapels piped crimson; with solid crimson cuffs, cuff flaps, piping, lining and turnbacks. Dependent on grade, full dress rank was distinguished by gold bullion epaulettes, or brass shoulder scales, bearing the engineer device consisting of serated pioneer's sword crossed by a spade and an axe. The waist sash was light blue. Trousers were blue-grey with crimson seam stripes, or gold button conchos. Shakos were plain and surmounted by a red pompon, underneath which was a tricolour cockade and gold loop, and a plate. Those officers attached to the staff wore tufts on their pompons. Engineer officers also carried a special model sword, and a cane the same as senior infantry officers. A grey frock coat was worn for undress.

The Sapper Battalion was used mostly as infantry or artillery, which was a waste of their special skills. In theory, this unit was to consist of approximately 600 men in six companies. Each company was composed of three officers, five non-commissioned officers, two drummers, a fifer and 78 sappers. The First and Second companies were miners and pontoniers respectively, with four buglers. In practice, this battalion was greatly undermanned, there being only 304 men in the battalion under Colonel José M. Carrasco at Palo Alto in May 1846, although this number had risen to 400 by the following February. The Battalion manned a battery of sixteen guns at Buena Vista. One hundred men from the unit, commanded by José María Para, formed part of the garrison at Vera Cruz during March 1847.

For full dress, sapper officers dressed in a similar coat to that worn by engineers, with crimson facings and black lapels. Headgear consisted of a black bicorne hat edged with gold lace, and decorated with a cockade and loop.

Non-commissioned officers and privates of the Sapper Battalion wore a black bearskin cap with red cords and flounders, and minus cap plate. The turkish blue tail-coat was trimmed on collar, cuffs, and turnbacks with crimson piped yellow, with crimson epaulettes, and crossed 'axe and mallet' insignia embroidered in crimson piped yellow on the left upper arm. Trousers were blue-grey with crimson seam stripes. Over this was worn a white leather apron, on top of which were white waist and cross belts. The gilt waist belt plate bore a flaming grenade, whilst the cross belt plate displayed the crossed axe and mallet device. Gauntlets were white leather. In the European tradition, beards were to be worn by Sappers for full dress. As many members of Mexican Army were of Indian extract, and did not usually grow thick facial hair, false beards were ordered to be worn! As with engineers, sappers wore grey frock coats for undress and in the field.

Mexican Military Academy

The cadets of the Mexican Military Academy, under Engineer Corps jurisdiction, wore a full dress uniform adopted on 8 December 1843, which consisted of a turkish blue tail-coat with a single row of gilt buttons stamped *Colegio Militar*, and crimson collar, cuffs, piping and turnback lining. Trousers were a lighter blue. All pupils up to the rank of Cadet-Lieutenant had a one inch-wide gold lace edging around the collar and cuffs, and gold lace shoulder straps. Their black cylindrical leather shako had a crimson top, an elongated red pompon, and a brass grenade insignia. On special occasions they carried a parade sword similar to those of regular army officers.

For daily service on Academy grounds, they wore a medium blue frock coat with red collar, and cuffs, dark blue trousers in winter and white drill in summer; a blue visored cap or a blue barracks cap with red lace and tassel; and black belt with brass plate.

Forty Cadets, remembered with pride in Mexico today as the *Niños Héroes*, or 'Heroic Children', were involved in the defence of the Chapultepec Castle, on 13 September 1847. Six were killed, and 3 were gravely wounded. On this occasion they were wearing a service uniform adopted by November 1846, which comprised a frock coat, trousers and barracks cap of grey cloth. The coat was trimmed on collar and cuffs with crimson patches and piping. Trousers were plain, under which were grey gaiters over black shoes. The cap was embellished with a yellow band, piping, and tassel.

They were armed with British 'Tower' muskets, plus some Baker carbines and American made rifles (possibly M1841 ['Mississippi'] Rifles), cut down to the stature requirements of the Cadets. They wore black leather waist and shoulder belts, the latter supporting a cartridge box.

By this time the Cadets also had a drill or fatigue uniform consisting of a short, grey, round jacket trimmed with crimson, and grey or white sailcloth trousers.

Marine Infantry Regiment

This regiment was formed on 19 September 1842, and adopted a dark green tail-coat with collar, cuffs, and turnbacks of the same colour. The collar was piped on top and front edges with crimson, and yellow on the bottom seam, with a two-inch high yellow anchor embroidered either side. Lapels were crimson with two sets of nine yellow lace false button holes. Cuffs were trimmed around with two rows of yellow lace, whilst sleeves were embellished with three diagonal yellow lace half chevrons running from the inner cuff to the outer elbow seams. Coat tails were piped with

crimson, and decorated with three horizontal yellow lace loops and buttons, and terminated in two crimson silk embroidered two-inch anchor devices. All buttons were gilt and bore an anchor. Epaulettes were yellow worsted. Headgear consisted of a crimson shako with yellow lace cinch bands around top and bottom, and three diagonal yellow strips of lace forming a V at the back; a yellow worsted safety cord attached to the top cinch band; a gilt scale chin strap; a yellow anchor emblem in front, above which was a national cockade under a metal loop, and a worsted yellow pompon with green falling plume. Trousers were crimson with yellow piping at the seams. Accoutrements consisted of a white shoulder belt supporting a black leather cartridge box bearing a gilt anchor.

Officers wore the same dress but of finer material, with gold lace or embroidery for all that was silk in the rank and file. Swords were brass hilted with a crimson sword knot, and were carried in a black scabbard with brass fittings.

At the beginning of the war the Mexican Marines were stationed at Tampico, and were marched north to assist in the defence of Matamoros during April 1846. Eighty enlisted men of the Marines, under the command of First Lieutenant Sebastian Holzinger, manned Battery Santa Barbara during the siege of Vera Cruz on 25 March 1847. Twice the Mexican flag flying over this position was shot away by the opposing U.S. Navy guns, and twice Lieutenant Holtzinger replaced it with his own hands. Much to the credit of the Mexican Marines, their 24-pounders were not silenced until early afternoon when their ammunition failed.

Mexican Militia and National Guard

The Mexican militia system of Spanish colonial days was re-organised under the Republic in 1827, while the National Guard was established separately shortly thereafter. Until the Zacatecas revolt of 1834, the National Guard was controlled by the various states, whilst the Active Militia was under the chief of staff of the army. After the Zacatecas rising had been crushed, Santa Anna reduced the power of the states and ensured that the National Guard was placed under direct army control. Hence, these two organisations were officially considered to be one on the eve of war in 1846, and are treated as such in this study

In 1846, this body consisted of five regiments and 15 battalions of infantry, plus 14 battalions as Coast Guards, and eight veteran companies of Coast Guards. The cavalry was composed of seven regiments, 19 squadrons, four coast guard squadrons, six coast guard companies, and 12 Presidial companies.

The infantry regiments consisted of the 1st and 2nd Mexico, 1st and 2nd Guanajuato, and Puebla. The battalions included the 1st and 2nd Celaya, Guadalara, Zacatecas, Michoacan, Sur, San Luis Potosi, Queretaro, Tehuantepec, Oaxaca, Aguascalientes, Lagos, Sinaloa, Chihuahua, and Sonora. Further battalions raised in Mexico City included the Victoria Battalion, composed of young commercial men of the wealthiest families; the Hidalgo Battalion, consisting of 'exempts, of ardent youths, and of old men that had passed their lives in sedentary occupations'; the Indepencia Battalion, under Colonel Pedro María Anaya, and the Bravo Battalion, both drawn from 'the laboring artisans and mechanics' of the capital.[131]

Inexperienced in action compared with the veterans of the Army of the North, the militia/National Guard units had mixed fortune in battle. The Independcia Battalion accidently fired down into the ranks of the Bravo Battalion during the defense of the convent at Churubusco. Lucas Balderas, colonel of the Mina Battalion, fell dead leading his unit at Molino del Rey, after having already been shot in the foot.

Meanwhile a wounded officer of the same unit saved the battalion colour from capture by twining it around his waist and escaping under fire as the remainder of his command was destroyed by enemy fire.

The battalions of Orizava, Veracruz, and Coatepec, under the command of General Manuel G. Zamora, played a valuable part in the defense of Veracruz. The San Blas Battalion, commanded by Lieutenant Colonel Xicoténcal, formed part of Rangel's brigade, Army of the North during August 1847, and were later cut to pieces during the storming of Chapultepec Castle.

As a result of the Decrees of 19 January and 27 April 1842, these units, plus the Coast Guard battalions, were prescribed a uniform consisting of a:

'Dark blue coat, red collar, cuffs, turnbacks and lapels, yellow piping; brass buttons with the name and/or number of the unit on them; tripointed false pockets with a button at the end of each point; the turnback ornament consisted of two yellow quivers two inches long, united at the lower ends each containing three arrows of the corresponding size. Sky blue trousers with red piping down the outer seam. Shako with chinstraps, a strap in the crown, a plate with the national coat of arms and the name or number of the unit, and a red pompon.'[132]

Although militia units were often poorly clothed and equipped, there were some exceptions. The Victoria Battalion was described as wearing 'rich uniforms' during August 1847, whilst the Independcia and Bravo battalions mustered in a 'modest dress'.[133] The San Blas Battalion were well equipped with the uniform decreed in 1842.

Militia buglers wore a black shako with a red top cinch band and a white bottom cinch band; a red pompon; a scarlet single-breasted coatee with dark blue collar, cuffs and turnbacks, all piped in white; silver lace diagonal sleeve stripes, three above the cuff, and two on the upper arm; silver epaulettes; white cartouche belt and waist belt; and light blue trousers with white seam stripes.

A number of militia units did not adopt the uniform decreed in 1842. The 1st Active Regiment of Mexico wore the facings of the 1st Regular Infantry, comprising yellow lapels and piping, with deep red collars, cuffs and turnbacks; and blue or white waistcoats. The Foot Artillery of Jalapa sported a long red pompon in their shako; whilst their dark blue coat had black lapels, emblazoned with six yellow blind button holes terminating in gilt 'Brüstlizen' buttons; red epaulettes; and red collar and cuffs, with yellow piping. The Grenadiers of Toluca wore a similar uniform to that of the Grenadier Guards of the Supreme Powers. Minor differences included the absence of plume and cords in their bearskin, which bore a simple gilt flaming grenade plate, whilst their light blue cuffs displayed no less than four *sardinatas* apiece!

The campaign uniform generally adopted by militia infantry consisted of grey frock coats and sky blue trousers trimmed with red piping. The medium-dark grey frock coat worn by the San Blas Battalion had red patches on the collar front, solid red cuffs and flaps. Shoulder knots and epaulettes were also red. Shakos were black with yellow cinch bands, and a red pompon. Barrack caps were dark blue with red piping and tassel. Shoulder and waist belts were black leather. Trousers were medium blue with red seam stripes. Lieutenant Colonel Xicoténcal wore a French-style red kepi with dark blue top, red band, and gold piping. His grey trimmed red collar was edged with gold piping. Red cuffs and flaps were also trimmed with gold. Epaulettes were gold, whilst his waist sash was crimson silk. Trousers were medium blue with gold seam stripes. His sword scabbard was suspended from a wide black leather shoulder belt.

Regarding militia cavalry, the regiments of Queretaro, Guanajuato, San Luis Potosi, Oajaca, Morelia, and Active Commerce Regiment of Mexico, adopted the uniform of the Regular Light Mounted Regiment of Mexico. The Queretaro Regiment was renamed the 2nd Cavalry Regiment, and subsequently wore a yellow tail-coat with crimson collar, lapels, cuffs and turnbacks; green pants with white seam stripes; a red shako; and red horse furniture with a white border.[134]

Mounted Rifles

Originally raised on 12 June 1840 as Light Cavalry, the Mounted Rifles were renamed and given a new uniform on 20 September 1843 which consisted of a black fur busby with an oval brass plate bearing the Mexican Eagle and Serpent, with the inscription

'VICTORIA' above it, brass scale chin strap, crimson bag with white piping, and crimson plume; a dark green jacket with crimson lapels, pointed cuffs, and cuff flaps, piped with white; two rows of 12 white metal ball buttons trimmed with white lace false button holes for troopers, and silver for officers; crimson epaulettes; grey pants with crimson seam stripes and black leather knee boots. Waist and shoulder belts were white leather. They also wore a yellow cape. The saddle blanket, holsters and roll were green with crimson border and edging. This regiment fought at Buena Vista.

Jalisco Lancers

The Jalisco Lancers were raised on 19 July 1843 and organised into two squadrons. This unit formed part of the Army of the North which garrisoned Monterey in September 1846. On the 21st of that month their commander, Lieutenant Colonel Juan N. Nájera, was killed in a skirmish with U.S. Dragoons. The Lancers subsequently took part in fighting at Veracruz within the cavalry led by Division General J. V. Miñon.

The uniform of the Jalisco Lancers consisted of a Polish-style Czapska with red top, black leather base, and silver central band, with silver lace trim around the black leather visor; silver cap plate bearing a large Mexican eagle and serpent sweated to a sun ray background. Officers wore a red fountain plume attached to the left side of the mortarboard, underneath which was a National cockade, and yellow safety cord. The plume worn by troopers was red horsehair. The silver chain chin strap, with red velvet lining, was secured to hooks either side via silver lion-head attachments. The single-breasted coatee was deep red with dark green collar, cuffs and bars, and turnbacks, with piping in opposite colour. Epaulettes were yellow and fringeless. Pants were dark blue with red seam stripes. Those worn by troopers had black antelope skin seat lining and 'false boots'. Waist and shoulder belts were white leather, as were sword knots. The saddle blanket and holster covers were green with white edging, whilst the saddle roll was green with red cover. Their lances carried red fork-tailed pennon.

San Patricio Battalion

This unique unit evolved from an artillery company organised largely from Catholic deserters from the U.S. Army, and appears to have been originally formed as the San Patricio volunteer militia artillery by November 1846. Also known as the Irish Volunteers, it was part of troops, also consisting of the Battalion of Sappers and three foot artillery companies, which manned 14 pieces of artillery at

Buena Vista. On this occasion the unit was commanded by Captain Francisco Rosendo Moreno, who was wounded in the battle.

By late May/early June 1847, the San Patricio artillery had been incorporated into a unit attached to the Army of the East called 'The Foreign Legion', or the Red Company due to their ruddy complexions, which was commanded by Captain Saturnino O'Leary. Nothing is known of the organisation of this short-lived unit. On 1 July 1847, it was replaced via the following decree which once again established a unit utilising the San Patricio designation:

Art. 1: Two infantry companies of territorial militia are to be formed from the unit known as the Foreign Legion. They are to be named the First and Second territorial militia companies of San Patricio.

Art. 2: Each company will consist of a captain, a first lieutenant, two second lieutenants, a sergeant first class, nine corporals, four buglers and 80 privates.

Art. 3: The uniform they are to wear is the uniform prescribed for the territorial infantry.[135]

Nothing further is known of the activities of the San Patricio infantry companies, by this time commanded by John Riley, or Reilly, a deserter from Co. K, 5th U.S. Infantry, until August 1847, when they composed a part of the brigade under General Rangel stationed in the environs of Mexico City. On the 20th of that month, they were involved in the defense of the Convent of San Mateo at Churubusco, on which occasion their British 'Tower' rifles were the only Mexican weapons for which a sufficient amount of ammunition was available. Hence they kept up a sustained fire throughout the entire action, whilst their Mexican comrades attempted in desperation to force balls of a larger calibre down the muzzle of their muskets.[136]

During this action the San Patricios suffered 35 killed, whilst the remainder were either captured or dispersed. Twenty-nine of those captured were tried by court martial and sentenced to be hanged. But after a careful review of the individual cases, General Scott commuted the sentences of seven to 'fifty lashes each on their naked backs, and to be branded with the letter "D" high up on the cheek-bone, near the eye, but without jeapardizing its sight'. Two men were subsequently pardoned for being legitimately captured and forced into the battalion where they had refused to fight. A further 36 prisoners were tried by another court-martial and, of these, 30 were hanged at Mixcoac on 13 September 1847, on a hilltop which overlooked the storming of Chapultepec Castle. The gallows trap was sprung the very moment that the Stars and Stripes replaced the Eagle and Serpent on the flagpole of the Castle!

The San Patricio remnants who managed to escape from Churubusco had gathered together to form a new company by December 1847. Enough survivors and new deserters had joined them by March 1848 to organise a second company. Thus a San Patricio Battalion survived the war, and became involved in the revolt under General Paredes in June 1848.

Nothing is known of the uniform worn by the San Patricios in late 1846 and early 1847, although it may well have been that of the active, or territorial militia, officially prescribed above. After the battle of Churubusco, the unit seems to have worn various forms of undress, consisting of either grey frock coats or white canvas jackets. The following items of uniform were issued to the San Patricio Battalion in 1848: 200 cloth jackets, 210 pairs of trousers, 400 linen shirts, 200 stocks, 200 blankets, 200 forage caps, 232 pairs of shoes, 100 drawers, 19 sets of straps for carrying overcoats.[137]

Despite their small numbers, and most likely for propaganda purposes, the San Patricios carried their own colour, which was borne at Buena Vista, and apparently used until after the dispersal of the unit at Churubusco. Sam Chamberlain referred to 'the glittering cross that waved over the deserters' guns' as the 1st U.S. Dragoons charged them on 23 May, 1847.[138] According to San Patricio member John Riley, their flag was green and had painted or embroidered on it a figure of Saint Patrick, the harp of Erin, and a shamrock.

Footnotes

1   Edward Waldo Emerson and Waldo Emerson Forbes, eds., *Journals of Ralph Waldo Emerson*, 10 vols. (Boston, 1909-14), 7: p. 206.

2   George Ballentine, *Autobiography of an English Soldier in the United States Army* (New York, 1853), p. 35.

3   Samuel E. Chamberlain, *My Confession* (manuscript ca. 1855, published with introduction and postscript by Roger Butterfield, New York; 1956), pp. 67-68.

4   Jacques Noel Jacobsen, Jr., editor, *Regulations and Notes for the Uniform of the Army of the United States, 1847* (New York, 1977). Barna Upton, 'Our First Foreign War', edited by William F. Goetzmann; *American Heritage*, Vol. 17, No. 4 (1966), p. 20.

5   'Account of Clothing Issued to Volunteers and Remaining on Hand at Vera Cruz, Dec. 6, 1847.' Original document at US National Archives, Washington, D.C.; data supplied by Ross Kimmel. Hereafter referred to as 'Account of Clothing', 6 Dec., 1847.

6   Erna Risch, *Quartermaster Support of the Army: A History of the Corps, 1775-1939* (Washington, 1989), p. 255: quoting Record Group 92, CGP Irwin, Letters Sent, No. 97, n.p., National Archives, Washington, D.C.

7   Robert H. Ferrell, ed., *Monterrey Is Ours! The Mexican War Letters of Lieutenant Dana, 1845-1847* (Lexington, Kentucky: 1990), pp. 83, 87, 97, 112. The author is indebted to Ross M. Kimmel for much of the uniform data in this section, which was published in 'American Forces in the War with Mexico, 1846-48 (2)', *Military Illustrated*, No. 42 (November 1991), pp.34-41.

8   Albert G. Brackett, M.D., *General Lane's Brigade in Central Mexico* (Cincinnati, 1854), p. 313.

9   John R. Kenly, *Memoirs of a Maryland Volunteer...* (Philadelphia, 1873), p. 154.

10 George Winston Smith & Charles Judah, *Chronicles of the Gringos* (Albuquerque, 1968), p. 381.

11 *Ibid.*

12 *Ibid.*

13 Brackett, *op. cit.*, p. 286.

14 Capt. W. S. Henry (3rd Inf.), U.S. Army, *Campaign Sketches of the War with Mexico* (New York, 1847), p. 276.

15 George C. Furber, *The Twelve Months Volunteer...* (Cincinnati, 1850), p. 329.

16 Brackett, *op. cit.*, p. 313.

17 Upton, *op. cit.*, 21.

18 Kenly, *op. cit.*, p. 98.

19 'Account of Clothing', 6 Dec., 1847.

20 Kenly, *op. cit.*, p. 98

21 Clyde A. Risley & John R. Elting, 'Company C (Ringgold's Battery), 3rd Artillery Regiment, 1837-1847', *Military Collector & Historian*, Vol. XLIV, No. 4 (Winter, 1992), pp. 178-79.

22 Chamberlain, *op. cit.*, p. 90.

23 Cited in Philip Katcher & G.A. Embleton, *The Mexican-American War, 1846-1848* (London, 1976), p. 14.

24 Cited in Katcher & Embleton, *Ibid.*, p. 15.

25 Lt. J. P. Hatch, camp near Corpus Christi, to his sister, Oct. 14, 1845, John Porter Hatch Papers, Manuscript Division, Library of Congress, Washington, D.C. Cited in Smith & Judah, pp. 25-26.

26 Chamberlain, *op. cit.*, pp. 240 & 245.

27 Gustavus W. Smith, 'Company A - Engineers in Mexico, 1846-1847', *The Military Engineer*, Vol. LVI (September-October 1964).

28 Smith, *ibid.*

29 H. Charles McBarron, Jr. & John R. Elting, 'U.S. Company of Sappers, Miners, and Pontoniers, Winter Full Dress, 1846-1851', *Military Uniforms in America, Vol. II, Years of Growth, 1796-1851* [Presidio Press, 1977], p. 128.

30 *Ibid.*

31 Frederick Zeh, *An Immigrant Soldier in the Mexican War* (Texas, 1995), p. 14 & 66.

32 Isaac D. Toll, 'Michigan Soldiers in Mexico', *Pioneer Society of Michigan Papers*, Vol. 7 (1884), p. 119.

33 'A Marylander in the Mexican War: Some Letters of J. J. Archer', ed. C. A. Porter Hopkins, *Maryland Historical Magazine*, Vol. 54, No. 4 (1959), pp. 409 & 416.

34 Katcher & Embleton, *op. cit.*, p. 13.

35 Order No. 26, H.Q. 1st Dragoons, Fort Leavenworth [Kansas], 31 Dec. 1846, in U.S. Army Comds., Regtl. Records, Order Book, H.Q. 1st Drags., 13 Jan. 1841-18 Apr. 1850, p. 147, Record Group 98, National Archives, Washington, D.C.

36 Orders No. 33, H.Q. 10th Infantry, Camp near Matamoros, Mexico; John E. Wool Papers- JT-12777, Box 11, Folder 4, State Archives, Albany, N.Y.

37 U.S. Navy Department. *General Order*, 1 May 1830, effective 31 December 1830, effective 31 December 1830; James Till. 'A Reproduction of the 1830 Naval Uniform Regulations', *Military Collector & Historians*, Vol. XI, No.2 (1959), pp. 45-50.

This engraving of Mexican guerillas was published in the *Illustrated London News* in 1847. Irregular bands of guerillas, led by officers commissioned by the Mexican government, harassed American supply lines throughout most of the war. Guerilla bands were established in the Mexican States of Puebla, Mexico, Vera Cruz, and Tamaulipas. Note the uniformed officer in gala dress commands a mixed force of cavalry and infantry. Courtesy of Cheltenham Reference Library.

38 Robert Debs Heinl, Jr., *Soldiers of the Sea: The United States Marine Corps, 1775-1962* (Annapolis, 1962), pp. 45-56.

39 Robert M. Reilly, *United States Military Small Arms, 1816-1865* Baton Rouge, 1970, pp. 29-31.

40 S.F. Nunnelee to Dr. W.S. Wyman, June 14, 1906, in 'Alabama in Mexico War,' *Alabama Historical Quarterly* 19 (1957): p. 417.

41 Walter Lee Brown, 'The Mexican War Experiences of Albert Pike and the "Mounted Devils" of Arkansas, *The Arkansas Historical Quarterly*, Vol. XII, No. 4 (Winter, 1953), p. 310.

42 Kenly, *op. cit.*, pp. 77-78.

43 Kenly, *Ibid.*, p. 237.

44 *Ibid.*, p. 375.

45 T. Frederick Davis, 'Florida's Part in the War with Mexico', *Florida Historical Quarterly*, Vol. 20

(January 1942), pp. 235-259.

46 Wilbur G. Kurtz, Jr., 'The First Regiment of Georgia Volunteers in the Mexican War', *The Georgia Historical Quarterly*, Vol. XXVII, No. 4 (December, 1943), pp. 301-323.

47 A[lexander] K[onze], Alton, Illinois, to Editor, Milwaukee *Wisconsin Banner*, 2 July 1846, cited in Milwaukee *Wisconsin Banner*, 18 July 1846 [typescript only], Alexander Konze Papers, State Historical Society of Wisconsin, Madison, Wisconsin.

48 Chamberlain, *op. cit.*, p. 32.

49 John F. Graf, 'Our Grand Regimental Flourish: The Uniforms and Equipment of the Fourth Regiment of Illinois Volunteers, 1846-47', *Military Collector & Historian*, Vol. XXIII, No. 3 (Fall, 1971), pp. 83-84.

50 Oran Perry, *Indiana in the Mexican War* (Indianapolis, 1908), p. 24.

51 *Ibid.*, p. 31.

52 *Ibid.*, 61. The cotton shirts were probably white; the flannel, shirts, red.

53 H.C. Duncan, 'Munroe County in the Mexican War', *Indiana Magazine of History*, Vol. XII, No. 4 (December, 1916), p. 291.

54 *Ibid.*, p. 42.

55 Lloyd Lewis, *Captain Sam Grant* (Boston, 1950), p. 161.

56 John T. Hughes, *Doniphan's Expedition, containing an account of the Conquest of New Mexico* (Cincinnati: 1850), p. 135.

57 'Extracts from the Journal of Henry W. Bigler', *Utah Historical Quarterly*, Vol. 5, No. 2 (April 1932), pp. 36-37, 41.

58 'Journal of Robert S. Bliss with the Mormon Battalion,' *Utah Historical Quarterly*, Vol. 4 (July-Oct. 1931), pp. 76-77.

59 'Volunteer Army', *Nile's National Register*, Vol. 70 (Aug. 22, 1846), p. 386.

60 'From the Kentucky Observer of October,' *Niles' National Register*, Vol. 71 (24 October, 1846), p. 122.

61 D. Allsop, *The Texan War of Independence & the US - Mexican War 1846-48* (Frei Korps 15, 1983), p. 8.

62 See Reuben Davis, *Recollections of Mississippi and Mississippians* (Uni. Col. of Miss. Press, 1972), pp. 223-251 for a short history of the service of this regiment.

63 William Burr Howell and Family Collection, Department of Archives & History, Jackson, Mississippi.

64 Chamberlain, *op. cit.*, pp. 122-23.

65 *Vicksburg Whig* (Mississippi), 28 April 1847.

66 Tho[ma]s N. Lowe, 'Remarks on Some of the Diseases Which Prevailed in the 2d Regt. Mississippi Rifles for the First Six Months of Its Service', *The New Orleans Medical and Surgical Journal*, Vol. 5 (July, 1848), pp. 3-6.

67 Powell A. Casey, 'Early History of the Washington Artillery of New Orleans', *Louisiana Historical Quarterly*, Vol. 23, No. 2 (April 1940), pp. 476-77.

68 K. Jack Bauer, *The Mexican War 1846-1848* (New York, 1974), p. 87.

69 [Private Andrew T. McClure?], Company E, 1st Regiment of Missouri Mounted Volunteers, Rio Vigita, to his wife, 22 August 1846, Getty Papers, New Mexico State Records Centre & Archives, Santa Fe, New Mexico.

70 Frank S. Edwards, *A Campaign in New Mexico with Colonel Doniphan* (Philadelphia, 1847), 21.

71 William B. McGroarty, editor, 'William H. Richardson's Journal of Doniphan's Expedition' *Missouri Historical Review*, Vol. 22, # 2 (1928), 209.

72 John Taylor Hughes, *Doniphan's expedition, containing an account of the conquest of New Mexico* (Cincinnati, 1850), p. 28.

73 McGroarty, *op. cit.*, p. 22.

74 *Ibid.*, Vol. 22, # 4 [1928], 533.

75 Daniel J. Ryan, 'Ohio in the Mexican War', *Ohio Archaeological & Historical Quarterly*, Vol. XXI (April-July, 1912), 277-290.

76 'Adolphus Heiman', *Tennessee Historical Quarterly*, Vol. I (1915) p. 49.

77 'The Militia Law of the State of Tennessee, passed January 28, 1840', p. 31; Tennessee State Library & Archives, Nashville, courtesy of Charles A. Sherrill.

78 Smith & Judah, *op. cit.*, p. 42.

79 George Wilkins Kendall, *Narrative of the Texan Santa Fe Expedition* (New York, 1856), pp. 295-96, 381.

80 Samuel C. Reid, *Scouting Expeditions of McCullogh's Texas Rangers: Or, the Summer and Fall Campaigns of the Army of the United States in Mexico—1846...* (Philadelphia, 1860), p. 38.

81 Justin H. Smith, *The War with Mexico* (New York, 1919), vol. 1, p. 236.

82 Brackett, *op. cit.*, pp. 173-174.

83 James Madison Cutts, *Conquest of California and New Mexico* (Philadelphia, 1847), pp. 71, 211 & 264.

84 Cutts, *Ibid.*, p. 71. The self-portait of Lieutenant Hollingsworth is in the collection of the California Historical Society.

85 Zeh, *op. cit.*, p. 69

86 Data courtesy of Howard Michael Madaus.

87 *Richmond Daily Whig*, 22 December 1846.

88 Virginia Regiment Letter Book, 1st Infantry Mex. War (1846-47), Record Group 92, U.S. National Archives, n.p.

89 *Ibid.*

90 John Francis Hamtramck Papers, Duke University, N.C.

91 *The Republican* (Petersburg, Va.), 26 July 1848.

92 Lee A. Wallace, 'Raising a Volunteer Regiment for Mexico, 1846-47', *North Carolina Historical Review*, Vol. 35, No. 1 (January 1958), pp. 20-33.

93 *North Carolina Standard* (Raleigh), 27 May 1846.

94 *Anderson Gazette* (South Carolina),18 December 1846.

95 *Ibid.*, 12 February 1847.

96 *Lancaster Ledger* (S. C.), 3 February 1858.

97 'From the Palmetto Regiment', letter signed 'Dan', dated 9 March 1847, published in the *Charleston Mercury*, 1 April 1847.

98 *Lancaster Ledger* (South Carolina), 18 November 1857.

99 *Ibid.*, 5 May, 1858.

100 Caleb Cushing, Boston, to Gov. George N. Briggs, Boston, Feb. 5, 1847, Caleb Cushing Papers, DLC.

101 Romeyn B. Ayres journal, (September 1847), Romeyn B. Ayres Collection, University of North Carolina.

102 *Daily Free Press* (Detroit), 19 October 1847.

103 Sergeant Thomas Barclay's Diary (2nd Pennsylvania Volunteer Infantry, Westmoreland Guards), Manuscript Division, Westmoreland County Historical Society, 1 January 1847 - 14 July 1848.

104 Gene Annette Burger, 'A Mexican War Roundabout', *Military Collector & Historian*, Vol. XLII, No. 4 (Winter, 1990), pp. 160-162.

105 'Mexican War Battle-Flags Presented to the Historical Society of Pennsylvania', *Pennsylvania Magazine of History and Biography*, Vol. 17, No. 2 (1893), pp. 185.

106 Richard A. Sauers, *Advance the Colors! Pennsylvania Civil War Battle Flags* (Pennsylvania: 1987), p. 6.

107 Ramon Alcaraz, *The Other Side: or, Notes for the history of the war between Mexico and the United States* (New York, 1850), p. 299.

108 Otto Zirckel, *Tagebuch Geschrieben Während der Nordamerikanischen-Mexikanischen. Campagne in den Jahren 1847 und 1848 Auf Beiden Operationslinien* (Halle: H. W. Schmidt, 1849), pp. 116-117.

109 Smith, *op. cit.*, vol. 1, p. 106.

110 *Ibid.*, p. 10.

111 *Ibid.*, pp. 9-10.

112 Ulysses S. Grant, *Memoirs of U.S. Grant*, ed. E. B. Long (Cleveland, 1952), vol. 1, 168-69.

113 Beauregard, P. G. T., 'Reminiscences': Claiborne papers, Mississippi Dept. of History.

114 Roswell Sabine Ripley, *The War with Mexico* (New York: 1849), 87.

115 Alcaraz, *op. cit.* pp. 90,173 & 262.

116 A. S. Brown, J. Hefter, and A. Nieto, *The Mexican Soldier; 1837 - 1847* (Mexico City, 1958), p. 72.

117 Brown, *et al.*, p. 72.

118 James Henry Carleton, *The Battle of Buena Vista* (New York: 1848), p. 229.

119 Smith, *op. cit.*, vol. 1, p. 462.

120 Ballentine, *op. cit.*, p. 199.

121 Gary Zaboly, 'Mexican Army Riflemen, Texas Campaigns', 1835-36, *Military Collector & Historian*, Vol. XLV, No. 4 (Winter 1993), 180-81.

122 Katcher & Embleton, *op. cit.*, p. 24.

123 *Carolina Spartan* (Spartanburg), 23 July 1857.

124 James K. Holland, 'Diary of a Texan Volunteer in the Mexican War', *Southwestern Historical Quarterly*, Vol. 30, No. 1 (July 1926), p. 31.

125 *Reglamento sobre la Organazion del Cuerpo de Artilleria* (Mexico, 26 July 1846), p.1.

126 Eric I. Manders & Albert W. Haarmann, 'Mexican Army: Artillery Officers, 1840-1848, *Military Collector & Historian*, Vol. XLVI, No. 2 (Summer, 1994), pp. 84-85.

127 Will Wallace to George, March 1, 1847, Wallace-Dickey Collection, Illinois.

128 Kendall, Vol. II, *op. cit.*, p. 104 & 107.

129 Cutts, *op. cit.*, p. 44.

130 Richard Pourade, ed., *The Sign of the Eagle* (San Diego, 1970), p. 87; Alcaraz, *op. cit.*, pp. 355 & 363.

131 Alcaraz, *op. cit.*, pp 88 & 248.

132 *Diaro del gobierno de la Republica Mexicano* (hereafter *Diaro*), Tomo XXII, Num. 2415 and 2500.

133 Alcaraz, *op. cit.*, p. 248.

134 Letter from Detmar H. Finke to Lt. Col. J. B. R. Nicholson, 16 December 1974.

135 *Diaro*, Tomo III, Num. 155, Mexico [Imprenta del Aguila], 1847, 'Estado de corte...Ejército del Norte', 2 December 1846.

136 Alcarez, pp. 294-95.

137 *Memoria de guerra y Marina*, Mexico, Estado, Num. 10.

138 Chamberlain, *op. cit.*, p. 124.

Bibliography

Manuscripts

Official Records in the National Archives

Virginia Regiment Letter Book, Record Group 92.

Regtl. Records, Order Book, Record Group 98.

LIBRARY OF CONGRESS

John Porter Hatch Papers

Caleb Cushing Papers

STATE ARCHIVES, ALBANY, NEW YORK.

John E. Wool Papers

DUKE UNIVERSITY

John Francis Hamtramck Papers

STATE HISTORICAL SOCIETY OF WISCONSIN

Alexander Konze Papers

MISSISSIPPI DEPARTMENT OF ARCHIVES & HISTORY

Claiborne papers

William Burr Howell and Family Collection

NEW MEXICO STATE RECORDS CENTRE & ARCHIVES

Getty Papers

UNIVERSITY OF NORTH CAROLINA

Romeyn B. Ayres Collection

WESTMORELAND COUNTY HISTORICAL SOCIETY

Thomas Barclay's Diary

Printed documents

'The Militia Law of the State of Tennessee, passed January 28, 1840'; Tennessee State Library & Archives.

Reglamento sobre la Organazion del Cuerpo de Artilleria; Mexico.

Diaro del gobierno de la Republica Mexicano; Mexico.

Newspapers

Anderson *Gazette*

Baltimore *Niles National Register*

Charleston *Mercury*

Detroit *Daily Free Press*

Lancaster *Ledger*

New York *Herald*

Petersburg *Republican*

Raleigh *North Carolina Standard*

Richmond *Daily Whig*

Spartanburg *Carolina Spartan*

Vicksburg *Whig*

Accounts of participants

George Winston Smith & Charles Judah (editors), *Chronicles of the Gringos* (Albuquerque, 1968)

George Ballentine, *Autobiography of an English Soldier in the United States Army* (New York, 1853)

Samuel E. Chamberlain, *My Confession* (manuscript ca. 1855, published with introduction and postscript by Roger Butterfield, New York; 1956)

Robert H. Ferrell, ed., *Monterrey Is Ours! The Mexican War Letters of Lieutenant Dana, 1845-1847* (Lexington, Kentucky: 1990)

Frederick Zeh, *An Immigrant Soldier in the Mexican War* (Texas, 1995)

John R. Kenly, *Memoirs of a Maryland Volunteer...* (Philadelphia, 1873)

Capt. W. S. Henry (3rd Inf.), U.S. Army, *Campaign Sketches of the War with Mexico* (New York, 1847)

George C. Furber, *The Twelve Months Volunteer...* (Cincinnati, 1850)

Frank S. Edwards, *A Campaign in New Mexico with Colonel Doniphan* (Philadelphia, 1847)

John Taylor Hughes, *Doniphan's expedition, containing an account of the conquest of New Mexico* (Cincinnati, 1850)

Francis D. Clark, *The First Regiment of New York Volunteers* (New York, 1882)

George Wilkins Kendall, *Narrative of the Texan Santa Fe Expedition* (New York, 1856)

Samuel C. Reid, *Scouting Expeditions of McCullogh's Texas Rangers: Or, the Summer and Fall Campaigns of the Army of the United States in Mexico—1846...* (Philadelphia, 1860)

James Madison Cutts, *Conquest of California and New Mexico* (Philadelphia, 1847)

John T. Hughes, *Doniphan's Expedition, containing an account of the Conquest of New Mexico* (Cincinnati:

1850)

Roswell Sabine Ripley, *The War with Mexico* (New York: 1849)

Otto Zirckel, *Tagebuch Geschrieben Während der Nordamerikanischen-Mexikanischen. Campagne in den Jahren 1847 und 1848 Auf Beiden Operationslinien* (Halle: H. W. Schmidt, 1849)

Ulysses S. Grant, *Memoirs of U.S. Grant*, ed. E. B. Long (Cleveland, 1952)

'Extracts from the Journal of Henry W. Bigler', *Utah Historical Quarterly*, Vol. 5, No. 2 (April 1932), pp. 36-37, 41.

'Journal of Robert S. Bliss with the Mormon Battalion,' *Utah Historical Quarterly*, Vol. 4 (July-Oct. 1931)

'A Marylander in the Mexican War: Some Letters of J. J. Archer', ed. C. A. Porter Hopkins, *Maryland Historical Magazine*, Vol. 54, No. 4 (1959)

James K. Holland, 'Diary of a Texan Volunteer in the Mexican War', *Southwestern Historical Quarterly*, Vol. 30, No. 1 (July 1926)

Tho[ma]s N. Lowe, 'Remarks on Some of the Diseases Which Prevailed in the 2d Regt. Mississippi Rifles for the First Six Months of Its Service', *The New Orleans Medical and Surgical Journal*, Vol. 5 (July, 1848)

William B. McGroarty, editor, 'William H. Richardson's Journal of Doniphan's Expedition' *Missouri Historical Review*, Vol. 22, No. 2 (1928)

Secondary sources

A. S. Brown, J. Hefter, and A. Nieto, *The Mexican Soldier, 1837 - 1847* (Mexico City, 1958)

K. Jack Bauer, *The Mexican War 1846-1848* (New York, 1974)

Justin H. Smith, *The War with Mexico* (New York, 1919), vols. 1 & 2.

Philip Katcher & G.A. Embleton, *The Mexican-American War, 1846-1848* (London, 1976)

H. Charles McBarron, Jr. & John R. Elting, 'U.S. Company of Sappers, Miners, and Pontoniers, Winter Full Dress, 1846-1851', *Military Uniforms in America, Vol. II, Years of Growth, 1796-1851* (Presidio Press, 1977)

Jacques Noel Jacobsen, Jr., editor, *Regulations and Notes for the Uniform of the Army of the United States, 1847* (New York, 1977)

Erna Risch, *Quartermaster Support of the Army: A History of the Corps, 1775-1939* (Washington, 1989)

Richard A. Sauers, *Advance the Colors! Pennsylvania Civil War Battle Flags* (Pennsylvania: 1987)

Robert Debs Heinl, Jr., *Soldiers of the Sea: The United States Marine Corps, 1775-1962* (Annapolis, 1962)

Robert M. Reilly, *United States Military Small Arms, 1816-1865* (Baton Rouge, 1970)

Oran Perry, *Indiana in the Mexican War* (Indianapolis, 1908)

Lloyd Lewis, *Captain Sam Grant* (Boston, 1950)

D. Allsop, *The Texan War of Independence & the US - Mexican War 1846-48* (Frei Korps 15, 1983)

Reuben Davis, *Recollections of Mississippi and Mississippians* (Uni. Col. of Miss. Press, 1972)

Ramon Alcaraz, *The Other Side: or, Notes for the history of the war between Mexico and the United States* (New York, 1850)

James Henry Carleton, *The Battle of Buena Vista* (New York: 1848)

Richard Pourade, ed., *The Sign of the Eagle* (San Diego, 1970)

Clyde A. Risley & John R. Elting, 'Company C (Ringgold's Battery), 3rd Artillery Regiment, 1837-1847', *Military Collector & Historian*, Vol. XLIV, No. 4 (Winter, 1992)

Gustavus W. Smith, 'Company A - Engineers in Mexico, 1846-1847', *The Military Engineer*, Vol. LVI (September-October 1964)

Isaac D. Toll, 'Michigan Soldiers in Mexico', *Pioneer Society of Michigan Papers*, Vol. 7 (1884)

James Till. 'A Reproduction of the 1830 Naval Uniform Regulations', *Military Collector & Historians*, Vol. XI, No.2 (1959)

S.F. Nunnelee to Dr. W.S. Wyman, June 14, 1906, in 'Alabama in Mexico War,' *Alabama Historical Quarterly* 19 (1957)

Walter Lee Brown, 'The Mexican War Experiences of Albert Pike and the "Mounted Devils" of Arkansas, *The Arkansas Historical Quarterly*, Vol. XII, No. 4 (Winter, 1953)

T. Frederick Davis, 'Florida's Part in the War with Mexico', *Florida Historical Quarterly*, Vol. 20 (January 1942), pp. 235-259.

Wilbur G. Kurtz, Jr., 'The First Regiment of Georgia Volunteers in the Mexican War', *The Georgia Historical Quarterly*, Vol. XXVII, No. 4 (December, 1943)

John F. Graf, 'Our Grand Regimental Flourish: The Uniforms and Equipment of the Fourth Regiment of Illinois Volunteers, 1846-47', *Military Collector & Historian*, Vol. XXIII, No. 3 (Fall, 1971)

H.C. Duncan, 'Munroe County in the Mexican War', *Indiana Magazine of History*, Vol. XII, No. 4 (December, 1916)

Powell A. Casey, 'Early History of the Washington Artillery of New Orleans', *Louisiana Historical Quarterly*, Vol. 23, No. 2 (April 1940)

Daniel J. Ryan, 'Ohio in the Mexican War', *Ohio*

Archaeological & Historical Quarterly, Vol. XXI (April-July, 1912)

'Adolphus Heiman', *Tennessee Historical Quarterly*, Vol. I (1915)

Gene Annette Burger, 'A Mexican War Roundabout', *Military Collector & Historian*, Vol. XLII, No. 4 (Winter, 1990)

'Mexican War Battle-Flags Presented to the Historical Society of Pennsylvania', *Pennsylvania Magazine of History and Biography*, Vol. 17, No. 2 (1893)

Gary Zaboly, 'Mexican Army Riflemen, Texas Campaigns', 1835-36, *Military Collector & Historian*, Vol. XLV, No. 4 (Winter 1993)

Eric I. Manders & Albert W. Haarmann, 'Mexican Army: Artillery Officers, 1840-1848, *Military Collector & Historian*, Vol. XLVI, No. 2 (Summer, 1994)

Detmar H. Finke, 'The Organization and Uniforms of the San Patricio Units of the Mexican Army, 1846-1848', *Military Collector & Historian*, Vol. IX, No. 2 (1957)

Mexican-American War Directory

This directory is a comprehensive guide for Mexican-American War re-enactors, historians, modellers and wargamers.

Museums and Battlefields

During the First World World the American Department of the Army, searching for desperately needed space, cleared out the U.S. Quartermaster Corps Museum in Philadelphia and sent the contents to the Smithsonian Institute in Washington. After the war, at General John J. Pershing's urging, the army decided to reserve the re-opened space for relics of the Great War; and in 1919 the earlier material was permanently consigned to the Smithsonian. Among this material are a number of uniform coats and fatigue jackets of the Mexican War period. Through the enterprise and initiative of Ross Kimmel, representative examples from this unique collection were photgraphed and published in *Military Illustrated* in 1991-92. Further previously unpublished examples from this collection appear in the pages of this volume. Some specimens have size markings in the sleeve linings indicative of the Schuylkill Arsenal. Though showing some deterioration from age, these garments exhibit few, if any, signs of actual wear. They are probably sample pieces made up by the Quartermaster; indeed, they may be the sample garments occasionally referred to in the 1847 regulations. For further information on this unique collection, contact the Smithsonian Institution, 14th & Constitution Ave. NW, Washington, D.C. 20560, U.S.A. (phone 202 357-1883).

West Point Museum, situated at the United States Military Academy, West Point, New York 10996, U.S.A., has an excellent collection of uniforms, weapons and flags of the Mexican War period.

San Jacinto Museum of History, situated 3800 Park Road 1836, La Porte, Texas 77571 (phone 713 479-2421) has a collection designed to preserve and revisualize the early history of Texas, and includes Mexican-American War exhibits.

Museo Nacional de Historia, Mexico, D.F. (phone 0052 5 286-9920), has the best collection of uniforms, flags, and accoutrements appertaining to the Mexican army of the period.

A small number of Mexican-American War exhibits may be seen at the North Carolina Museum of History, 109 East Jones Street, Raleigh, North Carolina 27601-2807, U.S.A. (phone 919 715-0200).

The James K. Polk Memorial State Historic Site, at Pineville, North Carolina (phone 704 889-7145) has several Mexican-American War exhibits, including a hat associated with Santa Anna.

Palo Alto Battlefield National Historic Site, 1623

Central Boulevard, Suite 213, Brownsville, Texas 78520, U.S.A. (phone 210 541-2785), contains a visitor centre and exhibits on the war and the battles of Palo Alto, Resaca de la Palma, Fort Brown, and Carricitos.

San Pasqual Battlefield State Historic Park, 8 miles south of Escondido, California, on Hwy 78 (phone 619 220-5430 or 220-5431). Open Fri through Sun. The forces of Kearny and Andres Pico both claimed victory in the bloody engagement at this location in 1846.

Fort Scott National Historic Site, Old Blvd., Fort Scott, Kansas 66701, U.S.A., was established in 1842, and named after General Winfield Scott. A well restored and reconstructed example of a frontier fort, companies of the 1st Dragoons from Fort Scott served in the ranks of Kearny's expedition, and with Taylor in northern Mexico. The fort's first commander, Captain Benjamin D. Moore, was killed at San Pasqual, near San Diego, in late 1846.

Bent's Old Fort National Historic Site, 35110 Highway East La Junta, Colorado 81050, U.S.A., boasts a reconstruction of the original adobe fort built in 1833. Serving as a way station on the Santa Fe Trail, and advanced post in the war with Mexico, Bent's Fort was burned and abandoned by its owner, William Bent, in 1849.

Sutter's Fort, 28th & Lower Streets, Sacramento, Cailifornia, contains a reconstructed fort and restored adobe house, originally built in 1839. Frémont's expedition first arrived at this post in December 1845.

Re-enactment Groups

The Hispanic American Military History Preservation Society is dedicated to the study and interpretation of the Mexican army of the mid-19th century, including 2nd and 3rd Regiments Infanteria Permanente, and 1st Regiment Caballeria. Contact: Marco Gonzalez, La Guardia Civil del Rancho San Pablo, Alta California National Headquarters, 1050 - 36th Street, Richmond, Ca. 94804, U.S.A. (phone 510 235-7845; fax 510 235-3337). Branches within this society include Bat^n. Act^o. del Presidio de Tuscon, 2531 W. Tolosa Circle, Tucson, Arizona 85746; Bat^n. Act^o. de Contra Costa, 1050 - 36th Street, Richmond, California 94804; and Bat^n. Act^o. de Santa Clara, 1666 Rarringdon Drive, San Jose, California 95127.

The Alamo Legacy and Missions Association portrays the 4th Mexican Light Infantry Regiment, circa 1846, plus various Texian, Tejano and Mexican soldado impressions for the 1835-1836 period. Contact: Charles Lara, Route 3, Box 3112, Lakehills, Texas 78063, U.S.A. (phone 210 612-3457).

Co. A, 7th Regiment U.S. Infantry - portrays U.S. Regular infantrymen from 1812-1851, covering the War of 1812, the Seminole War, and Mexican-American War. Contact: Steve Abolt, 3927 Mattison Ave., Fort Worth, Texas 76107, U.S.A. (phone 817 737-7513).

Captain Sarshall Cooper's Company of Missouri Rangers & Captain Eli B. Clemson's Company of 1st U.S. Infantry - re-enacts Missouri Militia from 1810-1848. Contact: Dave Bennett, 5401 Haymeadow Place, Apartment 3a, Peoria, Illinois 61615, U.S.A. (phone 309 691-4951).

Duncan's Battery. Contact: Dan Lawrence, 809 Goshawk, Norman, Oklahoma 73072, U.S.A.

Re-enactment Suppliers

Britain's largest supplier of re-enactment equipment for the period encompassing the Mexican-American War is The Sutler's Store. Contact: Alan Thrower, 16 Howlett Drive, Hailsham, East Sussex, BN27 1QW (phone 01323 840973).

C. & D. Jarnagan Company produce a full complement of uniforms and equipment for American troops for the Mexican War period.

County Cloth, 13797-C, Georgetown Street NE, Paris, Ohio 44669, U.S.A (phone 330 862-3307). Run by Charles R. Childs, this company deals mostly in fabrics, patterns and cut kits to be sewn by the customers.

Caps & Kepis, 2665 Longfellow Drive, Wilmington, DE 19808, U.S.A. (phone 302 994-6428) specialise headgear for the period, including M1839 Regular Army caps.

Dixie Leather Works, P.O. Box 8221, Paducah, KY 42002-8221, U.S.A. (phone 502 442-1058; fax 502 442-1049), supplies Historic Military & Civilian Museum Quality Reproductions covering the period 1833 to 1872.

Ordnance Park Corp., 657 20½ Road, Grand Junction, Colorado 81503, U.S.A (fax 303 243-5980). Deals in accoutrements and other ordnance supplies.

Mexican-American War Organisations

Descendants of Mexican War Veterans. Chartered by the State of Texas, this national lineage society has nearly 300 members scattered across the U.S., Mexico and Canada. It offers an organisational newsletter, *The American Eagle*; a quarterly *Mexican War Journal*; publications, including *How to Find Your Mexican War Veteran Ancestor*; meetings; special events; and a genealogical research service. Contact: DMWV National Office, P.O. Box 830482, Richardson, Texas 75083-0482, U.S.A. (E-mail address: DMWV@aol,com).

The South and Central American Military Historians Society produces the bi-monthly journal *El Dorado*, plus *El Dorado Books*, and devotes much of its attention to the study of the Mexican army of the 1830s and 1840s. Contact: Terry Hooker, 27 Hallgate, Cottingham, North Humberside, HU16 4DN (phone 01482 847068).

The Company of Military Historians has published many articles on the Mexican-American War period in its quarterly journal, *Military Collector & Historian*. This society has also produced numerous colour plates on the subject in its series 'Military Uniforms in America'. For details on membership write to The Company of Military Historians, North Main Street, Connecticut 06498, U.S.A.

On the Internet - aepm@servido.unam.mx, the Mexican-American War Memorial Homepage has been established to exchange information on the period.

Mexican-American War Book Suppliers

The Military Bookman, 29 East 93rd Street, New York, NY 10128, U.S.A. (phone 212 348-1280), specializes in rare and out-of-print books of the period.

Michael Haynes, 46 Farnaby Road, Bromley, Kent BR1 4BJ (phone 01814 601672) sells a limited range of Mexican-American War books, both new & second hand.

The following bookshops specialise in Latin American books:

Libros Latinos, P.O. Box 1103, Redlands, California 92373, U.S.A.

Howard Karno Books, P.O. Box 2100, Valley Center, California 92082, U.S.A.

Mexican-American War Model soldier & Wargame Suppliers

Frei Korps 15, 25 Princetown Road, Bangor, Co. Down, BT20 3TA, Northern Ireland (phone 01247 883187) - offers a wide range of Mexican-American War 15 mil. wargame figures.

Miniature Militaria of Montana, P.O. Box 1166, Wolf Point, MT 59201, U.S.A. (phone 406 6533 & fax 406 6533510) has books and figures relating to the period.

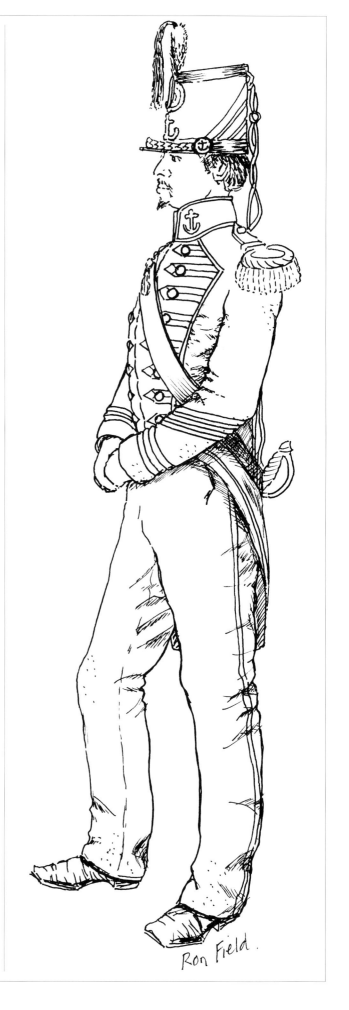

A Mexican Marine. From descriptions, by Ron Field.

Index

Acknowledgements

The author would like to thank the following without whose assistance this book would not have been possible: Michael J. McAfee, Curator of Uniforms & History, West Point Museum; Robert Fish, Curator of Arms, West Point Museum; Margaret Vining, Armed Forces Collections, Smithsonian Institution; Maricela Fonseca Larios, Subdirectora Técnica, Museo Nacional de Historia, Mexico City; Julie Causey, Associate Registrar, Amon Carter Museum; Allen R. Hoilman, Curatorial Specialist, and Eric N. Blevins, Photographic Research, North Carolina Museum of History; Ron Read, Museum of Church History & Art, The Church of the Latter Day Saints; John Bigham, Curator of Education, South Carolina Confederate Relic Room & Museum; Brian Butcher, Editor and Director of Research, San Jacinto Museum of History Association; Marco Gonzalez, Hispanic American Military History Preservation Society; Kay Bost, Curator, DeGolyer Library, Southern Methodist University; Mary Michas, Illinois State Historical Library; Elizabeth P. Bilderback, Assistant Manuscripts Librarian, Caroliniana Library, University of South Carolina; Mary Stuart, Cass County Historical Society; Cindy Krimmel, San Diego Historical Society; Patty Dean, Minnesota Historical Society; Richard Brown, Westmoreland County Historical Society; Joyce White, Curator, James K. Polk Memorial State Historic Site; Ken Tilly, Reference Archivist, Alabama Department of Archives and History; Charles A. Sherrill, Director of Public Services, Tennessee State Library & Archives; Mark Greenough, Living History Associates; John Pinfold, Librarian, Rhodes House, Oxford; Jane Wright, Gloucestershire Library Service; Rubén Garcia Velázquez de Leon; the late J. Domingo Ramirez Garrido; Alberto Guerra y Portugal; Michael F. Bremer; William J. Schultz, M.D.; David Wynn Vaughan; Jeff Patrick; Helda Costa; Dale S. Snair; John M. Hightower; William Dunniway; Herb Peck, Jr.; Phil Katcher; Lee A. Wallace, Jr.; the late Detmar H. Finke; Eric I. Manders; Albert W. Haarman; Robin Smith; Peter Milne; Harry Roach; David M. Sullivan; Albert J. Ott; John F. Graf; William B. Bynum; Alan McBrayer; Richard Warren; Mike Blake; Alan Thrower; Jim Enos; Dennis A. Waters; Don & Sandy Nielson; Robin Forsey; Peter Newark; Rosemary Scott-Smith; Judith Wray; Robin & Carol Wichard; and lastly to Terry D. Hooker, President of the South and Central American Military Historians Society, and to Ross M. Kimmel, for so generously sharing with me their files, knowledge and expertise on this fascinating period of study.